Best Wishes
Prof. Howard N. Tuttle
Univ. of Utah SLC

**human life
is radical reality**

PETER LANG
New York • Washington, D.C./Baltimore • Bern
Frankfurt am Main • Berlin • Brussels • Vienna • Oxford

Howard N. Tuttle

HOWARD N. TUTTLE
939 Donner Way Apt. 108
Salt Lake City, UT 84108

human life
is radical reality

An Idea Developed from the Conceptions of Dilthey, Heidegger, and Ortega y Gasset

PETER LANG
New York • Washington, D.C./Baltimore • Bern
Frankfurt am Main • Berlin • Brussels • Vienna • Oxford

Library of Congress Cataloging-in-Publication Data

Tuttle, Howard N. (Howard Nelson).
Human life is radical reality: an idea developed from the conceptions of
Dilthey, Heidegger, and Ortega y Gasset / Howard N. Tuttle.
p. cm.
Includes bibliographical references.
1. Life. 2. Dilthey, Wilhelm, 1833–1911. 3. Heidegger, Martin, 1889–1976.
4. Ortega y Gasset, José, 1883–1955. I. Title.
BD431.T88   128—dc22   2004018809
ISBN 978-0-8204-7604-9

Bibliographic information published by **Die Deutsche Bibliothek**.
Die Deutsche Bibliothek lists this publication in the "Deutsche
Nationalbibliografie"; detailed bibliographic data is available
on the Internet at http://dnb.ddb.de/.

Cover design by Sophie Boorsch Appel

The paper in this book meets the guidelines for permanence and durability
of the Committee on Production Guidelines for Book Longevity
of the Council of Library Resources.

© 2005, 2007 Peter Lang Publishing, Inc., New York
29 Broadway, 18th Floor, New York, NY 10006
www.peterlang.com

All rights reserved.
Reprint or reproduction, even partially, in all forms such as microfilm,
xerography, microfiche, microcard, and offset strictly prohibited.

Printed in Germany

For Emily

"Human beings are never simply original,
but successors and inheritors of the
human life that has preceded them."

> Goethe

"After thirty we want to reach beyond received opinions,
reach for an insubornable depth which is within us,
and stand in ourselves to carry out the project that we are."

> Ortega y Gasset

Contents

Introduction   1

Chapter One: Wilhelm Dilthey and the Idea of Human Life   13

Chapter Two: The Question of Being in Martin Heidegger and Ortega y Gasset   23

Chapter Three: Human Life: an Overview   31

Chapter Four: The Concept of Categories   43
   Historical Development of the Concept   43
   World and Circumstances   45
   The "I" and Its Circumstances   47

Chapter Five: Historical Time and Care   51
   Clock Time and Lived Time   51
   The Care Structure   56

Chapter Six: Historicity   61
   Defining Historicity   61
   Historicity, Constant and Changing   64
   Heidegger's Historicity   68
   Historicity and Freedom   71

Chapter Seven: The Inner Experience of Human Life   75
   Lived Experience   75
   Embodiment   79
   Thinking   81
   Truth   85
   Knowledge   87

x   Contents

    Meaning   88
    Perspective   90
    Beliefs   93

Chapter Eight: Reason   97
    Vital Reason   97
    Historical Reason   100
    Narration and Prophecy   102

Chapter Nine: The Social Dimension   109
    The "I" and the Other   109
    Dilthey's *Verstehen*   112
    Heidegger's Understanding   118
    Interpretation   120
    Language   122
    The Anonymous "They"   123
    The Vital Elite   127
    Culture   132
    Mood   133

Chapter Ten: The Directions of Human Life   135
    Will, Motives, and Ends   135
    Possibility and Self-Determination   137
    Man the Technician   138
    Generations   146
    Death   149

Chapter Eleven: Summary of Human Life as Radical Reality   153
    Dilthey's Idea of Human Life   153
    Ortega y Gasset and the Radical Reality of Human Life   156
    The New Being of Human Life   159
    A Comparison of Dilthey, Ortega, and Heidegger   161

Chapter Twelve: Conclusions on the Fundamental Datum of Human Life   171

Notes   181

Bibliography   187

Introduction

Human beings in the twenty-first century have many needs, and one of the most prominent of these is to discover a reality that is objective to themselves. It is the contention of this essay that if we look at the world as carefully and immediately as we are able, that is, if we look within ourselves to the world of our life, we shall find that the radical fact of our experience, the most transparent given that we possess, is our life itself, the life of each one of us. While our life is not the only real thing, nor even perhaps the most important, it is the most primary and radical reality in the sense that whatever else we may call real must first or last make its appearance within human life itself. While our life may not be prior in time or greater in extent or power than the universe, matter, deity, or nature, our life is in fact experienced as prior to these, and the context in which these must appear. Our life is prior to all theory, reason, or explanation as the pre-cognitive and ultimate perspective through which the universe is given to us at all. All secondary realities must appear within the primary reality of our life. Even biological science and all other arts and sciences must first appear and be sustained within our life, and not the other way around. Truth itself is never outside of human life; rather, truth is the light carried within our life for the determination of the world.

In this essay I shall be concerned to show that while our life is the most immediate and transparent and familiar thing we experience, it is also the most problematical, obscure, and distant entity that contemporary humanity can attempt to know. Both of these claims are the case in spite of their apparent contradiction. Yet our life is present to us in such a way that we are constantly being informed about it and present to it. Human life is what we do and what happens to us when we are present to ourselves in the circumstances in which we must always find ourselves. By this I mean that our life is transparent to us in a surrounding world of circumstances about which we must care, if we are to be at all. Our life must be understood not only as a subjective or private state within ourselves, without worldly circumstances. To understand it so is to divide our life in half and to separate it from those things about which it must take account, and be occupied with. The other half of human life is the environment or circumstances in which we exist, as Ortega y Gasset stated the situation in his philosophical battle cry, "I am myself and my circumstances." Both in its inner and outer dimension our life is primarily experienced as something immediate, transparent, and our own-most possession, though a possession held on short lease. To lose this possession is to lose all that we are or may become. But in spite of its experiential primacy and import, our life has been largely assumed in the history of philosophy, even by Kant, as a "mere appearance," something subjective or even unreal. "My life," the life of each one of us, remains one of the least acknowledged or understood areas in Western and even Eastern philosophy since its inceptions in ancient Greece, India, or China. It has usually been understood in the West as soul, mind, spirit, or consciousness. A discursive idea of human life was not generated as a philosophical presupposition until the German philosopher Wilhelm Dilthey (1833–1911) presupposed and partly developed it in his writings and teachings. But so real and present is "my life" (a term Dilthey would simply call in its generic sense "human life" or *das Leben*) that it is the contention of this essay that human life as a philosophical concept must now replace the traditional notions of substance or being in the Western tradition. This is a thesis which is yet to be defended, but any philosophical arguments which I may use to support the status of the idea of human life do not necessarily depend upon traditional assumptions about the real in traditional Western metaphysics, science, or theology. Instead, the radical reality of human life must somehow be shown to be prior to any of these.

When we ask "What is my life?" we are not asking a scientific or biological question. Nor are we inquiring into a state of matter which is the opposite of death. Instead, human life is a philosophical concept which refers to the fundamental manner in which human beings exist for themselves as individual and collective entities through time. In this sense,

Dilthey's idea of human life was said by Ortega y Gasset to be "a new philosophical continent" and "the most important philosophical idea of the latter half of the nineteenth century." Yet Dilthey's idea has remained significantly vague and undeveloped, in spite of its enormous influence upon European thought. This idea will hopefully be developed and clarified in this essay by a method of description and interpretation which has been called phenomenological, i.e., a disciplined and persistent attempt to describe and interpret our experience as it is actually lived through time. The goal here is the description and interpretation of the essential properties and structures of human life as the definite and understandable things they actually are, what the philosopher Edmund Husserl (1859–1938) called "the things themselves" (*die Sachen selbst*). This implies that the descriptions and claims made in this treatise need not necessarily be referred to an "authority" who exclusively sanctions or rejects what is claimed here. Instead, it is my hope that thoughtful readers of good will can also be the judges, critics, and participators in the construction of the idea of human life. The subject here is in fact our own-most possession, namely our life, the life of each one of us. In spite of its ambiguities and repressions, our life reveals itself through its own transparency, and we are each witnesses to it as it is actually lived. With this in mind, I shall designate our method as a self-referential phenomenology, a participating description and interpretation by the reader of the lived experience of his or her life as it is actually lived.

The question "What is real?" is one which in ordinary language usually denotes a question about what is actually the case, or what is factually true. In the history of philosophy there is a related meaning of this first denotation, which asks after what has objective existence and is not merely a name, idea, or fiction. This sense of the question may inquire about that which is self-existent, independent, or ultimate and not in need of anything else in order to be the thing it is. In this latter sense the real has often been called substance or true being. As such, the question of the real was posed by Parmenides around 475 BC. Parmenides' great contribution to philosophy was his method of reasoned proof for his claims, and he began with the assertion that real being is the substance of which the universe is composed. It is the one eternal reality. He asked about what is truly one, unchanging, or eternal reality. Because all objects of sense experience are changing and temporal, they don't belong to the realm of the real at all. Only the One is real in its unchanging identity. For Plato (427–347 BC) the real was understood as the timeless and unchanging forms (*eide*) of all particular entities. Physical things with their motion and change were merely objects of sense in perpetual becoming. Consequently, they too were unreal. For Parmenides and Plato something as temporal and changing as human life could never qualify as the radically real, for when we speak of the real, it is usually our intent to assign something like human life to a realm of appearance. The term "appearance" usually means that there exists for some region or subject a negative implication for our basic and positive interests. But the term "radical reality" implies much more than an interest, preference, or popular usage. Radical reality means here that there has been a distinction made not about something which exists, but about the form of existence in which all else appears and from which they must be explained.

Reality is the basic category of metaphysics, and the one from which all other categories gain their meaning. Radical reality is the search for the criterion that provides the most adequate perspective of meaning for all the other categories. Radical reality is the question about what absolute presuppositions are at work, or in what sort of inquiry these presuppositions are at work. The great issue here is the intellectual construction of reality, which is to be distinguished from the judgments of fact about the natural world. Reality is always the great teacher of man, but if it seems to exist only as an idea, if it exists in our personal life only as a theory, we tend to lose any sense of our own reality, our own existence. There is needed a new revelation of what we are when most other absolutes have been abandoned. We are left with our life, our disillusioned life, as our only possession. We must, as Ortega y Gasset says, take our last stand in our life as the only thing left to us. Around 1870 Dilthey made the discovery of a new reality, human life. While this idea fathered many movements, it never really got born. For both Dilthey and Ortega y Gasset this idea of human life made its first appearance in the latter half of the nineteenth century.[1] They understood human life as that existence from which our presuppositions ultimately emerge, and as the ultimate perspective from which all secondary realities, theories, and facts take their grounding and ultimate significance.

The attempt to establish the existence and the nature of the radically real was a central mission of Western philosophy, from the presocratics to Nietzsche. But with the exception of such relatively recent philosophers as Dilthey, Bradley, Royce, Bergson, Whitehead, and Ortega y Gasset, this search has been significantly abandoned in recent philosophical scholarship. Since the early part of the twentieth century professional philosophy in the English-speaking countries has been largely concerned with logic, language, and the theory of knowledge. The search for the radically real has been given over to the analysis of internally generated philosophical "problems." This labor seems to exist for the consumption of a professional academic "they" who supposedly consume and legitimize such philosophical researches. It is usually claimed by these professionals that the traditional philosophical enterprise as it was understood at the turn of the last century is over; that the search for the radically real is a pseudo-problem, and bears no relation to philosophical research, science, or the humanities at large. In contemporary Continental philosophy there exists a more or less sustained effort to "deconstruct" the problem of the radically real. The tendency there has been to treat the issue of reality as a pseudo-problem from which we must uncover the political, economic, cultural, or gender bias which supposedly grounds such a notion. In any case, the question has usually been relegated to the decision procedures of politics and ideological and gender considerations, and the search for the radically real is dismissed as an impossible and utopian goal. The upshot is that in both Anglo-American and Continental thought the philosophical search for the radically real seems to have become a dead issue. But an unintended consequence of this situation has been that without any grounding in a theory of the real, professional philosophy has tended to become more a problem to itself than a solution to its "problems." As Nietzsche predicted at the end of the nineteenth century, philosophy that is not founded in the real will itself become part of the nihilism of the twentieth century and beyond. With this consideration in mind, the present essay is presented as an essay in fundamental ontology, i.e., the branch of philosophy which investigates the basic principles and categories of the radically real. Its purpose is to show that human life is the radically real, among secondary or derivative realities. Such a reality, once philosophically designated, must also be shown to be relevant to the needs of the human condition in the twenty-first century.

Part of our task is to utilize the work of three twentieth century thinkers, Wilhelm Dilthey (1833–1911), the founder of the philosophy of human life (*Lebensphilosophie*), Martin Heidegger (1889–1976), and the Spanish thinker José Ortega y Gasset (1883–1955). Dilthey, the earliest of these, devoted his life to what he called "a critique of historical reason." By this expression he intended a methodological, empirical, and epistemological analysis of the grounds of philosophy, history, social studies, and the humanities, or what is called in German the *Geisteswissenschaften*. He also would differentiate these studies from the natural sciences, the *Naturwissenschaften*. The idea of human life is implicit in this critique of historical reason. In this sense, Dilthey remains the most significant inaugurator of the philosophy of life school of thought in Germany. But his idea of life was appropriated by Martin Heidegger in his *Being and Time* (1927). Heidegger replaced Dilthey's term *das Leben* with *Dasein*, a more abstract expression for human life or existence. The term also signifies our human "there-being" in a world. Heidegger understood Dilthey's idea of human life as only a philosophical prelude to the final question of Being itself (*Sein*). This means for him that the original idea of human life exists only as a so-called "preliminary ontology," a means of ingression into the final question of the meaning of Being itself. Dilthey's idea of human life, then, was considered to be only another philosophical anthropology and not final Being or radical reality at all. Part of the purpose of this essay is to show that, contrary to Heidegger, human life is radical reality in so far as reality can be given to human beings at all. Further, our third thinker, Ortega y Gasset, pronounced the idea of human life, even in Dilthey's undeveloped and unsystematic presentation, to be the fundamental philosophical idea of the modern era. As in the case of Heidegger, Ortega assumed Dilthey's idea as a central element in his own work. While Ortega would develop and utilize the idea beyond Dilthey's uses, he too failed to write an extended or complete treatise upon the idea and its categories. In this essay we shall attempt to formalize and develop the notion of human life and its sources into an extended and categorical form. In other words, we shall draw upon certain of the writings of Dilthey, Heidegger, and Ortega, to the end of a formal and extended treatise.

There are many ways to approach the understanding of human life, one of which is to place the idea in the context of an earlier development in the history of thought. Such a crucial development is to be found in the seventeenth century with the rise of mathematical science and the response it received from thinkers in the humanities, social studies, and history. One thinker and scholar who responded was an obscure Neapolitan named Giambattista Vico (1668–1744). His importance has gone largely unrecognized until recently. He was ignored for one hundred years after his death, but he was among the first to grasp fully the relation of history and social studies to the rise of mathematical science, and by implication to the nature of human life and its works. Vico's thought informed a tradition in the history of ideas that is still in the process of unfolding in such diverse areas as philosophy of history and social studies, the thought of Herder, Goethe, Coleridge, Marx, Croce, and James Joyce. Vico also anticipated the intellectual life world not only of Dilthey but of historicism and existentialism in the twentieth century. Vico's goal was the creation of "a new science" which he believed could "penetrate the thick darkness" which obscures human life and its world. While a professor at the University of Naples, he published *On the Study Methods of Our Time* (1709). One of the first important critical reactions to the regnant rationalism of Descartes, Vico's book attacked the Cartesian tendency to place primary truth value upon mathematics and physics to the neglect of history and the humanities and ordinary human life. A new method of understanding was needed, he thought, for history and the humanistic studies. Aristotle had anticipated Vico's demand for a new method of understanding, with his notion of *phronesis* or the practical wisdom which is necessary for the conduct of ordinary human life, especially economics, rhetoric, social relations, and the practical arts of life. But Vico believed that with the rise of mathematical science in the seventeenth century Aristotle's older category of *phronesis* had been subverted. Descartes, rationalism, and mathematical science have granted a higher truth priority to another of Aristotle's means of knowing which he called *theoria*, or the knowing faculty and abstract thinking required for physics, mathematics and metaphysics. Because for Descartes Aristotle's *theoria* had subverted the common-sense, life-oriented faculty of *phronesis*, there was a tendency for mathematical science in the seventeenth century to ignore or despise those subjects which dealt with human life and history. Such subjects, it was believed, could not be understood with the rationality or authority of the abstract sciences of mathematics, physics, or metaphysics.

8   *Introduction*

Vico claimed that both the new mathematical physics and Cartesian rationalism which explained it were never able to achieve an authentic unity of method in understanding the world, but only one species of it, namely the mathematical-deductive formulation of the laws of physical nature. Contrary to this tendency, Vico's life was devoted to the formulation of a method that would be valid for the understanding of human life and its works, especially history and society. To this end, Vico advanced a new formula for the understanding of the nature of truth and the human life world, which he phrased in the Latin expression *Verum et factum convertuntur*. By this formula, which has since taken its place in the history of philosophy as one of the theories of truth, Vico meant that the idea of truth converts into what human beings have made or created in time. Opposing the anti-historical elements of the prevailing Cartesianism, he asserted that history is a valid object of human knowledge, because human beings have themselves constructed history and culture. Vico's thesis here implies that we have knowledge only of what we ourselves have made. He held the conviction that God is immanent in nature, and the reason present in nature is a creation of God's own being. But human beings can approach this inner nature of God's created world only externally through sense perception and hypothesis formation. The innermost meaning of God's creation remains unknowable to human beings, because they did not themselves create the innermost parts of the world and its meaning. Both history and culture, on the other hand, were created by human beings, and authentic knowledge is obtainable, because the sociohistorical world and its meanings were imputed to it by human beings. This means that human beings are the cause of their own meaningful effects in history and culture, and these "effects" for Vico are found in the modifications of our own minds. His thesis implies that our humanly created world actually possesses two aspects, which we may call an inner and outer dimension. One of these is material and the other is understandable as a form of human life. For example, the outer physical motions which accompany a human action, such as the sound waves of a speech act, or the paper and ink that compose a check we write for a hospital bill, are not sufficient conditions for understanding the whole sense of either a speech or the bank check. While it is true that these actions and creations always possess a material embodiment, such as sound waves or paper, the speech act and the creation of a check must possess what we contemporarily call intentionality; i.e., they are both products of human creation and understanding, and the whole check or speech act must involve other elements beyond its physical and material aspects, such as meanings, symbols, will, purpose, and value. This implies that our human actions and creations are always significant beyond their physical and sensate properties.

The goal of Vico's *New Science* (1744) was the establishment of the universal principles of history and culture. His theory of truth in this respect comes to the claim that the outer and material aspects of the historical and cultural world can be unified with its "inner" aspects, because in all human creations and actions the agent self-consciously performs the subjective and symbolic operations that compose the meanings, values, volitions and purposes, the subjective or inner significance, of his or her creations and actions in history. These elements are understandable because the human consciousness which recognizes itself in the objects made and actions performed is the cause of intelligibility in both. Put another way, human beings are both the makers and interpreters of history and culture. It is human beings who make history and culture, and it is human beings who understand them.

While Vico was the first to point to the methods and philosophical presuppositions for the understanding of the cultural-historical world, it was Dilthey who over one hundred years later would inhabit the new continent of human life with his vision of subject matter and method in his critique of historical reason. Vico's theory that the truth converts into what is made by man would come to expression in Dilthey's theory of understanding, or what he would call *Verstehen*. The concerns which animated Vico's life were to be shared by Dilthey, but the commanding and immediate issue which Dilthey faced was not the rise of mathematical science, as in Vico's case, but the nineteenth century positivist claim that all explanation in the sociohistorical studies must be founded in the methods and materials of the natural sciences.

As with Vico before him, Dilthey claimed that human life and its creations must be understood through a new science. The new science would attempt to interpret human life from its outer expressions, actions, and creations to its inner meaning. Dilthey called his new method of interpretation *Verstehen*, or the understanding of human life from its outer expressions (*Lebensäusserrungen*). For both Vico and Dilthey their respective sciences would act as viable alternatives to the assumptions and methods of seventeenth century mathematical sciences and the nineteenth century positivism which confronted Dilthey. While these assumptions and methods are complicated in their history and development, it is important to present in brief outline the following generalizations upon these two eras and their scientific forms. It is only then that we may comprehend the idea of human life as a response to their primary philosophical and scientific presuppositions, which we can briefly enumerate as follows:

(1) The world is composed of elemental material bodies whose motions and interrelations can be expressed mathematically as "the laws of nature." This claim implies that given any physical cause, such as the gravitational influence of one body on another, there can be determined a given and specific effect, such as the mathematically predictable orbit of a planet around the sun. Physical phenomena, when so understood, were usually believed to exhibit in their causal relations the same necessity that axioms bear to theorems.

(2) The real status of nature can only be authentically understood by reference to its quantitative and mathematically expressed properties. These were the so-called "primary qualities" of physical bodies, namely weight, velocity, figure, position, magnitude, and number. Such primary qualities were believed to be the essence of matter in that they are the elements of the external world of nature as it is in itself, apart from its perceptual and subjective appearance to human beings. Our ordinary sense experiences of nature, that is, the perceived sense qualities of physical things such as colors, smells, sounds, taste, and touch were designated as the "secondary qualities" of nature. Only the primary qualities were considered to be the essence of matter, in that they were the best subjects for mathematical quantification and consequently most available for use in formulating the laws of nature. These primary qualities were also considered the best expression of the nature of the material world as it is in itself, apart from the subjective apprehension of them through the senses. For example, Galileo (1564–1642) believed that our ordinary sensation of heat is actually a subjective illusion, an imperfect representation of heat as it exists in its primary state. Heat in its primary state of existence is only the friction of elementary atomic bodies in

motion. For Galileo reality applies only to nature in its primary status, such as the friction of atomic bodies. The qualities of our subjective feeling of a phenomenon like heat have only a mediated or secondary status as the real.

It is in the writings of Rene Descartes (1596–1650) that we begin to feel the impact of these philosophical assumptions for the idea of human life, the humanities, and history. In his *Meditations on First Philosophy* and *The Discourse on Method* he claimed that the humanities and history were both subrational and uncertain, because of their lack of a universally valid method. These studies provided no path to the discovery of self-evident and deductively ordered, mathematically formulated laws of nature. In all his writings he advocated what presently is called a monomethodological approach to knowledge and truth, the claim that there exists but one method of reasoned inquiry into reality: the comprehension of nature in her primary and mathematically quantifiable status. He equated all secondary qualities and subjective sense experience with subrational conscious states. It is no accident that Descartes' thought makes no adequate provision for the humanistic studies and history. Indeed, the implications of his assumptions and methods were fatal to them. The very subject matter of these studies is necessarily subjective, sensate, and human-life oriented. Humanistic and historical studies cannot be explicated in the clear and distinct quantitative terms of the primary qualities and quantitative mathematical terms, without seemingly eliminating everything the world of human life is about, e.g., deliberative human actions, first person emotional and volitional states, goals and values, ordinary subjective sense experiences, culture, symbols, social relations, records, artifacts, and the whole significance of ordinary language. In short, because Descartes' presuppositions about method and the ultimately real are incompatible with an understanding of our ordinary subjective life world, he confined human life, its works, history, and subjective mode of experience to a subrational and unreal status.

Descartes' assumptions about method and physical reality were incompatible with the entire idea of human life as we are trying to understand it. Both Vico and Dilthey contended that human life in historical time need not be necessarily subjective, nor can human life without distortion be explicated in the manner of the sciences of nature or reduced to the quantifiable status of material objects. But because the rationalistic and reductionistic assumptions of Descartes' mathematical science were incompatible with the understanding of human life and its works as they are actually lived, human life would tend to be confined by both the later rationalistic and positivistic traditions to a questionably real status. And there it tended to remain until the later nineteenth century with the work of Dilthey.

CHAPTER ONE

Wilhelm Dilthey and the Idea of Human Life

Wilhelm Dilthey, born in 1833, was the son of a Protestant minister in Germany's Rhineland. His rural and pietistic surroundings seem to have given him a sense of the inwardness which would later reveal itself in his belief that the immediacy of our inner life is the authentic ground of all philosophy. He studied history and philosophy at the University of Berlin, where he sat under such famous scholars as Jacob Grimm and Leopold von Ranke. It was under the influence of the latter, especially in his famous historical seminar, that Dilthey prepared for a career as a historian of ideas. He assisted in the editing of the letters of Friedrich Schleiermacher (1768–1834), and this theologian's methods of textual interpretation would influence Dilthey's theory of the hermeneutical understanding of human life through the interpretation of its outer expressions. He chose as his field of concentration the history of philosophical and literary ideas, and he is often seen as the founder of the history of ideas as an intellectual discipline. Dilthey's philosophical, literary, and historical inclinations would later help him to construct a critical foundation for the methods and subject matter of the human studies, which he would designate as "the critique of historical reason." While teaching at the University of Basel in 1867 he formed a friendship with Jacob Burckhardt (1818–1897), who was at that time the reigning monarch of historical and humanistic scholarship in Europe. It is interesting to note that Dilthey seems to have had no association with Nietzsche, who taught at Basel at that time. In 1882 he returned to the University of Berlin to occupy the chair of Hegel and Lotze in philosophy until his death in 1911. Dilthey's complete writings have been edited and published and they presently appear in over twenty volumes.

Yet there is not in these works an extended or formal philosophical treatise on the specific idea of human life per se. Rather, this idea remains in his work a pervasive notion, a background assumption that would inform his writings upon the critique of historical reason, history, methodology, biography, psychology, literature, and philosophy.[1]

Dilthey was also the prime inaugurator of the philosophy of life (*Lebensphilosophie*) school of thought in Germany. For him this meant that philosophy and indeed all thought and reason are ultimately grounded in the varieties of human life as it exists through historical time. His idea of human life also guides his scholarship in methodology, the history of metaphysical and literary thinking from ancient Greece through the seventeenth century, and finally his biographical studies of Schleiermacher and the young Hegel. Dilthey would claim in 1867 that the heart of his philosophy of human life had developed from the thought of Goethe and Schiller; and the influence of Kant, Hegel, Schelling, Schleiermacher, and the British empiricists can also be felt in his thought. Ortega y Gasset likened Dilthey's idea of human life to the founding of a new intellectual continent, which exerted a powerful force on the thought of Karl Jaspers, Karl Mannheim, Martin Buber, R.G. Collingwood, Ortega y Gasset, and Martin Heidegger. For Dilthey all of the *Geisteswissenschaften*, or the human studies of history, philosophy, literature, art, religion, law, social studies, music, psychology, and education, were founded in human life. Dilthey would attempt to show that human life is the ground of the autonomy of the human studies. These could be philosophically founded only in his method of understanding life's history and culture, which he called *Verstehen*. Part of his program was to show that the methods and materials of the natural sciences (*Naturwissenschaften*) were not efficacious for the understanding of the human studies. It must be noted here once again that Dilthey never achieved a conclusive ordering of his ideas upon human life and its method, and he fretted over this omission to the end of his career. Part of our work here will be the attempt to piece together his often scattered and suggestive ideas upon human life and its assertions. But in spite of its inchoate status, his thinking was developed enough that he considered it part of his critique of historical reason.

What then is Dilthey's idea of human life in its minimal senses? How can we approach it? We may begin by noting that in normal English usage the term "human life" usually applies to the biological status of *homo sapiens*, the opposite of death. But for Dilthey the German term for human life is *das Leben*, and it refers to human life as our lived experience, and to the meaningfully connected experiences of human beings in their individual and collective existence, past, present, and future. The collective totality of human life is history itself. Sometimes the term "human life" also refers to "the interaction of consciousness and nature in their achievement of purposes through historical time."[2] In this essay the idea of human life is understood as the life of each one of us, and it is the ultimate perspective through which human beings are in the universe. It is understood as the final horizon in which all thought, knowledge, and experience must show themselves. Not a "mere appearance" as Kant thought, but a positive and real thing, the reality of human life is an existence within whose context all else that we call real must first or last appear and be explained. Also for Dilthey the idea of human life is in part the acknowledgment that all philosophy, indeed all thinking, must somehow appear within the context of human life. It is human life and not the traditional philosophical category of substance which is for him the radically real. No rational, discursive, or factual thinking, and no intuition, can penetrate behind human life to a deeper explanatory or ontological ground. There is none. Dilthey claimed that the ruling notion of his career was to construct philosophy from the basis of human life itself.[3]

Human life, the life of each one of us, both appears to us and is given to us as a subjective phenomenon in the sense that it is lived (*erlebt*) as our own-most conscious state. It does not appear as a material, overt, or external thing in the physical world. Yet the external world is never presented to us apart from human life, and human life and its world always exist together in a bipolar intentional relation. But human life is always in the state of a givenness to itself, an object to itself that is lived and reflected upon from the inside. Transparent and immediately given, human life is lived in a definite state such as "X is painful," "Y is sweet," or "I fear z." Its givenness is equivalent to its being lived in such a way that the subject and object of experience become one. The person intends his or her state as an object of awareness (*innere Wahrnehmung*) that is transparent to itself. As George Berkeley (1685–1753) contended in another context, the actuality of human life is its being perceived of itself (*esse est percipi*), and it is lived or perceived as it is. Known to itself in its temporal connectedness, it is understood without hypothesis, proof, or derivation from the laws of the external world, and there is no need for outer sense perception to provide the empirical basis for our judgments. We comprehend human life as it is without the mediation of external sense perception.[4] In this sense, then, human life is understood as the totality of our inner experiences in their lived connectedness through time (*innen erlebten Zusammenhang*). As an immediacy which is our own unique possession, and not another's, our life is what is happening to us right now, what we are doing right now, what is before us in a now present. Yet human life retains its past in its memory and temporal construction, and it both projects and anticipates its future.

For Dilthey the experiences of human life are interconnected within a mental system, and in his *Ideas Concerning Descriptive and Analytical Psychology* he described the nature of such a system. The term "system" for him refers to the fact that the experiences of human life are given to us in the context of a part-whole relationship. Put another way, through introspection we can observe that our ideas, feelings, volitions, and desires are always given to us within a greater mental context of which they are parts. All judgments within our life presuppose the existence of such a mental system. Dilthey called the most general and identifiable relations between the parts and the whole of the mental system the "categories" of human life. He never developed a total theory of such categories, for each of them was only examined as it related to the topic he was immediately considering in his various works. Also he never attempted to develop the categories of life by means of the transcendental deduction which Kant developed for his *Critique of Pure Reason*. Nor did Dilthey attempt to derive the categories of human life from those which were only appropriate for the sciences of nature, as Kant had done. Instead, he formulated his categories from the structures already implicit in human life and immediately given to introspection. Dilthey's analysis of human life and its categories was for him part of his "critique of historical reason," and any authentic understanding of the human studies could only be achieved through such a critique.

In this introductory preface we shall consider only a few of his most prominent categories, and a more complete analysis of them must be reserved for the later categorical section of this essay. But for now we may briefly mention his primary category of temporality (*Zeitlichkeit*). Temporality, like all the categories of human life, designates a structure of life so essential and basic that without it human life could not be the entity it actually is. Temporality indicates that our life is lived as constant change, a process of unresting advance in which the present becomes the past, and the future is lived as a continual becoming of the present. We live in a continually advancing present, and the present is defined by Dilthey as the filling of a moment of time with reality. The present alone is fully experienced by us, but both the past and the future actually exist for us in the present as either remembered or anticipated. Also, any authentic understanding of our life's temporality requires that we make a distinction between an external clock time and the primordial lived time of human life. World time, the time of public clocks, is a secondary and derived mode of temporality by which we attempt to calibrate the flow of lived or inner duration by correlating it with the motions of spatial objects such as the earth, the sun, or the hands of a clock. Since Aristotle there has existed the tendency in philosophy to understand time as the counting or calibration of the motions of natural objects. The duration, flow, or stream of our life's lived time has been both measured and externalized by its translation into our counting of the motion of clock hands which indicate the seconds, minutes, and hours that have been previously correlated with the turning of the earth with respect to the sun. But while such time is crucial for our scientific, social, or economic existence, it is always a nominal and arbitrary derivation which derives its final significance from its correlation with the duration of human life in its flow from the past, to the present, to the future. The universal construction of world time has obscured the primacy and duration of lived time, and its premises can neither explain nor describe how lived time can retain the past in the present and project both upon the future. Clock time cannot, in short, account for the temporal structure of human experience in general. By understanding temporality only as clock time, we have obscured the true status of temporality. Only lived time assigns final significance to world time, and it remains philosophically prior to it. Through the artificially imposed priority of world time in the public sphere, lived time's real priority has been obscured or forgotten. Dilthey's thought is in part an attempt to construct the priority of lived time as history.

Another of Dilthey's fundamental categories of human life is world (*Welt*). This category does not imply that human life is necessarily related to the earth (*Erde*). Rather, it indicates that our life always exists in an intentional relation to circumstances. Put another way, the "I" always exists in relation to something not an "I," and this is an environment with which it must deal. In this sense our life exists as a bipolar relation between itself and its world, a relation which Dilthey called *Ich und Gegenstand*. Our "world" circumstances may include material things, other people, human creations, the earth, or even our universe at large. But in all these cases our life exists in constant relationship and orientation to some content outside itself. This relationship and orientation is so constant that even if we retreat into our own interiority exclusively, we still remain necessarily in a relation to what surrounds us. Dilthey understood this relation as an inner-outer dynamic which recognizes that while our life is lived within us, it nevertheless strives constantly to assert itself into a public, outer world. Human life reaches from its own interiority to the outer world through what Dilthey called "life assertions" (*Lebensäusserungen*). Such assertions include anything from language to gestures, cultural creations, institutions, overt actions such as writing a check or constructing a home—anything through which human life may externalize itself or control the outer environment through material means into a common outer world available to the senses. Human life assertions are one aspect of the I-world dialogue which transcends the individual through the life expressions of larger forms such as cultural objects, artistic creations, nations, cultures, or historical eras. These life assertions become the subject matter of all sociohistorical inquiry for Dilthey, who considered history as human life conceived from the viewpoint of the whole of mankind.[5] When so formulated, history becomes understood as the totality of human thought, feelings, volitions, actions, purposes, language, institutions, values, symbols, culture, art, religion, and philosophy in their interconnections through the whole of historical time. Dilthey thought of this interconnected whole as the *geistige Welt* or the mind-affected world in historical time. In this connection it was Dilthey who first used the term human life not with reference to a biological entity, but to the whole of human life as history.[6]

Our human life, then, becomes externalized in a public world of human history which is available to others for their recognition and interpretation. This fact brings us to the most famous of Dilthey's categories of human life, which he called *Verstehen* or understanding. Through this category Dilthey is telling us that the mind-affected world, the world of human history and culture, is not explained or understood by the laws, methods, and materials of the physical sciences (*Naturwissenschaften*), but by the understanding (*Verstehen*) of the life expressions of another through historical time. As such the category of *Verstehen* becomes for Dilthey a technical, methodological term which refers to the understanding of another's actions, creations, purposes to which any meaning can be assigned by an interpreting agent. In other words, *Verstehen* is the method of the human studies, the *Geisteswissenschaften*. *Verstehen* was for him the chief means of distinguishing the human studies from the natural sciences. The natural sciences explain (*erklären*) by reference to the laws of external nature, and the human studies understand human life through its outer expressions through historical time. Not only is human life understood from its life assertions through historical time, but human life is fundamentally historical by nature. This means that for Dilthey human life can never be adequately conceived without reference to its historical dimension. This aspect of our human life he called by another category, which he designated as *Geschictlichkeit*, or historicity.

In the later writings of Dilthey, history became the basis of his researches into human life. "Whatever human life may be," he wrote, "history will inform us of it." But Dilthey saw the idea of human life and its historicity threatened by the positivist attempt to subject human life and its expressions solely to the methods and materials of the natural sciences. As Vico before him noticed, the rise of mathematical science in the seventeenth century tended to promote the assumption that human life is merely a subjective or subrational phenomenon or "a mere presentation," as Kant would have it. The experience of human life was considered significant by many only in so far as it could be translated into the quantifiable and physical denominators that were demanded for the preconceptions of mathematical science. For both Vico and Dilthey these scientific preconceptions must be reconsidered for their relevance to the life world, and not the other way around. Finally, human life must be understood as a reality in its own right, one that precedes the whole construction of mathematical science in the seventeenth century.

In sum, the idea of human life became a formal object of philosophical research when Dilthey discovered it as the primary given in human experience which precedes all abstraction, theory, or metaphysics. As such, human life became for him the ground of all philosophical intuitions which may arise. All metaphysical systems in one way or another try to account for what happens when we attempt to comprehend the basic fact of human life and its categories. Further, all meaning, value, and purpose are grounded in the life experiences of those individuals who exist in the temporal duration and actual circumstances of human life. For this reason the general nature and specific properties of human life cannot for Dilthey be understood through metaphysical or scientific systems, yet human life is the starting point of both philosophy and the human studies. Dilthey also emphasized that the varieties of human life are experienced by human beings as history, and human life can never be grasped as merely the "knowing subject" of Locke, Hume, and Kant. Human life must also be comprehended as the whole of thinking, valuing, willing, and imaginative components of our nature. Finally, for Dilthey the means by which we understand human life is not through the methods and materials of the natural sciences but through *Verstehen*, the interpretation of human life through its life expressions.[7] Dilthey was the paramount philosopher of human life, and he formulated his idea from about 1860 to 1870. He established from the beginning that his subject was not biology, natural science, or even psychology. In this way he distinguished himself from such later thinkers as Bergson and Nietzsche. These men were overly involved with the subjective, personal, and psychological components of the individual.[8] As a counter to these tendencies he restricted the term "human life" to a technical philosophical expression for the aggregate of human consciousness through historical time. But Dilthey failed to extend and formalize his discovery. He left his idea as a general expression for the totality of life which precedes all theory, abstraction, world views, and explanations which have been advanced as solutions to the enigma of human life itself. The term "human life" becomes nothing less than the relation of the individual to the whole of humanity in its historical, social, and cultural continuity.

From the beginning Dilthey rejected any association of human life with Kant's critical analysis of the transcendental conditions of human experience. Kant's categories of the understanding are for Dilthey immanent in human life. Always transparent to itself, human life is understood out of its own givenness to itself through reflective self-observation (*Besinnung*) of its own properties and categories. Human life must appear within the human beings who live it and not in external nature. The task of philosophy is to interpret the structure and content of life's appearance to itself. Such self-interpretation preempts any scientific or psychological attempt to explain or construct human life from theories, materials, or presuppositions which are derived from outside of human life. The authentic *cogito*, the "I think" of Descartes, is always human life's understanding of itself, the attempt to grasp its nature through its own transparency to itself. Finally, Dilthey used the term human life to refer to his contention that we are radically historical beings, and by this he meant that the human agents who investigate history are identical in their human nature to those who have lived and acted in historical time. The term "human nature" becomes an expression for the medium which exists between those who make history and those who attempt to understand it, a general expression for the universal intelligibility of human life through historical time, past, present, and future.[9] We must now turn briefly to Martin Heidegger's so-called "question of Being" in its relation to what he called *Dasein*, or human life as a metaphysical problem, and briefly as well to Ortega y Gasset's relation to Heidegger.

CHAPTER TWO

The Question of Being in Martin Heidegger and Ortega y Gasset

Heidegger's thought, especially in his *Being and Time*, is both an appropriation and refusal of Dilthey's thinking upon human life. Ortega y Gasset, on the other hand, assumed the idea, developed it, and fashioned it to the special presuppositions of his thought. We may begin to unpack this situation by a look at the earlier Heidegger, who was the most influential and famous European philosopher of the twentieth century, and his relation to Dilthey is an important part of his significance.

Martin Heidegger was born at Messkirch, Baden, in the Black Forest area of Germany. He was the son of the sexton of St. Martin's Catholic Church. He attended the local Gymnasium in Constance, and the University of Freiburg, where he studied theology and philosophy. He had earlier been influenced by Franz Brentano's *On the Manifold Meaning of Being According to Aristotle* (1862), a work which started the philosopher on his life's task, the search for the meaning of Being. He read Husserl's *Logical Investigations*, and his interest in logic and medieval thought was expressed in his 1916 *Habilitation* thesis entitled *The Doctrine of Categories and Judgments in Duns Scotus*. After a brief service in World War II, Heidegger became Husserl's assistant at the University of Freiburg. At this time he became interested in Dilthey's work, which he regarded as an alternative to what he considered to be Husserl's excessive rationalism. From 1923 to 1928 he taught at Marburg University, and while there he developed friendships with Rudolf Bultmann, Paul Tillich, Max Scheler, and Karl Jaspers. During this period he built his cabin retreat in the Black Forest, where he wrote the material that would come to fruition in 1927 with the publication of the first half of *Being and Time* in Husserl's *Yearbook for Philosophy and Phenomenological Research*. This work would establish Heidegger as Germany's leading philosopher, and the rumor would spread that a "hidden king" had at last appeared in German philosophy. Though Heidegger became Husserl's successor at Freiburg, Husserl would later claim that Heidegger's *Being and Time* was only another variety of "life philosophy" (*Lebensphilosophie*). As though he were anticipating this appraisal, Heidegger's self-proclaimed plan in his *Being and Time* was to pursue an existential analysis of human existence in light of the question of the meaning of Being itself. This meant for Heidegger that human being could only gain an authentic understanding through his analysis of its relation to the idea of Being (*Sein*) itself. This, and not Dilthey's philosophy of life, was the task of his *Being and Time*.

Heidegger's thought drew from the earlier phenomenological movement in Germany, especially from the work of Edmund Husserl, and Heidegger would appropriate Husserl's phenomenological method in his *Being and Time*.[1] Husserl's earlier *Logical Investigations* (1900–1901) had purported to be a philosophical description of the "things themselves," or the objects of our immediate experience. Philosophical knowledge could only be attained by a disciplined method of "seeing" such phenomena. For Husserl the phenomenological method could attain a "pure reflection" upon what is given in consciousness, through a rigorous description of all immediate experience. Husserl held that all existence can in theory be reflected in consciousness, and consciousness is characterized by what Husserl's teacher Franz Brentano (1838–1907) would call intentionality. Intentionality is the thesis that all consciousness is consciousness of something; that consciousness has no status apart from that of which it is aware. We may even intend our consciousness itself and become aware of all that is immanent there. For Heidegger the phenomenological method was basically the disciplined examination of phenomena as they are given in and through themselves. He used this method in his *Being and Time*, and he understood phenomenology as the reflection upon all phenomena which reveal themselves to consciousness.

Heidegger's *Being and Time* is primarily a description of the basic structures of human existence as they are revealed in and through our human being (*Dasein*). The delineation of these structures (he called them *Existentialia*) was for him only a prelude to his search for the meaning of Being itself. The examination of our human being, he thought, was the means of ingression into the problem of Being itself.

Heidegger's philosophical goal was proposed on the title page of his *Being and Time* as follows: "The Interpretation of Dasein in Terms of Temporality and the Explication of Time as the Transcendental Horizon for the Question of Being." The part of this work which was actually published in 1927 as *Being and Time* was entitled "Preparatory Fundamental Analysis of Dasein and Temporality." The thesis here was not a new philosophical anthropology as Husserl claimed, nor a philosophy of human life, but a philosophical preparation for the question of the meaning of Being which he intended to pursue in all his later works.

In 1928 Heidegger assumed Husserl's chair at the University of Freiburg. But after the publication of his *Being and Time* it would come to light that the master and the pupil disagreed on such fundamental issues as Husserl's postulation of a so-called "transcendental ego." Further, Heidegger judged Husserl's work to be a modern recapitulation of the Cartesian "idealism" which would attempt to reduce human existence to a form of pure consciousness. Heidegger would also claim that human being (*Dasein*) does not actually exist in a transcendental realm, but in only a radically historical and worldly finitude which is philosophically prior to any transcendental realm of pure consciousness. Heidegger would search for the meaning of Being through the initial examination of human being in his *Being and Time*, and from this point he promised to advance to the examination of Being itself. His search for the meaning of Being itself, he claimed, is more fundamental than Husserl's project of searching for a pure transcendental consciousness. Prior to any such search there must take place a fundamental examination of our actual existence in historical time and worldly circumstances.[2]

Heidegger's philosophical project, then, was nothing less than the attempt to rethink the problem of the meaning of Being itself, an attempt to understand Being as a collective noun which names something both definite and real. The term Being here is supposed to serve as the most universal, simple, and inclusive term for "what there is." As such, it is supposed to transcend all the particular "things that are," and yet to remain the ground or common possession of them all. In this sense, the question of the meaning of Being remains the most authentic question that thought can undertake. For Heidegger the question of the meaning of Being was first posed by the presocratic philosophers. In Parmenides, for example, the question was undertaken as the problem of what is truly real. In his poem "On Truth" Parmenides intended by the question "What is real?" to designate the problem of naming the necessary characteristics of true Being itself. It must be an abstract, rationally conceived entity without reference to sense experience or motion. It must be understood as a unity, a oneness that is eternal. Only the One truly "is," and the "many things" of our sense experience were seen as unreal and changing. For Plato Being is to be understood as the unchanging and immaterial forms (*eide*) which can only be comprehended by the faculty of reason. For Aristotle Being becomes understood as substance (*ousia*), or that which possesses attributes, but is itself the attribute of nothing. Spinoza (1632–1677) also understood reality to be substance which is conceived in and through itself as absolute existence, and remains the cause of itself. It is the contention of this essay that the idea of substance, true being, or radical reality must be conceived in our era as human life. This was also the notion of Ortega y Gasset, who believed that the previous attempts to determine the real apart from human life must be abandoned.[3] Further, the idea of human life must replace the Parmenidean and Platonic assumption that the radically real can only be understood as a timeless and unchanging entity which exists apart from human sensation and volition, apart from sense experience and temporality. The idea of the radically real must be conceived within the lived time and immediacy of human life itself.

José Ortega y Gasset was the son of an editor and lawyer in Madrid. He was born in 1883 into the culture and privilege of the liberal upper classes. He attended a Jesuit school which educated him in Latin and Greek and granted him a bachelor's degree at fourteen. He went on to the University of Madrid and received his *licenciado* in philosophy and letters in 1902 and the doctorate degree in 1904. He was examined for the degree by Miguel Unamuno. Ortega held that the Spain of his youth was intellectually and culturally provincial, and he believed this to the end of his life. He saw his mission in life as one of bringing European culture and government to Spain, a mission opposed by his teacher Miguel Unamuno (1864–1936).

In 1905 he began postdoctoral studies in Germany at the University of Leipzig. Ortega's period in Germany was devoted both to the study of Kant's first *Critique* (Ortega believed that a grasp of Kant is the *sine qua non* of any claim to philosophical competence) and to the experimental psychology of Wilhelm Wundt (1832–1920). He gained a scholarship to continue his studies at the University of Berlin. Ortega later said that while he was there he never heard of or met Dilthey, the thinker he later claimed had changed both the intellectual mind of Europe and his own. (Dilthey had just retired from full-time teaching and was conducting private seminars in his home.) Dilthey's *Einleitung in die Geisteswissenschaften* (1883) and his Schleiermacher studies were then available in print, but Ortega claimed that this work was never available in the University library when he tried to read it. We may recall here that Dilthey never published during his lifetime many of the works for which he later became famous, and even a philosopher of Max Scheler's rank did not fully understand Dilthey's importance at this early period. Ortega became aware of the full import of Dilthey's work only in 1929, and he claimed that the four years required to learn it had caused him to lose ten years of intellectual development. Later he concluded that the manner in which Dilthey was a thinker would constitute the future of European philosophy. His reference here was probably to Dilthey's empirical account of human life and to his distinction between *Empire* and *Empirismus*, the former being the authentic and the latter only a sensate positivist account of human experience. In this sense Ortega saw Dilthey's empirical subjectivism as the major principle of his era.

In 1907 Ortega joined the neo-Kantian movement inaugurated by Hermann Cohen and Paul Natorp at the University of Marburg. These teachers influenced Ortega by their criticism of speculative metaphysics and by their methodological distinction between the natural and the human studies. It was through Cohen and Natorp that Ortega learned of a modern pedagogical program for public schools in Europe. It was at Marburg, too, that Ortega became aware of the incipient phenomenological movement. At first he was so impressed by this thought that he considered it as an alternative to neo-Kantianism. Later he would correct this early estimate. At this period he came to know the philosophers Nicolai Hartmann and Ernst Cassirer.

In 1908 he returned to the University of Madrid, married, and taught logic and ethics at the Escuela Superior del Magisterio, then returned for further study at Marburg. The following year he criticized Miguel Unamuno as a *hispanizante* who upheld Spanish educational traditionalism against the Europeanism which was then appearing in Spain. In 1911 he took the chair of metaphysics at the University of Madrid, where he taught until 1936 at the start of the Spanish Civil War. He founded the premier intellectual journal of contemporary Spain, *Revista de Occidente (Review of the West)*, a journal which continues to this day. In 1921 to 1922 he gave a course of lectures which he would publish as *The Modern Theme*, a work he considered the best single representation of his philosophical position. Yet this book is too early to be so considered, because it does not adequately reflect his idea of human life, the historicity of human life, or historical reason.

Ortega urged all his life the reformation of Spain by the *europeizantes*. This movement would model education after the empirical sciences and the politics of Europe since the industrial revolution. This outlook would assume concrete, institutional form with the founding of "The School of Madrid," a group of thinkers and writers which included Xavier Zubiri, José Gaos, José Mora, Julián Marías, and Ortega himself. Ortega was a member of the Constituent Assembly of the Second Spanish Republic in 1930 and following. He continued to publish his journal through the dictatorship of General Primo de Rívera, who would close the University of Madrid in 1929. Ortega resigned his professorship in protest of the closing, but he continued to lecture in a local theater on the subject "What Is Philosophy?" With the outbreak of the Spanish Civil War in 1936 he was forced into exile in Argentina and various European capitals. He went to Paris and was subsequently offered a position at Harvard, which he refused. In 1938 he lectured in Holland. He returned to the University of Buenos Aires, where he wrote *Man and People*, which he considered his major contribution to social studies. He then returned to Europe in 1942 and lived in Lisbon. He returned to Madrid in 1945 but did not participate in politics or teaching, because Franco refused him teaching and political rights. In 1948 he founded with his disciple Julián Marías the Institute of Humanities, which the government closed in 1950. He spent his last years in a rootless routine of travel and lecturing, and he was awarded honorary degrees from Marburg and Glasgow Universities. His last years were marred by homelessness, disappointment, and mental depression. He died of cancer in Madrid at the age of seventy-two. With his death contemporary Spain had lost her greatest son.

Ortega served many standards, philosophical, educational, political, journalistic, and literary. He was one of the twentieth century's greatest literary stylists, in terms of clarity and depth, two characteristics which do not often coincide. Albert Camus thought of him as one of the greatest stylists and writers in European history, though he remained Spanish to the core. Ortega believed that modern humanity has lost its orientation in history, and he sought to establish certainty, orientation, and clarity in the reality of human life. With Dilthey and Heidegger he believed that our era is in need of a philosophical principle objective to itself. The idea of human life was this principle.

Ortega's idea of human life bears an important relation to the early Heidegger's search for the meaning of Being as it is posed in his *Being and Time*. Heidegger had claimed that the question of human life or *Dasein* was only a preliminary issue to the whole question of the meaning of Being itself. But for Ortega y Gasset the question of Being must be confined to human life. For Ortega human life becomes the basic philosophic issue, and not only a point of departure for the further question of the meaning of Being as such. Heidegger's idea of Being would transcend human life and nullify its priority as radical reality. Further, Heidegger's understanding of the question of the meaning of Being was both unclarified and undeveloped, and his use of the technical term *Dasein* had only replaced the simpler and more natural expression of human life (*das Leben*) as it appears in Dilthey. Heidegger's question of the meaning of Being for Ortega is in fact only a modern equivalent for the scholastic doctrine of *Ens*. For the medievals *Ens* was an abstract noun which designated the most general, simple, and inclusive characteristics that could be applied to anything, and the Heideggerean term *Dasein* is only a subordinate typology of the medieval concept of Being. It is never clear how *Dasein* or human being could ever lead us to the meaning of Being itself. *Dasein* remains always in an unfinished relation to Being itself, and Ortega believed that Heidegger should have confined the question of Being to human life. Had he done so, his search for the meaning of Being would have ended in the idea of human life. Ortega rightly predicted that there would be no second half to *Being and Time*, because Heidegger's search had "ended in a blind alley." His search for the meaning of Being was only a *furor teutonicus* which ended in the separation of Being or radical reality from its natural place as human life itself. According to Ortega, Heidegger had entered into the idea of human life as deeply as anyone, but he would never accept it as radical reality or the starting point of philosophy. In this sense, Heidegger avoided the great theme of philosophy since Dilthey's discovery. Not only was human life placed in a secondary position to the more abstract question of Being, but Heidegger considered Dilthey's doctrine of human life (*Lebensphilosophie*) to be only another form of philosophical anthropology, and not fundamental ontology.[4] The reader may recall that this is what Husserl had called the *Being and Time* of the young Heidegger. Ortega went on to claim that there were few of Heidegger's ideas that had not appeared *in ovo* in his own work prior to the publication of *Being and Time* in 1927. In Ortega's lectures "What Is Philosophy?" he claimed that Heidegger's doctrines of truth, world, perspective, and *das Man* were his by ideological priority since 1914 with the publication of his *Meditations on Quixote*.[5]

In sum, the idea of human life was for Ortega the proper subject of twentieth century philosophy, whereas Heidegger had seen human life as only an initial means of penetrating to the question of the meaning of Being itself. For Ortega and Dilthey human life is radical reality in so far as human beings can understand reality at all. For Ortega specifically, the task of philosophy is to grasp human life, and to establish a so-called "historical reason" or the understanding, interpretation, and description of human life through historical time. While Dilthey's idea of human life would inform the thought of Heidegger, especially his notions of *Dasein* and historicity, Heidegger would claim that Dilthey had never defined human life in "an ontologically distinct manner," because it failed to answer the question "What kind of Being is human life?" We shall attempt to answer this question in the subsequent portions of this essay. Heidegger's antipathy to Dilthey's purportedly flawed understanding and expression of the idea of human life had misled Heidegger and caused him not to confront the idea of human life as the authentic question it is.[6] We must now turn to a closer examination of human life itself.

CHAPTER THREE

Human Life: an Overview

When we ask the question "What is my life?" it is not sufficient to reply only by reference to our bodies or to objects at hand. Nor is it enough to consult a science textbook or to refer to the writings of wise men of the past. Neither the question nor an answer to it can be derived from sources outside of our life itself. We are fundamentally our life, and this life that we actually are is composed of all we have done, all that has happened to us, and all we have made of ourselves. While this claim is perhaps oppressively platitudinous, it is, I believe, both self-evident and true. My life now consists of writing and reading these sentences, and your life presently consists of reading them. But our life is more than these present behaviors; it is also our being present at what we do and what acts upon us. The term "my life" is at once an individual thing, be it applied to myself or another, and a general thing in the sense that it is applied to many individual lives. This radical reality is both individual and general. Such a being was called by Hegel the "concrete universal," something both concrete and individual, but also an inclusive term that refers to a plurality of such individual concrete entities. Each of our lives is a revelation to us as our own event. This presence of our life to itself is analogous to what we do when we stand over or preside over something which is apparent to us. Such a "standing over" our life may also take the form of noticing what happens to us, and noticing what we are doing. You and I do not preside over, possess, or experience our life by having a prior theory about it, nor do we derive it from physical or biological facts. Instead, our lives are ours prior to all external facts and considerations. Indeed, all theories and presuppositions about ourselves or anything else will in fact appear within our lives, and not our lives within our theories and presuppositions.

Yet our life, the life of each one of us, exists as something which is enclosed within itself, an inner thing which is always situated in the face of outer things. Leibniz spoke of life's self-enclosure as a monad, as a self possessing its truth and disclosure to itself within itself. But my life is never directly disclosed to you, and your life is never directly disclosed to me. While we have spoken up to this point of "our life" as a generic and "shared" entity, it is actually the case that individuals experience their life only as their very own. It is "my life" which is the primary reality. I can experience the life of another only in a secondary and derived sense, and your life can appear to me only within the context and priority of my own life. My life, in turn, can appear to you only within the primacy and context of your life. Each of us is presented with the interiority of another's life only by means of what Wilhelm Dilthey has designated as "life assertions" (*Lebensäusserungen*). Dilthey's claim was that we can understand another's life, thoughts, feelings, and actions only through the outward, empirical expressions of gestures, behaviors, actions, creations, symbols, texts, and especially language. These expressions, these life assertions from within to without, are also interpreted through what Dilthey called *Verstehen*, or the understanding, from another's life assertions, of their lived significance in the life of that other. Such an understanding of another's life by means of its outer, empirical expression was what Max Weber also called *Verstehen*, or the interpretation of another's life through the meanings, values, and purposes which were originally assigned to them by the agent from which they originally emanated.

For Dilthey this life of mine does not depend upon me alone as my private possession, but my human life is also composed of that which is the life of another, which is real for another, so human life is also the relationship that an individual life has to the life of another.[1] Dilthey contributes the notion that our fundamental life experience is duality, that our life is not simply a subject or an object, that a bipolar relation is the minimum requirement that can be truly asserted of the reality of human life. The togetherness of both subject and object is the irreducibly minimum requirement for the radically real.

This life of ours, this inner thing which attempts to get outside itself through its expressions to the world, has been for modern philosophy largely forgotten. Since the early twentieth century primary emphasis in philosophy has been placed not upon human life and its nature, but upon the theory of knowledge, logic, science, and language. Since Descartes the concern has been to know clearly, distinctly, and without presupposition how knowledge of the objective world is possible. But it must also be noted that since Dilthey important segments of European philosophy have recognized that any approach to the real, to the problems of philosophy in general, is impossible without reference to the primary fact of human life. While the *Lebensphilosophie* school since Dilthey has questioned the dominance of both realism and idealism in the modern period, since Descartes it has tended to accept the realist claim that the objective world is not simply a construction of the mind; that our sense experience reports a true, if limited, account of the world. But at the same time it has accepted the idealist thesis that the objects of the world must be understood as objects of consciousness or idea; that our awareness of the objective world is not the world itself, but a presentation to the mind of which we are aware. Further, the self or the "I" is but one element of experience, and the other is the world to which the "I" must relate. Human life is composed within itself of both "I" and world, and an adequate thinking of human life is partly the recognition that whenever we speak of an "I," whenever we try to identify or locate it, we always discover it in the context of something which is not an "I." This was the case even for Descartes, who had to admit both the "I" thinking and extended things as separate substances. The "I" always exists in the context of what it is not, and Ortega y Gasset has called this "what the 'I' is not" context the circumstances which always surround it. These circumstances come to be recognized as the definite entities they are only when they are in relation to something for which they are circumstances.

Yet circumstances are not simply our thoughts, nor is our awareness of our circumstances the circumstantial entity itself. Our life, the life of each one of us, is in fact the coexistence of both an "I" and its circumstances, as Ortega would express it, in a sort of philosophical battle cry. For him this means that the one fact which carries its own assurance and immediacy is the bipolar existence of both self and world. This is to say that the "I" always finds itself as a part of a dual fact whose other part is the world of circumstances which surround it. Ortega understood the circumstantial component of human life from the two Latin terms *circum* and *stare*, or that which surrounds us and is over against us. The coexistence of "I" and that which surrounds us is a bipolar fact which expresses a mutual need. On the one hand, circumstances need to be completed through their being known as what they are. In other words, circumstances remain incomplete and lacking identity without a subject for whom they exist, and for whom they are identifiable facts. On the other hand, the "I" or the subject of the interaction stands in constant need of and relation to circumstances to which it can relate and ascribe meaning. Because it is in need of circumstances from which it cannot be separated and to which it cannot be indifferent, the "I" must remain in continual orientation to that which is not itself, and this is its actual living. In this sense human life cannot even be conceived as separated from what it is suffering and doing in a world.

At this point it is important to describe in at least an abbreviated and preliminary manner the basic structures which we shall here designate as the "categories of human life." These categories are a crucial element in the idea we are developing, and they will be fully and more formally treated in Chapter Four and from there on in this essay. For our immediate purposes we may note that the term "human life" is used in two different ways, expressing two differing dimensions. The first refers to a living human organism, an object of biological and medical science. This outer, bodily sense of the term must be distinguished from its inner or "lived" dimension, which is of chief interest for our inquiry. The second sense of the term "human life" is not simply another abstraction derived from something our life is not, but it is the most immediate and transparent fact we know. It is that fact in which all secondary facts must appear, and it is to this sense of human life that we must now turn.

We may begin by sketching the categories of human life, those essential structures and meanings that human life actually exhibits in its journey through time. Here it becomes the reader's task to examine, re-experience, and judge our claims of the basic data of human life, according to his or her experience of life itself. The first datum of human life, its first category, is that it is transparent to itself. This transparency refers to the immediate apprehension that our life is both what is happening to us here and now and what we are doing here and now. The implication of such an apprehension is that we are actually a subject to ourselves, an existence for ourselves. Such transparency is exemplified in our knowing that we are having a pain, or that we are running to catch a plane. This knowing that we are both what is happening to us and what we are doing is most pointedly what a stone, for example, does not possess. The constant revelation of our life to ourselves and our being informed about ourselves are the primary features of our life's transparency. This self-transparency has traditionally been designated as self-consciousness, a condition which indicates a presiding over and a possession of our lives. But this life over which we preside and which belongs to us is not simply enclosed within itself. In fact, it exists in bipolar relation to its circumstances which are not itself, but which affect it. Because our life must be concerned about and occupied with circumstances, it can never be an independent subject which exists apart from a world.

This inseparability of our life from the world or circumstances is the second categorical fact about it. It remains the fate of our life that it exists in constant interaction with that which it is not. Because our life consists of finding ourselves in the midst of both the facilities and difficulties of our circumstances, it is imperative that it constantly do something with itself. Even my body exists as a circumstance of my life. I am an embodied subject, and I exist in the world by means of this embodied life, which I must put to use in the world in order to continue to exist. So inevitable is our being in circumstances that even if we were to conduct a thought-experiment in which we were to attempt to conceive a life void of circumstances, then even this empty state would be the environment to which we must still relate. This is another way of saying that from its beginning our life has been forced to be in circumstances which it did not create or choose.

Martin Heidegger claimed in this respect that still another categorical condition of human life is its being "thrown into" a world (*Geworfenheit*) it did not choose. Such a condition is more than just another philosophical oddity, for a theoretical suspension of belief in an external world would theoretically void the bipolar interaction of my life and its circumstances.

Because we are surrounded by a world to which we must respond, we exist under still another categorical imperative, i.e., the requirement that we must orient ourselves to that which surrounds us on pain of suffering, failure, and eventually non-existence. It is a paradox of our life that we must somehow become what we are by dealing with what we are not. Our life consists not only of its present constitution, but also of its possibilities for the future. Our life exists under the imperative of deciding itself into the possibilities of the future. Always present to our life is the question "What am I going to do?" In our various attempts to answer this question we decide not to remain identical with what we presently are, but to project ourselves into new future circumstances. Because we are in a constant orientation into our future, our not-yet, it belongs categorically to the structure of our life that it cannot be separated from its becoming something different than it presently is, through its decisions. Even a life which refuses, waits, avoids, or hesitates is actually deciding itself in a manner. The paradox of our decisions is that our life's projection into the future by means of its decisions and behaviors is an inevitability so long as it is life. Even deciding not to decide is covertly to decide. William James spoke to this paradox through the following example. Suppose yourself to be riding a cable car down a steep hill, when the cable suddenly snaps. In such a condition we possess various possibilities. We may, for example, decide to brace ourselves for a crash, to jump, or to ride passively to our fate. In any of these perhaps overly-dramatic possibilities, we have decided ourselves, done something with ourselves in our inevitable orientation into the future. In this circumstance and in all our circumstances we explicitly or implicitly ask of ourselves the question "What am I going to do with this time at my disposal?"

Human life exists under two different forms of temporality, which can be designated as its inner and outer dimensions. The inner dimension of human temporality has been variously called duration, lived time, or inner time. Such time takes the form of a lived present, a "now" which has arisen from the past and is tending to the future. Time's outer dimension is sometimes called world time, or clock time, or solar time. It is a characteristic of human life when it is conceived as a physical object, an organic body perceived through the senses. In clock time temporality is measured by reference to the counting or measuring of units indicated by the pointers on the face of a dial. The measurement indicated by these pointers corresponds to outer spatial motions, such as the earth's rotation on its axis, or its journey around the sun. In this manner clock time corresponds to the perceived motions of pointers which represent the motions of terrestrial or celestial bodies in space. In this manner clock time becomes united with both space and the motions of spatial bodies. Since Aristotle outer or clock time has been understood by reference to the counting of the motion of physical bodies. More recently this counting has been made correspondent to the position of pointers and dials which are divided into seconds, minutes, hours, days, and years. Clock time has tended to become the *sine qua non* of all temporality, the condition without which physics and spatial motion generally could not be understood, a dimension with which every physical existent must be measured and located. Such clock or world time also has become the looming abstraction which regulates and measures the performance of the socio-economic world. Since the rise of mathematical science in the seventeenth century, world time has tended to replace, even to nullify, the concrete and immediate experience of temporality's other dimension, namely inner time or duration.

While clock time is something external in its reference to the motions of bodies in space, lived time is primordially characteristic of human life as an inner event. Our inner time is the lived experience of change within our life itself, an awareness in which we advance from the past through the present to the future. For such thinkers as Dilthey, Heidegger, and Ortega y Gasset lived time is both the ground and experiential referent of the derived mode of temporality we have previously indicated as clock, world, or external time. Lived time can be measured by clock time, but it can never be simply equated to clock time. Such an equation would be trying to understand, count, or represent the lived duration of the suffering of a terminal cancer patient merely and only by reference to the four months, sixteen days and seven minutes required for him or her to expire. Further, the dominance of clock time in the modern era has tended to relegate the temporality of lived experience to a comparative unimportance or to a mere subjectivity without an authentic philosophical status of its own. The modern emphasis upon world time has also tended to abrogate an understanding of the structure of lived time's duration from past to present to future. In other words, the thesis of clock time is unable to reveal the status of lived time as that temporality in which decisions are made, and in which feelings, orientations, volitions, memory and cognition take place in our life's advance into its future from out of its past and present. As noted before, while such lived time can be measured by clock time, the lived temporality of our human life cannot be reduced to or derived from the temporality of clock time without a total distortion of its nature. In sum, clock time as it is derived from the counting of the motion of physical bodies is indifferent to the tendential structure of lived time with its comportment to future circumstantial possibilities. The advance of human life upon itself is lived time, and such an advance is experienced as lived duration and history and not as the counting of the external motion of physical bodies.

As a constant temporal advance upon itself, my life exists always under the lived imperative of a question, namely, "What am I going to do?" This question, whether covertly or explicitly posed, demands that I know more or less what I will do, where I will go, and why. This life of mine, or of any one of us, stands in constant need of orientation into my future and my circumstances. Such a need speaks the fact that my life is always more or less disoriented, even lost, in its temporal advance into the future, into its "not-yet." As I sit writing in my cabin study in Utah, I steal a glance at the calm of the mountains, those natural symbols of eternity, while I attempt to put these sentences down. No sooner is one sentence completed than I must join it to the next one in some meaningful connection. All of this must be somehow oriented to the future with its looming possibilities of success, indifference, or failure. Always more or less indeterminate and insecure, my projects exist as a sort of soft threat in the face of the future and its circumstances. I am in only relative possession of what is required for my advance into the future. Lasting orientation seems never attained, and any anticipation of such a state is usually utopian. My life is never guaranteed except relatively, and while both religion and metaphysics often claim perfect orientation for individuals and society, even the universe at large, such a condition seems always to elude me.

In marked contrast to human life, however, a stone neither possesses nor needs an orientation into anything. Never seeking or avoiding a way into the future and its circumstances, a stone is not a problem to itself. Human life, by contrast, carries within itself a constant and pervading concern for its existence in time and circumstances. Such concern remains a central category of human life, and it is in its concern for the onrushing "not-yet" of its future that our life reveals its fundamentally temporal structure. Because our existence is the constant and inevitable possibility of its "not-yet," the very core of our being is time and the passing of time. Martin Heidegger's *Being and Time* is arguably the attempt to reveal that the most vital dimension of human life is its possession of a future. The nature of our life, he claims, is more fully revealed through the possession of a future than through any of its other attributes. Because it is compelled to advance upon itself from out of its past to its "not-yet," our life is in fact its own self-construction through time. This autofabrication of our life is itself to be understood as part of the temporality of our existence. In this respect Nietzsche once remarked that human beings are the only animals which are "unfixated." Such a status indicated for this philosopher of human life that our being is self-constructed in time and not handed down to us ready-made or complete. Our life exists under the continual necessity of deciding, of fabricating what it will be. The demand that our life continually compose itself in time is a sort of lived imperative. As a continual composition and memory of what it does and what happens to it, our life's autofabrication is its history. While this life and its future are not causally determined by what has happened in its past, we are bound to the fact that we have done and suffered definite things; that we have composed a definite story of ourselves. Such a composition through time has been called the "drama" of our lives by Ortega y Gasset. Because our life is a temporal inevitability which we cannot resist or avoid so long as we exist, we must somehow fabricate our existence from out of the past and present to the future. We must become what we irremediably are, our life.

At this point we may summarize in a selective manner the categorical facts of our life, those general attributes and structures which may be identified through our inner reflection. Our life is first of all transparent to itself and aware of its nature through that transparency. In its self-awareness our life actually presides over itself and even "owns" itself. This presiding ownership is illustrated most finally and forcefully in the act of suicide, which is the relinquishing of its original deed, but with no recipient. Secondly, our life always exists within circumstances which are other than itself, and with which it must somehow deal. Our life must know what to do with itself in relation to what surrounds it. This is to say that our life must decide itself, orient itself, and construct itself in relation to what it is not. Thirdly, our life, though transparent to itself, is not transparent to others. It must reveal itself empirically and understandably in its outward expressions, creations, actions, moods, and above all through language. My life, in turn, must understand the life of others through their life expressions by an interpretive operation called *Verstehen*. Finally, because one of our life's most inclusive categories is care for itself and its circumstances, as it advances into its "not-yet," our care becomes an indication of the fact that our life is fundamentally and inevitably temporal. Our life's mode of temporality is history, the drama of its autofabrication through time.

Dilthey, Heidegger, and Ortega y Gasset understand our life as that immediate perspective through which radical reality is given to itself. The claim that our life is radical reality comes to the fact that our life is our primary being and possession; that our life has objective existence for us, and is not derived from or dependent upon another notion or abstraction prior to it; that all else that is called real must appear or arise within it. In these senses human life is its own ultimate fact. Other traditional candidates for the radically real, such as the universe in its totality, matter, nature, atoms, or even God, have claimed for themselves this status, yet they are actually secondary realities in that they must all appear to us within our life as part of our circumstances; they must be related to and dependent upon our knowing that they are of a specific nature and not something else. None of our other purported candidates for the real can be simply and automatically independent of the primary fact of our life. Were this so, I could say nothing or know nothing about them, for anything that is real for human life must be something that is kept in view, and dealt with as part of our circumstances. Anything that is called real must somehow be made known to us in some aspect of human life, individually or collectively. Real things must appear within something for which they can be real, and this is human life. The alternative candidates for reality do not exist as facts in themselves, but as secondary realities which appear within human life. This human life is always someone's life, and it is but one of the two basic components of experience. The other component is circumstances. But if real circumstances depend upon us for their being known and kept in view, it is also the case that our life is dependent upon circumstances which are also real. Human life exists as an interdependent polarity of both "I" and its circumstances. We shall employ the term "I" here to mean an actual person living his or her unique life. This is the usual, everyday usage of the term "I." That which we call radically real is the life of an "I," and all realities other than my life must first appear within it, including the life of another.

Yet the claim that our life is the radically real is not meant to imply that any secondary candidates for the real, such as matter or even God, somehow depend for their status as secondary realities upon human life in all respects. The claim to the radical reality of human life does not imply, for example, that if you or I were to die, matter or nature would cease to exist. Further, we do not here imply that human life is somehow prior in importance, power, extent, or age to the other candidates. In fact, the existence of human life has been created and sustained by and within matter and nature. Still, even granting the existence of a being like God, for example, however we may define Him, Her or It as the creator and source of human life, God would be a secondary reality for human life, appearing within the priority of human life itself. In other words, even such a being as God must depend upon appearing within our life as a being who is in view of human life, a being of a definite kind with identifiable meanings and characteristics. Such a being would also be required to appear for us in a definite time and tradition of human life, Judeo-Christian for example. But our position here should not imply or claim that beings like God or matter depend upon human life which "made them up" in some Feuerbachean sense. Instead, the claim is that God or matter, however conceived, existent or nonexistent, is not independent of its appearance in the human life in which it has revealed itself as a secondary reality. In this sense, even an orthodox Christian position has recognized that God must first appear as a human life within human lives in order to be relevant to humanity. Implicit here is the notion that divinity can never utterly transcend human life in some actual historical time and place. In this respect Kierkegaard thought that the most significant thing about Christianity is the "absurd" fact that the eternal should become human at all. This is to say in our context here that God must somehow become one of the circumstances of human life to which it could relate and which it could hold in view. Of course it remains possible to claim, as the religious often do, that God is infinite, eternal, omniscient and omnipotent. It is also possible to argue for God's existence or nonexistence, yet it must be remembered that radical reality is not first experienced as God, but God, if experienced at all, appears as a secondary reality within the radical reality of human life itself.

My life, your life, the life of each one of us is prior to the beliefs, theories, explanations, concepts, and traditions that appear within it. Even our body appears within human life. The toes and fingers of the baby, even the socially aspiring adult's ability to dance the rumba, must appear within his or her life. The science of experimental physiology first appeared within the lives and life worlds of Hippocrates (460 BC) and Galen (150 AD). Our life is the general fact which is prior to knowledge, science, religion, society, or culture. Our life is so fundamental and presupposed that we cannot, even in theory, "get behind it" or inquire into it without assuming its priority to all inquiry. Even the claim of an external world existing independently of human life must still presuppose a life for which such a status is already a possibility or question. Yet even in the face of such a universal presupposition, our life in its transparency and immediacy has tended to remain that entity which is still furthest away.

Since the rise of mathematical science in the seventeenth century human life has become as a philosophical issue increasingly forgotten, obscured, or passed off, even by Kant, as a mere "subjective appearance." Ironically, human life is in fact subjective, still obscure, and an appearance, but not in the senses usually presupposed. It is against the spirit of such presuppositions that Ortega y Gasset maintained against Descartes' *cogito ergo sum* thesis not "I think, therefore I am" but *cogito quia vivo*, "I think because, and only because, I first live."

The idea of human life was not explicitly present in Europe until the later nineteenth century. The Anglo-American world never found the idea a philosophical concern, with the possible exceptions of William James, John Dewey, and Alfred North Whitehead. Also, if we exclude Goethe, Maine de Biran, and Nietzsche, the only one of Dilthey's contemporaries to have even approximated a *Lebensphilosophie* was Kierkegaard (1813- 1855). It was he who generated the thesis that our actual existence is prior to all theory and abstraction; that "truth is subjectivity." This I understand to mean that our life is neither given in nor comprehended through epistemological theories, scientific hypotheses, or the abstract universals of Hegelian philosophy. But for Kierkegaard human life is always understood in the context of a theological problematic, and not as fundamental ontology. It is first in Dilthey that the philosophy of human life is understood in the context of a "critique of historical reason," which has as its end the empirical and secular understanding of the categories of human life as they exist in time. Human life for Dilthey is to be understood by means of its expressions through history, descriptive psychology, and the methodology of *Verstehen*. For Dilthey human life and its categories remain the presuppositions that terminate all presuppositions.[2] It is now to the more complete description of categories that we must turn.

CHAPTER FOUR

The Concept of Categories

Historical Development of the Concept

When we reflect upon the nature of our life, we find that it is not only significantly intelligible, but it is informed by very definite properties, structures, and meanings. Dilthey referred to these elements as the categories of human life (*Kategorien des Lebens*). In this respect he followed Kant's attempt to show that the categories of our life are always involved in any knowledge of existence. More specifically, Dilthey had understood Kant's task in his *Critique of Pure Reason* to be the development of the categories required for an understanding of the physical world. Dilthey is generally considered to be a neo-Kantian, but for Dilthey the categories of human life are not obtained through Kant's transcendental deduction of the categories required for the science of nature. Instead, they are derived from an immediate experience of how our life is revealed to itself. The categorical structure already present in human life provides it with coherence and meaning and does not derive from a pure categorical reason imposed upon it. Human life for Dilthey is best understood through a description of human life's elemental properties through historical time. Dilthey also maintained in this respect that because of Kant's emphasis upon the categories that are appropriate for natural science Kant could never have achieved "a critique of historical reason." For Dilthey the entire question of human life's historical nature was subverted by Kant's sole emphasis upon the critique of pure reason and search for the grounds of the general validity of the natural sciences. While Fichte had already expressed the need for an elaboration of the categories of human life, Dilthey would be significantly the first to develop those categories necessary for a critique of the human studies and historical reason.

The notion of philosophical categories such as those employed by Kant and Dilthey first appeared in the thought of Plato, Aristotle, and Plotinus, when they determined that all being possesses fixed and definite characteristics, which they designated as *kategoriae*, those elemental and necessary characteristics which were implicit in all that is. For Aristotle a category was a property which every real being, simply by the fact of its being real, carries within itself. These characteristics included substance, quantity, quality, relation, place, time, position, state, and that which acts and that which is acted upon. But for Dilthey such a conceptual list seemed more relevant to physical things than to human life. Also, since Kant, the classical conception of the categories had been developed into a theory about the forms of judgment, and not simply the characteristics of being itself. In Dilthey's development of the categories of human life there was never any attempt to employ Kant's transcendental forms of the mind, which synthesize our percepts into universal judgments of nature. Instead Dilthey would extend the categories to include the unique characteristics of human life, such elements as purpose, value, historicity, and *Verstehen*. These categories, he maintained, can be understood only through our inner reflection (*Besinnung*) upon the cognitive processes of our life. For example, in his *Ideas Concerning a Descriptive and Analytical Psychology*, Dilthey observed that the parts of mental life are organized into meaningful wholes or categorical form by our "silent thought." He further maintained that the categorical structures of mental life have already been interpreted by human beings who have presupposed and acted upon the categories through historical time. In this sense, the source of the knowledge of our life's structure and meaning is human life itself.[1] This means for Dilthey that there is no need for a Kantian transcendental deduction of the categories, because they are both given and presupposed within our life. Because these categories emerge from life itself, each human being is at once both the subject and the object of knowledge of his or her own non-transferable life. Human life is lived as its own given, remembered, and anticipated account of itself.

Our task is now to follow Dilthey's lead, along with the subsequent contributions of Heidegger and Ortega y Gasset, and attempt to describe, interpret, and clarify the categorical structures of human life as it is lived. While this task will continue to the end of our entire essay, we may begin with the fundamental categorical fact that we are beings in a world, that we are ourselves and our circumstances.

World and Circumstances

When we hear the statement "I am a being in the world," it is not necessarily a trite commonplace that is advanced. If this claim is philosophically considered, it becomes both a profound and important matter, the fundamental category in the idea of human life. It means that my life is lived in conjunction with things outside of itself; that we are surrounded by what is not ourselves; that we are constantly over against something; that we exist within something else. In the thought of Dilthey the term "world" or *Welt* does not refer to the fact that we live on the planet earth (*Erde*). For him it means that my life is never complete solely within myself. The fundamental datum of my life is that I live in a world. This primordial fact, the one that grounds all others, indicates that I possess my life within the context of a world. My life is not a hermetic substance which exists as a pure interiority. It can never remain identical with its internal nature alone, but must orient itself to a world of things which suggest significance and value for it. Because our life is in constant need of an environment for its survival and satisfaction, it remains incomplete without a world which it can relate to, use, and absorb. Our life is the story of what we do in a world, and what the world does to us. But whatever we do or do not accomplish, the world remains always present to us, and a prerequisite of all orientation and behavior. Our life comprises a bipolar relation and constant correlation to what is outside of it, an "I" and its circumstances. Everything in our life depends upon how we humanize and incorporate our circumstances into our life. It is only in the coexistence of "I" and circumstances that we attain to the conception of the radical reality of our human life, and a new meaning to the phrase "to be real" emerges.

The first consideration about our life, then, is that it happens in an environment that is of interest and concern to it. More than this, the nature of our experience itself is largely determined by the world which surrounds it. Our surroundings are never simply neutral objects, but they exist for us as important or unimportant, useful or worthless, alien or familiar. Even though we are thrown into our circumstances without our consent, we are nevertheless required to respond to them, to decide about them, to do something about them. Any refusal or inability to orient ourselves to our circumstances brings us to a danger of "falling short" before the requirements they pose for us. I am required to do something definite with my life in the face of its circumstances, even if it is only to get off an uncomfortable chair, stay on it, or adjust a bodily part to it. Circumstances exist as an imperative to action. In this sense they are entities about which I must care and which I must use as something serviceable in the context of my life. They are never present as things in themselves entirely apart from my life, never simply "pure" objects in my spatio-temporal field.

There is a tendency even in professional philosophy to pretend in the name of objectivity that the world is composed of absolutely independent entities which are "simply what they are," independently of any observer. They are posed as disinterested abstractions of a so-called "natural standpoint." But in various degrees our circumstances are precisely what we are interested in, what is not neutral. Simply put, we are required to act and be acted upon by circumstances so long as we live; required to behave in the light of beliefs and presuppositions with respect to them. Our life in circumstances is the one indubitable thing. Not to acknowledge these circumstances, or to assume for them only a theoretical nature, is to be in danger of disorientation and failure, to fall short before the world.

In Greek philosophy those actions and tasks which must be accomplished in order for us to achieve our ends were termed *pragmata*. In modern terms we would say that we can live only through something other than ourselves or through circumstances which are serviceable to our ends. Our circumstances, so understood, form an implicit denial of any assumption that our life is only to be seen as an internal or subjective entity removed from a world. In our actual existence circumstances happen to us without cessation, and human life happens to them. Neither I nor my circumstances can achieve independence of each other; neither can be fully real apart from this reciprocity.

The "I" and Its Circumstances

The "I" has been understood in the history of philosophy as the ultimate conscious subject. Descartes called this subject a *res cogitans*, or the thinking thing. This thinking thing exists entirely separated from a second type of substance which he designated as *res extensa*, or extended physical space considered as a single continuum. He considered the "I" as an immaterial thinking substance removed from the world of extended things, and unrelated to anything but itself. He derived the "I" out of a philosophical argument which he expressed in terms of *cogito ergo sum*, "I think, therefore I am." In this formulation any act of thinking was supposed to establish without doubt the existence of an "I" which thinks. Immanuel Kant, following Descartes, understood the "I" not as a thinking substance in opposition to a world of extension, but as the functional dynamic unity of consciousness, a necessary condition of all experience. The "I" there underlies the passing succession of all our conscious states. For Dilthey and Ortega y Gasset the "I" is the element that coexists with worldly circumstances. It exists as a distinct first person subject whose identity is composed in interaction with its circumstances through time. For Dilthey this "I" is formed from its dynamic interaction (*Wirkungszusammenhang*) with physical nature and history. This means that the "I" is formed through its relation to the greater historical life which surrounds it, and to the physical environment with which it exists in dialectical relation. This interaction of the "I" with its historical and physical circumstances is the event of human life. The "I" is the pole for which the process of the world takes place, and the world is never given apart from the "I" for which it is a world. As a self composed of specific events, actions, and circumstances, the "I" becomes that entity which encounters a world of historical and physical circumstances from within itself.

The "I" can also be understood as the name of the self or agent which "keeps in view" all that appears within its life. The "I" "stands over" its life from a transcending point of view. In this manner it judges, identifies, and remembers what it has been, and anticipates what it will become. Yet never an objective thing in the world, nor a separate Cartesian substance utterly apart from its circumstances, the "I" and its circumstances may never be separated from each other except by some forced and arbitrary abstraction. Human life remains inseparable from its confrontation with a world which exists as something serviceable for the mediation of what hinders or advances it. Neither the "I" not its circumstances can be authentically understood as independent "things in themselves" which are each independent of the other. Also, neither the "I" nor its circumstantial world enjoys any absolute priority over the other. As the ultimate structure of experience, the "I" and its circumstances are always bonded together in a dialectical bipolar relation. This polarity is neither the pure "outside world" of realism nor the pure "inside world" of idealism. The failure to comprehend this bipolar conception of both "I" and world has led to the split between traditional realism and idealism. These positions by themselves constitute two positions on the real which are incomplete and misleading.

We may define realism here as the position that all objects of perception are real in their own right, and exist independently of their being known by or related to the "I" which perceives them. Here in this position the world is considered the primary pole of experience. Realism found its first expression in the Greek thought which treated abstract terms or universals after the model of objective things which exist independently of the knowing or perceiving subject. In Plato, for example, the idea or form (*eidos*) possesses a real and objective status that is independent of its being known or perceived by the subject. For a philosopher of human life like Ortega, this entire prototype of thought is called realism.[2] The counterposition of realism is idealism. In one form or another idealism is the thesis that identifies reality with perceptibility or knowability. All objects of apprehension are subjective and privately possessed, and the basic object of knowledge is our mental life. Idealism can also refer to the belief that we cannot know the nature of anything except what is clearly or distinctly perceived, as in the thought of Descartes. Here the thinking thing (*res cogitans*) is considered primary being.

From the publication of his *Meditations on Quixote*, Ortega y Gasset considered both realism and idealism to be the two great prototypes of philosophy, but both positions, he maintained, possess a limited perspective on the real. His analysis of the self and the world was intended to repair the philosophical split between the doctrines of realism and idealism with the idea of human life. The fundamental reality proposed by realism and idealism can be neither the primacy of the independent and objective thing maintained by realism, nor the primacy of the subjective thinking thing as maintained by idealism. In his analysis of these two schools Ortega held that the objective and independent world proposed by realism can only exist when there is an "I" which perceives such a world to be the case; on the other hand, the idealist position that the real cannot refer to an independent, objective thing is also misleading. When it recognizes only a "pure indwelling consciousness" as real, it fails to recognize that our life is always "outside of itself" in circumstances. Realism omits the fact that the circumstantial world must exist within the perspective of the "I" or subject; the external world is not somehow real in itself, but it is real for a subject who also exists in a bipolar relation to it. An objective thing can be fully constituted only through the participation of a subject who endows it with significance.[3] The "I" and its circumstances exist together in the bipolar relation that is the radical reality of human life. In this sense human life is both immanent and transcendent, neither merely an indwelling subject nor merely an external object. When the bipolar fact of human life is forgotten we are led into the errors of idealistic and materialistic monism and the various forms of reductionism. The task of the philosophy of human life is to reveal the conjunction of the inner and the outer, of both the "I" and its circumstances.

The philosophy of human life is significantly the contention that when the "I" is subtracted from the world, or the world is subtracted from the "I," then an unreal and incomplete situation results. Out of this consideration the bipolar reality of both "I" and circumstance has been developed as the central category of the idea of human life. It is also the case that in the doctrine of human life there is the assumption that while both realism and idealism are incomplete positions in themselves, there yet remains a partial truth in both. The realists are correct in their claim that the external world is not an illusion, but a reality that is both present and real. The world actually confronts us and coexists with the "I." On the other hand, the idealist is right to assert a subjective pole in experience for which the objective world is a fact. But the new thesis of the idea of human life is that we can no longer separate realities but must recognize the correlation between them. It was Leibniz who first conceived this fact. For him the "I" and the world cannot exist without a relation of one to the other. To think of them apart as separate substances is only to think an abstraction.

In sum, the realist maintains that the real is an objective fact toward which the "I" always orients itself. The idealist hold that the real is fundamentally subjective or mental. What is inevitable about both of these positions is that human life possesses both components. It accepts the realist thesis that there exists a real and independent world and the idealist thesis that to be a human life is to be a subject in primary correspondence with a world. This is the event of human life as radical reality. Intelligent behavior in human life depends upon the adequate perception of the relation between what we do and what we undergo for the sake of the ends we desire to effect. Because all human action exists in the face of the need to decide what to do about circumstances, it is essential to our being in the world to establish adequate orientation, securities, and beliefs. The circumstances before which I stand in interest, fear, or perplexity always exist as definite possibilities for my behavior. My circumstances and my possibilities with respect to them are not transferable, and they exist as definite requirements for me alone. I am required to do that which completes my own life.

CHAPTER FIVE

Historical Time and Care

Clock Time and Lived Time

Whereas for Ortega the primary category is "I and my circumstances," for Dilthey and Heidegger the primary category is involved with time, and both time and world are experienced as constant flux, an advancing change that arises in the past and progresses through the present into the future. As the most constant characteristic of life's intelligibility, unity, and advancing content, our life is for Dilthey time itself. Our life is lived as a process, an advance upon itself through an ongoing present which leaves its past and anticipates the future.[1] Time does not exist for us as something which supports us or stands above or outside of us. Instead, human life is given to itself as the very existence of time, and it is only in the context of time that we are able to think and experience at all.

As a constant advance upon itself to something which it will subsequently become, the present "now" of human life which is our primary experience will dispose of itself into a "not yet" which will become the "now" of our future. Yet our temporal existence is not the cosmic time of natural science, but the very stuff of our existence itself. The clock time that is presupposed in the theories of the natural sciences is not the time that we directly and immediately live. The clock or world time of the natural sciences and the public world exists only as the measuring of clock pointers with respect to their relation to the motions of external bodies. The units of such measurements are seconds, minutes, hours, days, months, and years. But the movement and measurement of bodies in space does not correspond to the duration of the lived time of human life, nor to the meaning it has for itself. Lived time is immediately given as the forward, irreversible, and indivisible succession of conscious states in meaningful relation. Such a concrete and immediate process is experienced as a duration and an emergence from a lived past into the reality of the present and the anticipation of the future.

Maine de Biran (1766–1824) and Henri Bergson (1859–1941) have also identified this emergent duration as directly intuited, and not to be understood as something that is apart from our life. Philosophy, for them, is a disciplined reflection upon the reality of human life as it is given and lived in the subjectivity of persons. For Bergson it is because human beings already possess time as their lived experience that they are able to tell time, or to fabricate a clock time at all. The temporal structure of lived time is not equivalent to cosmic motion or physiological process, nor can it simply be identified with the calibration of the pointers of clock time. For Dilthey, too, the primordial temporality of human life is not experienced as the simple succession of identical moments. Such abstract time is only a continuum of successive units of measurement which do not reveal what actually fills the moments of lived experience. Lived experience is given to us as something which fills our present moment with reality, and it is only in the ongoing present of human life that the fullness of the real is actually experienced. Dilthey, Heidegger, and Ortega y Gasset all maintain that our actual life alone possesses the authentic and original mode of temporality, the one from which abstract clock time is then derived. If we regard the filling of lived time as only abstract "nows" in successive continuity, then we ignore the fact that our actual duration consists of the continuous development of a meaningful whole of past becoming present in the anticipation of a future.

For Dilthey the implication of such a temporality is expressed in a unique manner: human life is actually experienced as an ongoing present which is always in a state of orientation out of a past and into a future. This means that our present contains within itself the memory of the past and an anticipation of the future. Such a present is also experienced as feeling, willing, memory, thinking, decision, and anticipation of the future in meaningful connection. Here again such experience is never to be understood as a succession of clock time units of calibration to measure the motion of bodies in space or clock pointers. Our immediate ongoing present possesses what he called an "acquired structure" of meanings, memories, impressions, values, feelings, and goals in a coherent relation.[2] Such a relation between parts and wholes he called an *Erlebnis*, or a lived, inner experience. *Erlebnis* is the self-perception of our inner life. For our experience of the outer material world of the natural sciences he used such expressions as *Erkennen* or *Verstandt*. Such external experience tends to grasp only the abstract and quantifiable traits of the natural world, and these traits are broken down by analysis into the most generalized quantifiable denominators. All the lived, inner experiences of an *Erlebnis*, such as feelings, volitions, inner time, development, and value, are (by that external analysis) either ignored or reduced to quantified "primary qualities" which can be measured by clock time. Meanings there are assigned only to such formal, external properties as extension, weight, motion, speed, and power.

For Dilthey *Erlebnis* refers primarily to the self-perceptions (*Selbstbesinnung*) of our inner life, as contrasted to the outer physical world. Here each individual experience relates to others in a meaningful manner as parts to wholes. Their aggregate whole may become the subject of historical inquiry. Put another way, *Erlebnis* is the manner through which the inner reality of human life exists for a subject. Here we are not dealing with the sense appearances of physical objects, but with a situation in which the subject intends his or her own inner life as an object. In human life's givenness to itself we have access to the fact that human life is radical reality as it is given to human beings. In this case there is no need to explain our immediate inner experience by reference to the outer experience of the senses. In the physical sciences our sense perceptions always intend the world as an appearance. For Dilthey this fact provides the real distinction between the natural sciences and the human studies, i.e., that the objects of science are mediated by outer sense experience, and the world of human life is self-evident.[3] While the inner experience of our actual life is a self-awareness, we can never "get behind" such an experience, for this would suppose that there is a lower or more real denominator than inner experience itself. It would be here as if we could direct the beam of a searchlight behind itself to observe itself. But we cannot penetrate to the "back side" of consciousness, or to the ultimate conditions of human life. Human life is itself the ultimate reality for human experience.

In his book *Ideas upon a Descriptive and Analytic Psychology* Dilthey held that the inner experience of our life has three components:

(1) a cognitive or meaningful (*bedeutsam*) aspect; (2) an emotional or affective component; (3) a teleological and developmental structure directed to the attainment or completion of life or the satisfaction of human needs. This three-part structure of an inner experience may hopefully be clarified by the following example of the lived experience of writing a check to pay for our child's academic tuition. Here we operate in the context of lived time in which the temporal predicates of memory, present awareness, and future expectations form a whole of meanings in lived time. Our past commitment to a college education for the child operates in dynamic connection with the present act of writing the check in the context of anticipations of a future career for the child. Our present sense impressions are generated in the context of the act of writing the check, together with feelings of anxiety, regret, or satisfaction, and the overarching, long-range experience of providing for a child. In the experience of writing a check we also observe a temporal relation between parts and wholes of the check-writing experience as it exists in time. The act of writing a check is a teleological structure of related parts and wholes. Such a teleology is temporal, yet it can never be expressed as a content composed of clock time alone. Nor is the overt behavior of the check writing understandable without reference to the meanings, values, and purposes of the lived experience itself. All of the interlocking parts of this lived experience are given as a memory of the past, the actuality of the present writing, and the anticipation of the future, within the meaningful whole of the lived experience itself.

Dilthey thought of human life as an advancing "now," a present which is always in the condition of having left another present which is now in the past. While he understood our life as a continuous present, it is a present which includes within itself all the possibilities of temporality, the before, the now, and what is to come. Because our life is an ongoing present, we tend not to apprehend the fact that the moving objects of experience are life's duration, its continuity into the future. The present is understood as "the filling of a moment of time with reality," the reality of human life itself.

In short, for Dilthey it is the present which is the dominant and most real aspect of all temporality. But it is in Heidegger's thought that the issue of time reaches its fullest expression, and Dilthey's emphasis upon the present gives way to Heidegger's emphasis on the future as the essential temporal mode of human existence. Heidegger's contributions to the idea of temporality in human life are important. We shall consider his ideas in the light of the accepted and traditional view of time. Western tradition since Aristotle has tended to understand the passage of time as a general medium in which events take place in a succession of points or perpetually shifting "nows" of the present. Time is often imagined, too, as something objective which automatically moves of itself toward a future. The present has somehow arisen in the past, and moves of itself into the future. Each now possesses a fixed position in an ordered arrangement of events which exist in terms of a before and after. Such objective time follows irreversibly in a forward direction from out of a past, through the present, into the future. The stages of time were assumed to exist independently of the human subject or a given perceptual standpoint. But many controversies and problems on this thesis have led philosophers to believe that this concept of time cannot achieve any general validity or acceptance, without making a distinction between objective time and a subjective time which includes the perceiving subject's unique identity as human life. Also it has come to be generally believed that the traditional position has never succeeded in telling us what time itself is.

Heidegger's *Being and Time* is in significant part the attempt to show that neither clock time nor lived time can be authentically comprehended without placing it in the receptacle of human life and existence. To this end Heidegger understands time as the most fundamental factor in human existence, the presence of which allows human life to be in the world in the manner that actually is the case. For Heidegger our human being exists temporally as a sort of "stretching" (*erstrecken*) from the past, through the present, to the future. The contention here is that we are not simply in a time which is outside of us. Rather, our very existence is itself something which "stretches" into its possibilities as past, present, future. These temporal dimensions through which we authentically exist Heidegger calls the "ecstases" of time. Authentic time, the time which is our very own, is not like the water which surrounds a fish. Rather, we are the very time of our past, present, and future as our nature temporalizes itself through its three ecstases. Put another way, human life is not an "inside," watching time slip by as something external. Our human being is its own time using itself up. Human being is its very future which it projects ahead of itself, and it is also the present and past which it has been. Unlike Dilthey, however, Heidegger maintains that it is not the present but the future which is the most essential and revealing aspect of our being, and that about which it cares most. This is because Heidegger considers human beings to be essentially their possibilities which are ahead of them in time. Possibilities cannot be achieved except as time. We fundamentally find ourselves, develop ourselves, and become that which is ahead of us. In being ahead of ourselves, we project even our past and present into our future. Further, while the parts of our temporal nature exist interdependently, they are not merely a mechanical succession of past, present, and future components, nor are we merely spectators of the time which seems to exist outside of ourselves. Instead, human beings exist primarily as unfinished possibilities that project into the future. The future becomes the mode of the possible, a possibility which is ourselves.

The authentic time of our life is not infinite, but radically finite and incomplete. Lived time is not an eternal succession of individual nows advancing in infinity. Rather, human time or lived time is "used up" in actual human life and ended by death, one's own death. Such time, the time of our life, can be understood only as a mode of our life. Time is the fundamental nature of human being, and the traditional view of time as a counting of the motion of physical bodies by the pointers of a clock is an inauthentic vision of our temporal existence. In authentic, lived time, our life exists as choices made into the future, and our responsibility for these choices. Yet human beings in fact want to avoid and forget this fact, and lose themselves in their present, in things at hand, and the happenings of a mass society which is filled with the expectations of an anonymous "they" which they observe as spectators. In such a state the "now," rather than the future and its possibilities, becomes their primary concern. It is to this category of concern that we must now turn as a major component of human life.

The Care Structure

For Heidegger the entire issue of time cannot be understood apart from the issue of Care (*Sorge*) and the so-called Care Structure of human life. It is care which allows the revealing of the nature and role of time in human life as a whole. It is care, and not reason, soul, or individuality, that is at the center of our being. Care is the most characteristic feature of human life, and all that the first half of *Being and Time* has revealed of our human being will become synthesized into the more comprehensive and incisive idea of Care and its structure. He intended the first half of *Being and Time* to be a phenomenological description of the *existentialia*, or what we here are calling the categories of human life. In "Division Two" of *Being and Time*, which he entitles "*Dasein* and Temporality," he developed time in its relation to human being. He meant to tell us that the whole structure and content of human existence is radically temporal, and our life as Care is composed of a threefold set of existential characteristics, themselves temporal, which will allow us to understand the unique manner in which human life or *Dasein* exists in time. These three characteristics include what Heidegger designates as facticity (*Faktizität*), falling (*Verfallen*), and possibility (*Möglichkeit*). These fundamental elements of human existence Heidegger correlated with what he calls the three basic ecstases or aspects of temporality, which we commonly call past, present, and future. In this way he laid bare our existence as a whole, its being and time.

The first component of our Care Structure, facticity, Heidegger correlates with the temporal element of the past. Facticity denotes that which is fixed, unchangeable, and not chosen, but simply given and final. The past element of our temporal structure is given, unchangeable, and not presently subject to volitional change. This part of our being reveals that our human existence has been previously thrown into a definite and fixed status over which we presently have no control or choice. The past is the unchangeable givenness which must be recognized as a prelude and inheritance of both our present and our future. Through both fantasy and forgetfulness the human being often attempts to avoid the fact that he or she has been thrown into factical conditions which were not chosen or anticipated: for example, to have been born with the AIDS virus, or born female, or of African parentage, and in the twenty-first century.

The second component of the Care Structure Heidegger calls falling, and he correlates it with the temporal present. By this he means to indicate that present human existence is always alongside things at hand about which we care in some way. Fire, a fearful snake, love of a woman, and global warming are examples of things at hand to which we extend care in our life. We are almost forcefully absorbed in the things about which we must care in order to survive. It is in this temporal present that our life may become alienated, turned away from, or indifferent to the mode of the future through our fascination with the present. Here we may fall into an exclusive orientation to a "they," the anonymous mode of the mass man (*das Man*). This is the inauthentic manner by which we lose our identity in a crowd which seems to be able to choose for us and value for us. In such a crowd state there is a tendency to forget our past and to be indifferent to our responsibility for the future. In this state human life tends to love appearances and the abstractions and irresponsibility of mass society. Human life tends to become indifferent to its able-to-be-ness, to its future. It becomes dispersed through its drifting into the future and its forgetfulness of its past.

The third component of the Care Structure Heidegger calls possibility, and he correlates this component of our being with the temporal future toward which we tend and about which we must decide. Possibility is the manner by which our existence moves ahead of itself into its not-yet, its future. In the mode of possibility our existence anticipates its oncoming future as something to be resolved, chosen, and achieved. This casting of our possibilities upon the future Heidegger calls the projective resolution (*vorläufende Entschlossenheit*) of human life. In sum, the three elements of the Care Structure of human life include the categories of facticity, falling, and possibility. These three elements of our being are then correlated with the three temporal ecstases of temporality, namely past, present, and future. These three modes of time, together with the three existentials of human life, compose the everyday existence of our life. Time here is the very ground of our life. Put another way, when the Care Structure is combined with the three modes of time, we have present the basic wholeness of human existence.

Other elements of our human being's existence in time include mood (*Stimmung*), anxiety (*Angst*), and conscience (*Gewissen*). All of these elements are related to Care in that our moods are indicators of how our human being and its feelings are actually present in the world. Our moods are in constant change, both in their content and in their temporal relation to each other. They cannot be at all, aside from their duration and relation to the other moods which have preceded and followed them. Anxiety (*Angst*) is brought into being through the presence of our life's time as it advances into the uncertain possibilities of its future. Conscience (*Gewissen*) is also made possible through the existence of human life's being in time, and the term refers to our human awareness of falling short of our possibilities as they arise in our flow of life into the future. Conscience refers to human beings feeling responsible for what they have done in time, and what they have omitted. In the time of our life we often wish to flee or tranquilize ourselves, when we realize what we have done or omitted, in the face of finitude and death. For Heidegger the authentic life is one which spends its time with resolution under the perspective and counselorship of our coming death. In sum, the very being of our life is made possible by its embeddedness in time. Time past, present, and future is the ground of our life's basic structure as Care. Further, the unity of our existence is given in time as the coherence of a past which becomes a present, and a present that connects with a future that is its own. It is only because our life's existence possesses the characteristic of temporality that it is possible for it to be a whole or complete being.[4]

Heidegger never asks, "What is time?" Such a question is bracketed from his theme and method. Instead, his *Being and Time* shows that the question of time has not been properly asked nor revealed by an adequate phenomenological disclosure. The question of authentic time must arise from a description of human Care and its structure, in other words the conditions of human being's temporality which make Care possible. This is the primordial time of human existence.[5] Such time is a central theme in Heidegger's thought, especially in his contention that man's existence is temporal in its own unique manner. Time is the inner movement of human life, and this unique movement, for him as for Dilthey and Ortega y Gasset, must never be understood as the mere motion of an object at hand. All of the inauthentic attempts to define time in terms of the motions of such objects have converted the search for the meaning of time into a measuring of time, into a sort of counting device which identifies the duration of our lived experience with the public time of the clock. Such world time has been the attempt since Aristotle to count external motion by reference to a series of identical nows. This interpretation of time has obscured the fact of primordial or lived time as it is revealed in the temporal Care Structure of human life. In sum, what has been understood as the primordiality of clock time is really founded in the temporality of human life and not the other way around. The authentic and original time of human life has been repressed and forgotten. The datability of *Dasein*'s primordial time is the very ground of clock time and ontologically prior to it. To equate time exclusively with public or world time obscures the fundamental nature of human life's lived time. It especially obscures the self-transcendent character of human life, or what is designated as historicality or the temporal mode of history. Only a phenomenological description of human being's historical existence will reveal the complete temporal nature of human life. We must now turn to the final category of human temporality, which we shall term historicity.

CHAPTER SIX

Historicity

Defining Historicity

Human beings, says Goethe, are never simply original, but successors and inheritors of the human life that has preceded them. Our life consists not only of what we each are in our knife-edged present, but of what we have been and may become. The past as an essential component of our life is not simply to be understood as an academic subject, consisting of records and artifacts which are old or famous. Rather, the historicity of human life refers to the fact that to be human is in significant part to possess a nature which exists as a "having-been." We are by nature both the makers and interpreters of this past portion of our lives. Further, the human being thinks, experiences, and acts out of a historical context. For example, our eating with a fork is an action with its own unique form and meaning that has been acquired through historical time and place. The manner of the fork's genesis and use makes of it not only a physical object but a cultural artifact with its historically acquired system of shared meanings, values, and uses. Not only do we share this system with others, but the common uses and meanings of the fork are possible only through the shared existence and intelligibility that obtains between those who have used the fork in the past and those who use it in the present and future.

It was the intent of Dilthey's work to show that both human beings and the human studies that make them understandable cannot be grasped apart from the historicity of our existence. This historicity of human life may be compared to a symphony in that all the thoughts and actions of our lives are like the various notes which compose it. Each note is a part of a meaningful whole which happens in temporal succession from beginning to middle to end. One implication of this analogy is that both our present and future existence cannot be meaningfully separated from that past life from which they have arisen. All of our actions in historical time exist for Dilthey as a temporal succession of events which have affected each other.[1]

Yet this very temporal existence of human life gives rise to the following enigma: while human life is significantly the story of what has happened to it in the past, our perception and understanding of that past always occur in the living present of an observer. Even the future of our life must be lived in this present as an anticipation of events that are to come but are "not yet." Our experience of a past and a future must be given in a "now" present which has moved from a prior moment to a present one, and which advances to a future that is presently anticipated. Dilthey's thesis that lived time is an "advancing now" from out of the past through the present to the future is an implicit rejection of Kant's doctrine of the ideality of time, as he proposed it in his *Transcendental Aesthetic*. For Dilthey the Kantian notion never fully grasped the immediately lived duration and progression of our life's passage from past to present to future. Kant's conception of time has remained an abstraction which he constructed to satisfy the presuppositions of the natural science of his day, i.e., that temporality is the calibration of the motion of objects in space or simply the counting of motions. Such a notion of time was supposed to be both objective and absolute.[2]

Historicity (*Geschichtlichkeit*) is the forbidding name for a category of human life that always seems in need of further clarification. But when we pull back the academic hood of this term, we see that it is not only recognizable to us but also relevant to our lives as we actually live them. This word seems first to have been used by Hegel in his *Phenomenology of Spirit*. The term also appears in Schleiermacher, and after this in the writings of Dilthey. In the latter the term often refers to the supposed intelligibility that exists between those who compose the historical process and those who understand it, between interpreters and interpretants. Yet the idea of historicity can be expressed as the claim also found in Dilthey, Heidegger, and Ortega y Gasset that human beings "happen" historically. Such a claim can be unpacked to mean that the temporality in the happening of human life must always be distinguished from the temporality supposed for natural phenomena. The lived time of human life "happens" as a duration which is not solely experienced as a succession of external events and motions which clock time counts as a succession of discrete moments, each following the one immediately before it. Historicity for them is the category of human life which refers to the claim that clock time is itself secondary and derived from the radical priority of lived time. The duration of lived time is immediately experienced as the meaningful connection between the past, present, and future of human life. This temporality of human life is irreversible and compelled by its very nature to advance upon itself in an aggregate of new meanings which can never revert to what they have previously been. Such an irreversible sequence is characteristic not only of a particular life's past, but also of the life of others who were before it and after it.

The historicity of human life implies that our being is a radically temporal happening. We are composed both by what has happened to us and what we have done through time. We are what we are because previous things have happened to us in certain ways, and we have also behaved and thought in particular and identifiable ways. At any given point our life takes its departure from events that have developed and cumulated in it previously. In this sense we are all mutually dependent upon the past in our lives. Not only have we come to our present status from our own past, but our present life is possible because and only because of the previous forms of human life which we inherited, the history before us which we did not have to create but only assume and proceed from.

As a categorical element of human life, historicity is understood as an essential, universal, and necessary component of our existence. Such categorical components of human life are not simply facts among other facts, but elements which compose the very being of our life. Historicity is the duration of human life which advances in time from past to present to future. The historicity of human life is not the arbitrary, variable, and contingent clock time of the socio-economic world, but the very stuff of human life as it advances into a future from out of its past. As an irreversible becoming that underlies our actual existence, the historicity of human life is a possession of all human being, a time whose nature cannot be understood through the assumptions of natural science. For Dilthey it is only through a critique of historical reason that we can reveal such a time's nature. Such a critique would provide to the human studies, especially to history, a generally valid foundation which Kant had previously attempted to construct for the natural sciences in his *Critique of Pure Reason*. Part of Dilthey's goal here was to construct such a foundation for human life as it exists in historical time.

Historicity, Constant and Changing

As we have seen, the concept of historicity can refer to the unique manner in which our life is temporal, and as such, it is conceived by Dilthey as a categorical property of that life. But in Dilthey's thought the term may also designate the state of intersubjective understandability that can exist between the individuals who compose the historical process of the past and those who presently attempt to understand that process. In this sense historicity is the relation that obtains between those who interpret and those who are interpreted, between interpreters and interpretants. This process of interpretation for Dilthey, between those who compose the past and those who attempt to understand it, is possible because both the knower and the known possess a common and understandable humanity. This is what Dilthey meant when he claimed that history and the human sciences possess a common subject matter, human life. Through time human beings think, make, and do mutually intelligible things and constitute common meanings, values, and purposes. Human life's common intelligibility is the base from which we can proceed to know others through historical time, and in different times.

It is at this point that there arises the epistemological question of how generally valid explanation and understanding are possible in the human studies and history generally. This question is in significant part what Dilthey intended by his phrase "the critique of historical reason." The intellectual tool which he provided for this critique was the method of *Verstehen* or understanding. This element of human life became in his thought the category through which he attempted to explain how it is possible to comprehend the behavior, thought, and creations of others in historical time. The term *Verstehen* in Dilthey's thought is a *terminus technicus* which refers to the methodologically disciplined interpretation of another's life through its outward expressions in actions, creations, gestures, symbols, and utterances. Such expressions Dilthey termed "life assertions" (*Lebensäusserungen*). Here the interpreter of these life expressions attempts to understand them by transposing his or her own inner life experience into the meanings, values, and purposes that composed the lived experience behind the life assertions of their creators. This transposing of the interpreter's experience is actually a simulated reliving of another's life (*nacherleben*) as it is inferred from these expressions. All interpretation of another's life expressions must be finally referred to some individual's lived experience which endowed these expressions with meanings and purposes in the first place.

Dilthey's historicity has still another sense which with some reservations we may designate as historicism, or the belief that the recounting of the history of anything is a sufficient explanation of it; that the meanings and values of anything are revealed in our understanding of its origin and development. In the case of human life the historicist would attempt to understand life's varieties in time as it interacts with the physical and sociohistorical worlds which surround it. This means that a concept of human life cannot be formulated prior to such an understanding of those interactions. So stated, this position seems to put Dilthey in the historicist camp, yet he cannot be so simply understood, for he explicitly denied the historicist contention that truth, meaning, value, and human nature itself are always relative to the historical stages through which they have developed. In opposition to that historicist contention, he claimed that a common human nature is constant and everywhere the same.[3] Further, there exists a constant mental and psychological intelligibility in human beings which cannot be simply relative to the historical stages through which they develop. If the criteria for the intelligibility of human phenomena were themselves in change, the human studies and history would become so relativized that a generally valid science would be impossible.

While for Dilthey human nature exhibits a uniformity and intelligibility that remain constant, he also recognized variabilities and individual characteristics that distinguish different groups of human beings through time. All general theories and empirical explanations of human nature, he thought, must be based upon the observation of the varying responses to the historical and physical environments of human life, and no concept of human life can be generalized higher than the typicalities of any period with which researchers are familiar. This means that no final metaphysical or historical synthesis of human nature and the historical process will in theory be possible until the end of history itself.

Dilthey believed that the creative capacity of human beings in time is a central historical fact. Humanity is not a fixed species with a finally composed nature, but a species capable of self-transcendence. We must understand human life not only in terms of its limits but as a possibility of itself.[4] This fact for Dilthey is expressed in two further categories of human life, namely possibility (*Möglichkeit*) and development (*Entwicklung*). Both of these categories are related to the historicity of human life in that they involve Dilthey's recognition of the autonomy and self-construction of human life through historical time. This autofabrication expresses the way we attain self-transcendence and freedom. Such freedom and self-transcendence are not the result of some inner faculty of free will or an indeterminacy in our nature. Instead, freedom in human life is expressed in the historicity of human existence. Dilthey joined the notion of human freedom to historicity, because he meant to indicate that our life does not exist simply as ready-made or finished. Instead, our life is both the possibility of self-construction and the actual behavior required for the attainment of such autofabrication.

It was also in the context of historicity that Dilthey understood the self. He tended all his life to refuse any thesis which identified the self with soul or mind substance. Instead, what he called "mind" or "experience" always appeared within the prior and radical reality of human life. Here the self is understood as that part of human life which bears the unity of lived experience as it has developed through time. Dilthey called this unity of lived experience the "acquired mental system of our life" as it is generated from the past through the present and into the future. The temporality of the self cannot be understood by reference to clock time alone. It is through lived time that the unique historicity of human life is comprehended as the integrated advance of our life from past to present to future. Such an understanding of the self can never be separated from its unique temporality. The duration of lived time is the most concrete and essential aspect of human life.[5] Kant seemed never to grasp the concrete reality of human life, and its unique time remained for him a sort of intuitive abstraction which he never integrated into a concept of radical reality.

Toward the end of his career Dilthey came to the conviction that what man is cannot be grasped through introspection or psychological experiment alone, but only through history.[6] His new emphasis upon history seems to contradict the earlier work of his psychological period, in which he had attempted to describe the entire psychic system and its structure. His new emphasis upon history appears a departure from any unified and consistent sense of human nature, and he seems here to have embraced a historicist position. The nineteenth century historicist school can be identified with at least the following claims. (1) There is a distinction between the methods and subject matter of the human studies (*Geisteswissenschaften*) and the natural sciences (*Naturwissenschaften*). (2) The assumption is that by our complete delineation of the history of something we have provided a sufficient explanation of it; that the meaning and value of some X in historical time is understood through a comprehension of the stages of its development. (3) The explanation of the human studies, especially history, must refer to the individual delineation of events and actions, and not to historical laws which are themselves instances of the more general covering laws of nature. (4) The truth, meaning, and value of human beings and their works through time, including human nature itself, are entirely relative to the historical stages through which they have developed.[7] Dilthey's qualification as a historicist fails at the fourth criterion, for he claimed that "A common human nature and its individuations stand in constant life relationships and these are everywhere the same."[8] This common human nature refers in Dilthey to both the like psychological constitution of human beings and the universal intelligibility of their nature. This common nature is not relative to the historical stages through which it has passed, for it is assumed to be transhistorical for the general validity of the human and historical sciences.

Dilthey's belief that "What man is, history will tell us" is actually his faith that human nature is something that is cumulatively and systematically given in the expressions of human life in historical time. While we may abstract such ideal types as "medieval man" or "the Protestant ethic" in our research, Dilthey would only allow that a total representation of human beings and their work cannot be completed until the end of historical time. Finally, Dilthey held the belief that there exists a creative element in human beings that must be noted as one of the central facts of our existence. Humanity is not bound to the condition of its past as a fixed species with a finally composed nature. Human beings are creatures of self-transcending capacities with open possibilities for themselves. This for him remains the central fact of historical man.

Heidegger's Historicity

Heidegger's main treatment of historicity is found in his *Being and Time* under Section 74, "The Basic Constitution of Historicality," and in the subsequent Section 77, "The Problem of Historicality in the Researches of Dilthey and Count Yorck." Both of these sections are included in Part V of *Being and Time* and are entitled "Temporality and Historicality." Here Heidegger used the term "history" (*Geschichte*) to refer to the actual process and events of history itself. He used the term *Historie* to refer to the methods of research appropriate to history. It is in his use of the term historicity (*Geschichtlichkeit*) that Heidegger's work seems an extension of Dilthey's project, for it is only because we are essentially historical beings that we can both study and make the historical past. This is basically Dilthey's position, but Heidegger developed this category in a more extensive and explicit manner than his predecessor. The assumptions of scholars like Karl Löwith that Heidegger only carried out Dilthey's projects to ends that were implicit in Dilthey himself are misleading. Heidegger believed that Dilthey's project was the understanding of human life as it expressed itself in historical time, but he believed that Dilthey's weakness grew out of his overemphasis upon the problem of knowledge in his work. He thought Dilthey's researches were carried out from the question of the general validity of the historical sciences, and not from the standpoint of a fundamental ontology of *Dasein*.[9] For Dilthey human life must be understood within the context of the human studies and their search for generally valid judgments. He would have rejected Heidegger's later claims that the historicity of human life, or human life itself, is philosophically secondary to a fundamental ontology of *Dasein*. Heidegger believed in this respect that authentic historical science (*Historie*) is only possible when we have established a general ontology of the historicity of *Dasein* itself.[10] Dilthey failed, he thought, to reveal the ontological constituents of human life. Heidegger believed it was Dilthey's friend Count Yorck who showed a more insightful understanding of the difference between an empirical science of history and the requirements of a fundamental ontology of *Dasein*. Dilthey's work was only part of the tendency of the whole historicist movement to focus on the methodological and factual concerns of historical research, producing an "ocular" or external view of historical science. Instead, Heidegger thought, philosophy must be brought to the task of working out a generic difference between the empirical science of history and the philosophically prior meaning of human being itself. Neither historical science nor human life itself can be understood simply through Dilthey's *Verstehen* method. We must understand that our human existence is primarily historical, and human life must be understood as the ability of *Dasein* to "historicize" itself into its own future. Further, Heidegger maintained in his *Kant and the Problem of Metaphysics* that the era of understanding human being as a mental or spiritual state had come to a close. Man's being in the world is not primarily understood through the historical sciences at all, and Dilthey's idea of human life does not disclose what sort of being human life actually is. His idea of human life can at best represent "mere aliveness" (*Nur nochleben*), but as such it does not answer the question of what sort of being we are.[11] Dilthey's work, in Heidegger's view, remained only an expression of the Cartesian theory of knowledge, and a more adequate notion of human being in time must be prior to all the thematizing sciences and the misleading influence of Descartes.

Heidegger approached historicity as a phenomenological description of how human life "happens," and how it discloses its own-most possibilities. For him the concrete and full disclosure of how human life happens is historicity itself. He describes the happening of human life as a "stretching" (*Strecke*) from a past to a future. As a "historizing" between our birth and death, our life is time itself. In the context of such lived time Heidegger locates the "who" or the self of *Dasein*. Such a self cannot be separated from its historicity. Its very existence is a combination of its past, present, and future as it stretches between birth and death.

For Heidegger the historicity of human life is composed of three elemental categories, which he designates as heritage (*Erbschaft*), fate (*Schicksal*), and destiny (*Geschick*). Heritage is defined as the totality of facts and events which constitute the temporal mode of our having-been, or what we have been before. Yet "what we have been before" is also part of the constitution of our present life as a whole. Our heritage is composed of those happenings which we cannot nullify or avoid, because they happened to us in the way they actually did and not another way. Our authentically conceived heritage demands of us our resolute acceptance of the prior existence that still constitutes our present life. While we cannot change what has happened to us and what we have done in the past, we are still able to change our attitude to our past and our interpretation of it. The heritage of our past is always there to be retrieved in our present and future. Our past, our having-been, exists as a possibility for ourselves and others to emulate or avoid.

The second characteristic of human life's historicity is fate. In the condition of its fate human life becomes aware of the limits of its past, present, and future possibilities. In our fate we come to recognize that our authentic behavior is composed as we decide for ourselves which of our possibilities we shall accept as our own. In this manner we create a fate appropriate to ourselves. But an irresolute life, the life actually chosen by most human beings, attempts not to decide anything. Such a life only floats from one possibility to another, usually by conformity to collective fashions and norms. It is only our resolute choices that are historically significant. Such resolute choice refers to the manner in which we release ourselves from the conformity to the collective coercion of the anonymous mass of humanity (*das Man*). Such resolution appears in human life through the call of conscience to be the self which consciously disjoins itself from the conformity, adjustments, and assumptions of the crowd. In this case our historicity is constituted by the authentic decisions we make in our stretching between part and future. The fateful historicity of human life is composed of the resolute deciding of our destiny in the face of finitudes and fallenness.

The third element of Heidegger's version of historicity is destiny (*Geschick*). This refers to the relation that human life has to collectives, groups, nations, peoples, and the historical eras of which it is a part. While our existence always remains our own, our life possesses the possibility of an existence in time with others. Such a relation is a shared historicity in which our individual lives can recognize and appropriate the larger destiny of groups, nations, and historical eras as our own. It is only in our relation to generational and collective existence that the full and authentic historicity of human life is revealed.[12] In other words, the historizing of human life between birth and death, along with its heritage, fate, and destiny, form for Heidegger the very wholeness of human life's historicity. Such a wholeness terminates only in death as the final horizon of our life. All historicity and historical science must find their subject matter within this wholeness. History in this sense is conceived as the critique of human life and the uncovering of its previously existing possibilities as individuals, groups, and nations.[13] Here history becomes the study of the humanly possible, and this means that what has been achieved and what can be repeated in the present and the future are still available to present and future humanity. The end of authentic historical science is the uncovering of such possibilities for human life in the unfolding of heritage, destiny, and fate. Here the Diltheyan search for the general validity of the historical sciences is replaced by the claim that the proper object of historiology is the study of the essential individual and group choices of human beings in historical time.

Historicity and Freedom

Our human life is historical, not because it possesses a chronological past, nor because of a special internal capacity for free choice. Rather, both historicity and freedom are consequences of the manner in which we are in time. It is because human beings possess a future with specific and identifiable possibilities that we are historical at all. It is through the capacity to orient and decide toward our future possibilities and to actualize them in time that human beings are free. It is through the unique manner that we are in time that our life possesses freedom or autofabrication. Unlike the existence of a thing at hand, the temporality of human life is not simply the passing of an object from one "now point" to the next which succeeds it. Instead, human time is lived as the capacity to appropriate a definite and specific future. It is through our temporal orientation to and our stretching toward future possibilities that we are historical beings possessing freedom. Our freedom is not a secret spiritual agency in the soul possessing a "free choice" through which we transcend our past and present actualities. Rather, freedom refers to the autofabrication of our life towards its possibilities in the future. Ortega maintained that because our life is our fundamental being, because we are our life in time and nothing more, our freedom is exhibited as our ability and decision to uphold and direct our being without rest or pause into the future. Our being both decides and makes itself. Here Ortega does not speak of a freedom of the will, nor is our life exempt from causal conditions. Human life is not an escape from causes, but is always the attempt to be the cause that executes our desires and intentions. Human life is a constitutive instability.[14] Such instability means that human life executes its existence in time by advancing into various circumstantial possibilities. In sum, to exist in circumstances we did not create or choose is our life's most vital characteristic. In this sense, our freedom refers to the inevitable task of our life's self-construction in time. Our life is a *faciendum*, a thing that must be made. It is in our life's constitutive ability to be other than it is, to have possibilities within itself, that we can identify its freedom. Freedom means that our life is not a fixed but a self-creating identity, a possibility of self-creation in time. We have in this sense no final identity. Human life has no fixed or static nature, like a stone, but a history.

Our life's freedom consists in its being a permanent possibility of itself. As with Dilthey before him, Ortega saw the possibility of our being as a self-constituting becoming. The claim that we are free refers to our ability to rise to the recognition and the execution of this possibility.[15] But the presence of possibility in human life and the fact that human life possesses no final identity do not imply that human beings are not both limited or fixed by unalterable conditions or compelled by causally determined factors that transcend choice. We are not free to become anything we desire, to be without circumstances, to be always young, or without limits, problems, or death. Also, our genetic and anatomical makeup is subject to the laws of the physical and biological sciences. But because the nature of human life is to advance upon itself into the future, its autonomy is best understood in its being lived, and not through its reduction to laws external to itself. The proper medium for the comprehension of human life is for Ortega the historical narration of its self-creation in time. History is the story of human life in time, the totality of what human being has done up to the very present.[16] It is only the historical past of human life which is unalterable and finished. The unalterable past is our one fixed and "Eleatic" aspect of our human being. Yet it is our historicity, our autofabrication in time, which allows us to add to our already finished past the new possibilities of our being. In this respect historicity is the triumph of human life over an unalterable and dead past.

As we saw earlier, for Dilthey the actuality of freedom is understood in the context of his two categories possibility and development, both of which are to be understood in the context of historicity. These categories are meant to account for both the autonomy and self-construction of human life in time. Human life is a constant possibility for itself, for human life is not a ready-made condition such as that of a stone. The freedom of human life is its capacity for development out of the past and present to its future possibilities. It is possible for human life to anticipate and imagine various forms of life for itself, then to concretize, work out, and attain specific possibilities. For example, if a given person were to set as a possibility for himself or herself the attaining of a new profession, he or she must achieve new experiences, education, and circumstances that constitute the new professional status. Here both the possibility and development of that person's life in time are required to transcend the previous forms of his or her life through the construction of the "new life" of the new professional status. It is in the possibility and development of a new life form that Dilthey locates freedom, and this creative capacity of our life cannot be separated from its historicity.[17]

In sum, it was through Dilthey's appropriation of the idea of historicity from Hegel that it became a significant conception both in German thought generally, in Heidegger's specifically, and in the work of Ortega y Gasset. Dilthey developed the notion that historicity must be a chief category of human life and the premier study of the human sciences. He also developed the methodology of *Verstehen* for carrying out such study. In the thought of Heidegger both truth and being take on a relation to the historicity of human existence, in that the truth of being is disclosed from its hiddenness through historical time. In Dilthey and Ortega the self-construction of human life through historical time is required for the development of the reality of human life itself. Because human beings have made history, it is in principle understandable by other human beings in other times and places. The thought of Dilthey, Heidegger, and Ortega y Gasset also contains the notion that there is a crucial relation of historicity to human freedom. Freedom can only be understood as our openness to the possibilities of our being in the world. Possibility, development, and human transcendence must be revealed in historical time, in the constant advance upon itself that is human life.

CHAPTER SEVEN

The Inner Experience of Human Life

Lived Experience

For Dilthey "human life" is a philosophical expression which refers to the inner experience of all humanity through time, and to the meaningful relationship that individual life has to all human beings, living and dead.[1] Our individual life is not given externally in the manner of our sense experience of the physical world. Our life is given to us from the inside. This inner experience of our life is called by Dilthey *Erlebnis*, or a lived experience. In this state of self-awareness we become merged with our own experience, because we intend it through what Dilthey called inner perception (*innere Wahrnehmung*). An *Erlebnis* is the most fundamental unit of experience. Such units relate to each other in a meaningful manner, and the aggregate of these experiences is the individual's life and the life of humanity. Because there is no transcendental self which somehow lives behind our lived experience, and because our lived experience is never the appearance of something anterior to itself, the human being experiences his or her life as a whole of lived experiences, and as reality itself. This means that human life accumulates itself with each new lived experience which it has in time, and it accumulates itself as a complex whole of life which is made up not only of the individual's lived experiences, but also of the experiences of the entire society and history of which the individual is a part.

Our life is more than only our private possession, for it is also an object that bears a relation to the life of another in a common world. It is both understandable and real for another, to whom it bears a meaningful relation. Our life in connection with other lives forms a body of knowledge, and this aggregate view is understood as a general *Weltanschauung* that reflects the things and meanings of the world.[2] For Dilthey our lived experience is generally contrasted to the outer experience of the senses. Our external sense perception of the outer world, and the judgments we make of this domain, do become part of human life's general experience, but the primary goal of Dilthey's work was to formulate a philosophy of the whole historical existence of human life from the lived experience of life itself.

We may also understand both internal lived experience and external sense experience as those mental acts by which we intend some specific content in the domains of human life and external nature. If our act of conscious intention is directed to the outer world through sense experience, then this act is called by Dilthey *Erfahrung* or empirical sense experience. Such experience is opposed to our lived experience in general. Outer sensate experience becomes in Dilthey's thought the basis of the natural sciences (*Naturwissenschaften*), and lived experience becomes the ground of the *Geisteswissenschaften* or the humanities, history, social studies, law, religion, philosophy, and psychology. Dilthey was indebted to the philosopher and theologian Friedrich Schleiermacher (1768–1834), who earlier had claimed that the lived experience of our life is reality itself, in so far as reality can be known by human beings at all. Dilthey went on to claim that while natural science is founded upon our judgments of the external world of nature, and the human studies are grounded in lived experience, the logical structure of both lived experience and sense experience remains identical. But for Dilthey outer sense experience of the world of natural science is always translated and expressed in abstract, material, and quantifiable units of thought. The outer experience that grounds the natural sciences must be expressed exclusively in the quantifiable meanings and denominators assigned to it by the methods and assumptions of the natural sciences. Such a perspective is opposed to the immediate and concrete lived experience of our life world (*Lebenswelt*). Here the objects of lived experience become the assumptions, meanings, values, volitions, and feelings of human life itself. The life world exists in our lived experience as it actually is, and not as a sense appearance that hides a deeper phenomenon. For Dilthey the fundamental difference between the world of natural science and that of human life is that the materials of natural science are presented to experience as sense data, which must somehow be expressed as laws generated from sense perception through hypothesis formation. But human life is given to itself as what it actually is through lived experience. Human life and the subjects of natural science are distinguished by the fact that the experience utilized by natural science is mediated by external sense experience, and the inner world of human life is not.[3]

Related to Dilthey's distinction between inner and outer experience is his differentiation between two kinds of science. He notes that while all science is understood as the search to the foundation of first principles, its methods and materials are different, and these are of two basic types: (a) explanatory (*erklärende*) and (b) descriptive science (*beschreibende Wissenschaft*). The former is devoted to the discovery of the general laws of nature through empirical observation and by hypothesis formation. The latter refers to the description of the inner data of human life itself. For Dilthey the prescribed method for this description of the life world was not strictly that of phenomenology, as Husserl had used the term, but that of "self-reflection" (*Selbstbesinnung*). Here the goal was to describe the data of human life as they are actually given to our self-reflection. These data are then formulated into such categories as lived experience, imagination, thought, meaning, etc. Our lived experience takes the form of personal self-reflection, and the central feature of such reflection is the ego or self conceived as the total meaningful connection of a life's individual experiences through time.

Dilthey's elaboration and critique of the experience of the inner reality of human life is perhaps best explained by reference to his 1894 essay entitled *Ideas Concerning a Descriptive and Analytical Psychology*. In this essay he introduced his concept of the structure system of the mind. Such a system is composed of the fundamental units of lived experience in coherent relationship with each other. Put another way, each unit of lived experience is fully significant only in relation to other lived experiences. The totality of the individual's lived experiences compose the whole of his or her life as it has existed through time. The totality of all individuals and their experiences in time form history itself.

For Dilthey a lived experience is made up of three central parts which are themselves subcategories of human life. The first of these is meaning or significance (*Bedeutung*). This is the component of lived experience which indicates the relationship that a part has for a larger whole in the network of our experience. All human life is a coherent collection of parts, and the parts take their meaning within a greater whole of which they are one element. Wholes likewise are what they are in reference to their parts. For example, a steering wheel takes its unique meaning only with respect to the functions and purposes of the automobile of which it is a part. The automobile itself takes its collective significance by reference to its parts and their purposes. Secondly, all lived experience is affective or emotive. This means that our conscious responses to inner and outer stimuli always exist as positive or negative feelings, states of attraction or repulsion, and as the assignment of worth or lack of worth to definite ends. All lived experience is composed of such elements. Thirdly, our lived experience is purposive or end-oriented. It is end-oriented in the sense that our intuitions are directed from some prior state of meanings, feelings, and volitions to an anticipated future state which completes the development of the experience through time. The identity of the lived experience is finally determined by the purpose or goal to which it is oriented. For example, the lived experience of writing a check for our child's education is of a different purpose, value, emotion, and meaning than writing a check for a tax return. Their difference is understandable by reference to their unlike ends in human life. Both express a likeness to each other, yet as we calculate a relation between the drawn sum and the remaining balance of the account, we also experience a meaningful part-whole relation between the account fund, the check sum, and the purpose for which it was drawn. Each check writing is a lived experience which combines specific and unique meanings, feeling, volitions, and ends that take their whole significance from the purpose of each experience. Each lived experience possesses a teleological structure composed of different meaningful, affective, volitional, and purposive elements. The basic denominators of human life are such lived experiences. The totality of these experiences is at once the whole of an individual's life, and the combined lived experiences of all individuals living and dead through time, experiences which constitute the human life of the historical world. They are both the fundamental units of all inquiry in the human studies and the "stuff" of which history is composed. History and society are in principle understandable because they are made up of the life experiences that are possessed and shared by both the researchers and the agents whom they study. This means that our lived experience is in principle the object of generally valid judgments in the historical, social, and human studies. In sum, the aggregate of life experiences through time is the historical being of human life. As such, neither human nature nor the human studies can be separated from their historicity.

Embodiment

We can conceive of a physical body without human life, but we cannot conceive of a human life that is not embodied. The question for the philosophy of human life is not to explain how human life is separate from a body, or how the body and human life are the same. Rather, it is to understand that our life exists in the world as an embodied subject. Our bodies are not to be understood simply as physiological pieces of matter, nor is our life to be understood as "body free." Our bodies are encountered from the beginning as "lived" from the inside. This means that our body is never separated from our life, and our life is always given to us as an embodiment over which we somehow preside. It is as an embodied subject that we exist in the world. Yet both physiology and traditional philosophy have misunderstood this manner of being in the world. Physiology tends to understand our body without a human life, and traditional philosophy has tended to understand our soul, mind, and life as disembodied, or as possessing a radically different nature than the body. But the idea of human life implies that we cannot understand our existence in the world if we remain locked in this dichotomy. Our body can never be understood as a mere object at hand, and our life cannot be understood as disembodied subject radically apart from a body of some sort. We are always in the world as a corporeal presence, or as a body inhabited by a life that is our own.

Our embodied life is understood by others through the life assertions of language, overt actions, and creations which are part of an interpretable and physical world. All life assertions are one way or another embodied projections of the meanings, values, and purposes of an inner human life. The need and ability of human life to project itself into the outer world is an implicit recognition that our life is hidden from others and must somehow be embodied and objectified in the world. Our life exists not only as a pure subject, for it must "be for others" through its public, physical manifestations or life assertions. All the outward manifestations of our life involve a body presence, in which thoughts, intuitions, feelings, and mental states are expressed through the assertions of human life. We are always trapped in our embodiment, yet the body is the means of a liberation out of itself through lips, vocal cords, eyes, and ears as they express and receive a world. But our bodies are not simply objects that others may perceive as they would a stone. Nor is our life to be understood as an invisible ego, soul, or mind apart from all embodiment, world, or history. We are not even present to ourselves apart from our bodies. We are embodied subjects.

It was Descartes who formulated the thesis that human beings and the world in general exist as two separate substances: bodily extension and mind. Such a bifurcation is radically misleading, for it forces the issue of the embodied subject into the false question of how two different substances interact at all, or how they can constitute the human being at all. The idea of human life as radical reality rejects this Cartesian approach to the question of both the lived body and human life. The idea of human life stands as the attempt to show our real human condition not as an external relation of two separate substances, but as embodied human life. Because there can here be awareness only in a subject who is aware, we must speak of the relation between a subject and his body as inner or "lived." This implies that our proper or lived body is not the same as a body we perceive from without. Our lived body belongs to us alone, because it is lived by ourselves alone. A distinction always exists to be made between our lived body and a biological body which is the object of the life sciences. This latter body exists as derivation and not as our ownness, or as our lived body. It is only by an abstract inference that it is to be associated with human life at all. It is not only the external body we live when we reach out to another for a handshake that may be experienced as firm, weak, or noncommittal. Such a handshake is not simply a matter of two bodies touching in space, but it also exists as a meaning in our life and the life of the other as a specific way of our being in the world. The external handshake here cannot be separated from its significance for human life. The "lived hand" of the two people involved exists as a perspective that our life may take on the world. In other words, our hands exist in at least two perspectives, outer and inner. The handshake is both an external biological body and a part of our bodies that we inhabit with our lives. Yet the biological hand and the "lived hand" are the same hand under two perspectives. One exists in the perspective of my hand as a body object in the world, a subject of biological science. The other is a "lived hand" that is an extension of my life as lived experience, an expression of the fact that we are embodied subjects.

All human life is embodied in one way or another. For example, the human brain is the embodied side of our lived experience and our thinking in general. Without our organs of perception we could not speak of spatial predicates such as "here" or "there," "high" or "low," "far" or "near," "heavy" or "light." These predicates "are" as they are given to the subject perceiver. All such variations are perceived through the body.

While we live our bodies from the inside, we can nevertheless be given to ourselves as an "outer" physiological body alone. A face deformed in an accident may seem not to be our "real life," yet that is how we are given to ourselves. As perceiving, thinking beings we live through our bodies and carry out all of our projects through a body just as it is. Our lived experience is not merely a matter of "pure mind" or transcendental ego, but as an embodied subject acting and suffering in a real world. The Cartesian distinction between an extended body and a non-extended consciousness does not exist for the embodied subject which must bear itself up in the world. This embodied subject cannot be defined without relating it to a body, and I cannot define my body without relating it to my life. This relation is the very system of how we are in the world.

Thinking

All thinking must be referred in the end to its status within human life. The categories of life are implicit within it and are not deduced a priori, as in the case of Kant's system of judgments. For Dilthey all categories are abstracted from the flow of human life itself and then formalized as philosophical expressions. Meaning, unity, multiplicity, cause, etc. are never simply present as sense data or Kant's a priori forms of understanding, but as elements which thought has previously organized in the flow of life. It is from this source, this flow of life, that the stuff of science, philosophy, and all discursive thinking is derived. It is through our reflection upon life's categories that we are made aware that they are the center of human life and its thought. Both thinking and the other categories of human life are present in our self-awareness, and they are describable as the forms and operations that are actually happening within us.

In the philosophy of human life thinking has been understood as that activity by which human beings attempt to decide upon justified grounds what is to be done in their circumstances. Previously Aristotle had defined two types of thinking, one a contemplation upon first principles through what he called theoretical reason, and the other a deliberative mental act applied to the practical conduct of our human life. In both of these forms of thinking human thought is always an activity which is internal to the subject but which therefore requires for its external expression objective life assertions in the forms of language, symbols, and creations. The intellectual content of our thought is made objective in such a way that it can be apprehended by someone who resides outside the interiority of our own thought processes. In this manner the content of our thought is given a recognizable "look" or "profile" to others in the world. Yet in a sense our thinking always remains within ourselves as a sort of self-performance of the mental content which awaits expression in the world. For Ortega our life is the first object of thought and incontrovertible knowledge that we possess. Our life "performs" itself as constantly present to us, and all that we call real must somehow appear or show itself within it. We are permanently self-attendant to our lives, and we "count on" and "live by" its constant presence to us in all of our beliefs and presuppositions. I "perform" my life and in so doing I am a pure actuality. My life is a performative, not an objective, being. Its constant self-presence is such that it cannot "step out of itself" into an objective physical presence for another.

Dilthey affirmed that the category of thinking remains the element without which human life can grasp nothing.[4] We organize and clarify the content of our lived experience through what he calls "silent thought." It is here that we find the prediscursive operations which organize the meanings which exist in human life. Here too are the mutual acts of separation and combination of the noticeable givens that exist in our awareness. Silent thought acts as the capacity of the subject to raise particulars to the status of universals, to utilize the imagination and memory for reproducing from the universals the ideas which compose our life.[5] In such a mental act we experience not just raw objects but meaningful relationships. Thinking, then, is something that always goes on in our life. At all times our life is a considered "gearing into" the world and its circumstances. All theory and knowledge must finally be grounded in thinking's relation to circumstances. Here thinking is oriented to the world in the attempt to determine what is essential and inseparable in the circumstances which surround it. It then represents those elements in abstract ideas or wholes which are formed with the aid of memory and imagination. In this way thinking becomes language, logic, and reason in general. The laws of thought, science, and philosophy are in the last analysis the expression of the materials and relations already present in the silent course of previous thought.

In all thinking, human beings first encounter in their lives a reality of some sort, and subsequently they form a concept of it. In this way a mental action is directed to a content that the subject encounters in his or her life. That part of our life in which thinking occurs is said to be "intentional," i.e., always directed to some object or content. Thought is that property of consciousness which always refers to a content. This is to say that our thought is always "about something." The subject matter that it is about may be a concrete object in the world, or an abstract concept such as "justice" or "number," or such definite characteristics as meanings, natures, references, and relations. Furthermore, the "objects" about which we think are not necessarily real or existent things; they may be about such nonexistent entities as square circles or the ninety-ninth president of the United States.

Once thinking has directed itself to some object or content, it then forms judgments and assumptions about that content, and attempts to decide what to do in the face of circumstances. The end of thought is the attempt to establish what is believable, warranted, or true about something with which we are concerned in our life. The need to think is constant, for we are perpetually in doubt, concern, or hesitation about our environment. Our thinking is not simply a contemplation of some raw object of sense perception, but an attempt to substitute for a mere object another thing which we may call the being or nature of the object in question. In other words, thinking is also what takes place in experience when we replace for a raw thing or presence a nature which can be conceived or recognized. In this manner the actual physical presence or circumstance is replaced by a thought form, symbol, or nature which lends an identity that is recognized, stable, and available for use in the concerns and decisions of our life.

When we think about something, our life becomes occupied with finding out what that thing is, or what its nature is. In this process we compose part of the life which is our own and form a cognitive system of experience. A thing or a circumstance does not show its nature in the absence of some thought or concept which intends it. If we are trying to express or conceive some nature, we use such locutions as "X is the case," or "Something is x." For this conceived thing to take its place in human life, it must be interpreted within a human life. Otherwise, it remains in the vague status of a thing in itself without an endowed identity. In this sense thinking is related to naming, for to think is to name the fact that some x possesses a nature which can be recognized and communicated within human life.

Yet this is not the end of the story, for we also think in order to be able to rely upon the constant and expected nature of something in our environment. In order to possess this reliance or belief about something in our circumstances we must establish for them a specific nature or expectation of "what it will do or be next." If our thinking fails to anticipate or identify what something is or what it will do, then our thinking life becomes disoriented. Indeed, thinking may even be defined as human life's attempt to emerge from disorientation to orientation into its circumstances; or life's attempt to decide itself, as Ortega would have it. Thinking is that about human life which allows for a progression out of disorientation into orientation. It is our attempt to establish a fixed nature for something, so that our expectations of that something do not fail or mislead us. When we have confidence and success in our dealings with our immediate world, then we have established for the moment what Ortega called "being in paradise." In such a state we have seemingly no failures, needs, or problems; there has been established at least a temporary understanding of what we can believe or take for granted. Truth becomes the warranted belief that we know what nature a given circumstance in our life possesses. Ignorance is an implicit faith that something must have a nature but that we do not know what that nature is. When we have knowledge of something, that its nature is secure and assumed for a prolonged period of time in our life, then our personal beliefs assume a social dimension. Society becomes our living in a world of common usages and meanings, until there occurs some failure or refutation of our belief system. Then the requirement arises that human life must reject some part of its tradition and establish new assumptions and beliefs about this part of the world of circumstances.

This "new truth" may be characterized by the following features. The nature that is now assumed and justified must be something more clear in identity and consistency than the former failed belief. The new nature or identity must be non-contradictory, and its oppositions and relations to the older belief must be both warranted and pronounced in the new position. Its claims must be detectable, apprehended, and expressed in a natural language. These features of thinking must become synonymous with judgments, purposes, and decisions made in actual human life. Such thinking is an active faculty which spontaneously apprehends the concept or nature implicit in the raw objects and circumstances of the world. For Dilthey all thinking must be developed and integrated into a larger mental system of human life which is acquired and built up over time as an expression of what we have lived through and understood. The result is a mental system growing through time as our total experience, remaining always with us, and conditioning everything we do. Such a total experience is designated as the structure system of the mind. But the inner connections of such a system can only be experienced in part, for our awareness can only raise a limited number of elements to direct a lived experience in given time. If one of our given ideas has been able to evoke a subsequent class of ideas, we may be said to have arrived at a given meaningful connection between whole classes of ideas. We are then able to generalize their meaning, function, and importance according to the likenesses, differences, separations, combinations, and uniformities of human life itself.[6]

Truth

The very substance of our life is to be found in the ways it can exist in the world. One of the ways it exists is as a being which both needs and seeks truth. It was Aristotle who advanced a traditional view of the nature of truth, when he claimed that the experiences of the soul are approximations of things in the world, an adequation of thought to things, or what the medieval thinkers called *adequatio intellectus et rei*. The assumption here was that truth resides in our judgments, and judgment can only consist of an agreement of the judgment with the objects that are judged. A true judgment consists in stating what something actually is. Knowledge exists when a judgment is verified by an experience that shows it to correspond to something as it "really is" in the world.

But in Heidegger's view the ultimate nature of truth is not established by constructing such criteria for truth as Aristotle's adequation theory attempted to do. For Heidegger all theories of truth since Aristotle make this error: i.e., they confuse the criteria of truth for truth itself. In his *Being and Time* there is the attempt to reveal the very essence or meaning of truth itself. The question of the meaning of truth itself, he claims, has been left essentially untouched and unexamined in the tradition of philosophy since Aristotle. Truth, says Heidegger, does not lie in judgments or propositions, but it lies in the "making unhidden" of something. This notion of truth, as the Greeks saw it, is called *aletheia*, or the revealing that shows something to be what it really is. This alone is primordial truth, a "letting be shown" what is really the case with respect to some aspect of the world. It belongs to the nature of human life itself to be open to the truth as it discloses itself. Truth cannot disclose itself to or in a stone, but the truth or nature of a stone is disclosed in human life.

Truth here is a characteristic not of objects at hand in the world, but of human life itself. This means that truth belongs primordially to human life as one of its essential properties or categories. Our life is a being which is open to the truth, yet it may also be closed to the truth. If there is a refusal to let things be disclosed as what they are, then we are in a state of untruth or even fallenness. For example, if we refuse to believe in the face of all contrary evidence and reasoning that a given black person is more intelligent and educated than a given white person, then we are in a state of untruth, even fallenness. We have not let the truth be shown.

All judgments of fact in order to be knowledge depend upon the fact that our openness to truth is a necessary precondition for knowledge. In other words, human life exists at least in part as a capacity to uncover and understand what is actually the case. Human life is the vehicle that allows truth to be shown at all. In this sense, truth cannot exist apart from human life. But it does not follow from this that truth is only relative to man, or that man is the measure of all truth (*homo mensura*). Rather, human life is the very "openness" that allows truth to be revealed. Human life here is a necessary condition for the appearance of truth. It is through the presence of truth in our lives that we are able to inquire into truth, falsity, or knowledge at all. Put another way, all judgments about the world presuppose that there is within human life a property or capacity for truth, which can never be independent of our life. When we say in this case that the truth exists, what is meant in this context is that the truth is a category of human life. This category is grounded in human life's capacity for being receptive to the disclosure of truth. Truth and human life are therefore bound together, and neither can be independent of the other. We both judge and understand because human life is capable in principle of both true judgments and true knowledge.

Knowledge

The nature of knowledge has been a formal problem of philosophy since Plato's *Theaetetus*. There Plato defined the concept in such a way that knowledge could only be "about" the trans-temporal and eternal forms which were contrasted to the unreal and changing particulars of sense. Plato believed, as Ortega did later, that one of the tasks of philosophy is to describe the nature of reality. For Plato the ultimately real was to be associated with the eternal forms, which are the legitimate objects of knowledge. But for a modern like Ortega all knowledge is to be apprehended within the context and priority of human life as radical reality. This is to say that while for him the universe in general is revealed from many perspectives—personal, social, historical, mathematical, scientific, etc.—there remains one reality which is prior to all other perspectives that may be called real, and this is our life, the life of each one of us. As we have seen, human life is not the only reality, but it is the prior and radical one, in that all others are rooted in it and understood through its categories. The question of the nature of knowledge itself arises first in human life, because when the beliefs of human beings fail or require the extension or criticism of subsequent insight, knowledge itself is called forth as an essential requirement of human life. All other realities besides human life become interpreted through the needs, meanings, values, purposes, and ends already present in human life itself. Our life is experienced in relation to real things, and all that is real for us must be seen within the context of human life itself. In spite of the plurality of realities there remains one radical reality which is prior to all the others in explanatory power and presupposition and perspective—the life of each one of us. The term radical is derived here from its Latin form which means "root" or rooted. We have stressed that human life is not the only reality, but all the others must be seen through its meanings, need, presuppositions, and perspectives. While the universe may contain realities unknown to human beings, realities perhaps more important and primordial, all that can be experienced or known must come to us first through the perspectives of our life. In Ortega's idea of human life knowledge is generated through a re-translation of our beliefs into facts or empirically verified theory. Knowledge arises in the inner mental life of the individual when he or she proposes an answer to the question, "What is this thing?" The validity of such a question is actually based on a more covert or prior question of the "being" of this or that thing. When we are able to grasp the question of the "being" of something, there occurs a sort of transference of the essential characteristics of the thing in question into the mind of the subject. In this transference the subject receives the thing's conceptual identity into his or her mental life. The nature or truth of this concept is an instance of knowledge when it corresponds with what the given thing really is, its characteristics of a definite nature. The knowledge process is a constant search for the being of the thing in question. Ignorance is defined as our "being in need" of the "being" of something. Human life is always in need of the knowledge of many things, but primary among them is the need to know. To know is to abide with security and clarity with some concept or idea of what is the case in the world of our inner experience and outer circumstances. To know the meaning of something is to grasp the relation that thing has to us and how it functions in our life. For Ortega the question "What is x?" is equal to the solution of the question "How does it function in the context of our life and its circumstances?"

Meaning

While meaning is an ambiguous term it clearly supposes at least the following senses: (1) it has purpose or intention, (2) it designates or refers to some understandable entity, (3) it has an established definition, and (4) we can understand its causal antecedents or consequences. Within the traditions of the philosophies of human life meaning has been generally understood as what life expressions express and understanding understands. But meaning (*Bedeutung* or *Sinn*) is also used here to intend (a) that mental content which exhibits relations between parts and wholes, and (b) that which one intends to convey by an action, creation, or other life expressions such as language. For Dilthey meaning is the most basic and inclusive, the most pervasive and important category of human life.[7]

For the most part Dilthey used the term "meaning" as the sense in which something is understood as a related aggregate of parts, or the relation that obtains between parts and wholes. All meanings for him exist as parts of more inclusive systems of meaning. But the understanding of larger contexts of meaning does not refer to something outside of human life, for life does not mean something entirely outside of itself.[8] The "I" understands all life expressions as a sign of specific mental content. In this sense meaning becomes a sort of pointer to the relations between outer objects and events and the inner connections which are the inherent forms of human life. Such meaning can only arise within the life of individuals who stand in interaction with the world. For Ortega y Gasset a thing's meaning is the highest form of its coexistence with other things.

Dilthey also pointed out for the first time in the philosophy of life tradition that meaning can never be separated from the temporality of human life. The flow of lived time through the constant present of our awareness is the source of meaning in our life. Time for him becomes the specific context through which we understand the relations of part-whole, and the temporal sequence of human life itself. It is the particular kind of relationship that exists between all the temporal parts of life. Such a relationship is not only inherent within our life, but we can neither understand nor describe human life without reference to such relations. The actual events of life can be neither remembered nor reproduced in isolation, nor made without reference to a temporal context. Any concept of human life is always dependent upon how its significant parts relate to each other, especially through historical time. The meaning of any idea, experience, anticipation, or remembrance must be revealed in the temporal relations with other things. Put another way, all meanings point to the connectedness of human life itself, and the most extensive connectedness that exists for it is its history. History is life itself considered as the whole of human experience.[9]

Human life is only understandable in terms of its own elemental categories which it both possesses and presupposes. When we inquire into the world of human life, we ask after the significance of events, creations, gestures, and actions. The elemental meanings of human life are not only understandable, but they are pre-thematic and pre-discursive. Meanings exist primordially as the constituents of actions and creations and preferences which have arisen from human involvement in circumstances. Without the ground of such a supposed and pre-thematic world we would not possess any orientation for our existence. Meanings arise from the constant dialogue between self and world, and our dialogue with a world is not a theory but the very fact of existence itself. Our experience of the world is not a theory or an appearance but reality itself. The objects of the world are real in the sense that they aid, hinder, advance, or assure the enterprise of life itself. They are also pleasurable or painful, helpful or fulfilling in our will to power over objects, other life, and the environment in general. It is the circumstantial world, and not theoretical arguments, which assures us of the meanings and conditions of human life. No so-called objective reality is understandable apart from the fact that we are ourselves and our circumstances in constant relation. The very meaning of human life arises in the particular and definite ways in which we are involved with the world of circumstances.

Perspective

Our human life must perpetually exist under the condition of perspectives. Objects in the world generate perspectives in us in the sense that they possess differing qualities, such as colors and shapes, which are not intrinsic but relative properties. The table appears round from one perspective and elliptical from another. Sensible qualities are not possessed by things in an absolute sense; they exist relative to a point of view. We experience the world and any possibility in our life at each moment from some definite perspective. The perceiving subject always brings a point of view to the world that he or she perceives. The spilled salt on the tablecloth is one thing from the point of view of the waitress, but quite another from the point of view of the scientist, who may submit the salt to analysis under an electron microscope. There is no final point of view here. Both are real to the agents, and absolute priority cannot be assigned to only one of them. Also, the objects of the world are perceived not only through the senses but with different meanings, presuppositions, and interests on the part of the subjects who confront them.

Perspectivism is the thesis that we see from a limited perspective the parts of the circumstantial world. Each perspective is a part of reality that cannot be seen from another point of view. It is not to be inferred from this doctrine that truth and understanding are only relative. Both truth and reality are unchanging, but can be apprehended through an infinity of perspectives. A given reality is not relative but absolute. But human beings can never transcend their relative perspectives to absolute and final knowledge. Nothing can be known apart from the context of the perspective in which it appears. As Ortega established, perspective is a fundamental component or category of human life itself, and all that is real must appear in some determinate perspective.[10] In sum, the doctrine of perspectivism maintains that all knowledge of the universe is possible only through particular points of view, and particular points of view in aggregate. Yet the individual point of view is primary here, and there is no more basic denominator of reality than the individual human life.

One historical source for the doctrine of perspectivism was Leibniz (1646–1716). Ortega was a student of Leibniz and of his theory of the graduated perspectives of preconscious and conscious monads. These monads reach completion only in God, as a universal perspective. But whatever the source of the doctrine, Ortega clearly stated in his *The Modern Theme* (1923) that we can comprehend the world only through the definite perspectives of individual lives.[11] Yet it must be noted here that perspective is not a deformation of experience, but it is the point of view that is taken by any subject on a subject matter. For example, Flaubert's Madame Bovary is both a book and a character. Never a simple self-identity, the novel exists in the world through various possibilities, meanings, and points of view. It may be understood by the historian or sociologist as a naturalistic analysis of class relations. The psychologist may understand Emma as a perpetual child trying to live out childhood illusions. A feminist may perceive the book as chauvinistic. An American teenager may see it as something to be avoided, if he avoids all serious reading, and the book for him becomes a mere thing at hand. The novel can be all of these and none exclusively. There is no absolute perspective from which the novel can be meaningfully and finally constituted. Ortega understood falsehood as a single perspective which claims for itself universal validity to the exclusion of all other perspectives. It is typically the function of politics to generate such thinking. It is true, of course, that there are false or misleading perspectives. Some perspectives are more inclusive than others. Also, there may have been a time when a given perspective did not exist at all.

Ancient Greek philosophy developed the idea that it is possible to understand things as they really are in themselves. True being, for example, was conceived as substance (*ousia*) or that which "truly is" in and for itself. But perspectivism denies any final perspective to either our life or its circumstances. We shall never find something which is perspectiveless or simply a "thing in itself." Nor is there something that exists only "under the aspect of eternity" (*sub specie aeternitatis*). Such an entity simply cannot enter human life. Our human life is radically a being *sub specie temporis*, a being that is itself lived, finite time.

Any fact is not separate from its meaning as a fact, and its meaning is revealed in the perspective from which it is interpreted. Ortega claimed that the end of human life is to obtain clarity about the world through concepts gained through various perspectives. The end of human life is the illumination of circumstances. The "natural light" of our life is our openness to circumstances through the perspectives possible to human life. While the world reveals itself through our perspectives, the data are not random, meaningless confusions. Perspectives themselves form an order, because human beings attend to them through the demands of care, to address their most important circumstances. Such "chosen" perspectives act as our life's real possibilities as they actually exist in our environment and era of time.

Human beings form, or attempt to form, a perspective of the Absolute. This purported perspective is usually associated with the expression "God." Here God becomes identified with an ultimate perspective, or the sum of all perspectives, including all partial or less inclusive ones. For Ortega human life exists as "the sight of divinity," "a point on the path" to an envisioned absolute where all partial perspectives take their place. Yet human beings are not God, and they are not able to comprehend the absolute through reason or knowledge. Such a comprehension is only an envisioned status, and any status or identity we may assign to God must always appear within human life. God must appear within human life if He, She, or It would be known by human beings at all.

Beliefs

Beliefs are assumptions and presuppositions that arise not from reflective thinking, reason, or scientific evidence, but from the prolonged absence of these. For Ortega, to believe something does not mean to be aware of it or to think about it. Rather, when people believe something, they act as if their beliefs were reality itself, with no need of proof or reflection. Abstract and rational ideas are usually generated by the inner reflections of individuals, but beliefs are part of the collective, "vital" assumptions of human life as society.

As the vital assumptions of our life's self-performance, beliefs both support and facilitate collective actions and attitudes. The result of such a situation is that beliefs are able to achieve an accepted status in society until they become failed or abandoned. At that point they have ceased to be either vital or efficacious and they achieve a sort of retired status as "failed beliefs." When the failure of a belief becomes widespread, then a society or group falls into what Ortega calls "demoralization," the individual or collective state of life that results from the absence of definite standards of value and behavior. In such a demoralized state the concept of human life as a meaningful reality is so weakened that the demoralization may become a major characteristic of an era or society. Such a state implies that not only our beliefs themselves but also our sense of reality has failed with respect to the demands of human life and its circumstances. Vital beliefs must be present at the deepest level of consciousness whenever we attempt to decide or act at all. When our beliefs fail, we feel without security, support, or meaningful recourse in our environment. For example, when the Soviet Block in Eastern Europe was under the Communist system, the vital assumptions of personal security and recourse to rights under law became significantly nullified for individuals in that system and replaced by a feeling of personal unimportance, anonymity, and helplessness. The role of the state supplanted the importance of the individual. Such a demoralized state of a lack of assumed reality was described by Kafka in his novels.

Our beliefs are usually so subterranean and implicit in our life and society that they are at the root of our actions and attitudes. Our beliefs are not even justified to ourselves. We rarely think of supporting them or broadcasting them into the public arena. We find ourselves "placed" in our beliefs in such a way that they "possess us" and give us support, so long as we (or the beliefs) live. What we call knowledge usually rests upon or presupposes our unfailed and vital beliefs, not because they necessarily rest on good reason or evidence, but because our beliefs seem a reality that is assumed by everyone. As the collective assumptions about ourselves and our circumstances, our beliefs have persisted out of the past, and they will abide for a time as the basis of society's attitudes, culture, and personal behavior. For Ortega our ideational and socially sanctioned "knowledge" is in fact "secondary" in importance to our more primordial belief systems. The "reality" of belief in which we abide is not a rationally evident thing, but it is the base upon which knowledge is usually founded. Our normal life is more or less constantly independent of concepts, ideas, or reasons. In sum, our beliefs are the results of assumptions we did not consciously create, prove, or formulate. They are not knowledge, in the sense that knowledge may be defined as true judgment about what constitutes a given fact. A fact is a statement about something actually existing or accomplished. Such fact statements can in principle be falsified, and they are fully verified only in an incomplete and approximate sense; but facts can have verification, whereas our beliefs are not about verified states of existence. They are only assumed as real until they fail.

When a society becomes consciously aware of the fundamental beliefs that it possesses, it is usually the result of the fact that the beliefs are already non-vital or dead. If a society is forced to justify or rationalize its beliefs, they are usually ceasing to be vital. When beliefs are weakened, falsified, or forgotten, the demoralization that results always displays an absence of trustworthy attitudes in our personal lives and even in our historical era. However, in the case of the failure of either a belief or reason, Ortega reveals a possible positive outcome, for there is a tendency for human beings at such a time to retreat into their interiority, or what Ortega calls *ensimismamiento*, the condition of withdrawing or being within oneself. In this interior condition we may be led to our deeper and more authentic being. In this interior world resides our true authenticity and creative nature. It is in our interior selves that there resides all hope for the improvement of human life in its outer circumstances. Human progress does not ultimately depend upon politics, science, or society, but upon this ability of individuals to withdraw into meditation and self-creation.

This condition of *ensimismamiento* is the opposite of what Ortega calls *alteración*, a term coming from the Latin root *alter* or other, and signifying a state of living by external circumstances and whatever is other than the qualities of the interior life. In *alteración* life ceases to be our personal creation and becomes merely an outwardly socialized and conformed existence which is alienated from its more authentic and interior self. In that state our life tends to lose any ultimate meaning or decided existence. This external state is not necessarily abnormal or unimportant, because human beings are required to live with outer circumstances and things other than themselves, if they would prosper and survive. Our life is often a socialized, debased, exterior conformity to outer social behavior, however vulgar or inane. But for Ortega the important thing is not to forget utterly or to lose our true inner life and personal standards, which are authentically human.

CHAPTER EIGHT

Reason

Vital Reason

The term "reason" has various uses in the history of philosophy. In Ortega it denotes "every act of the intellect which brings us into contact with reality."[1] Yet he developed two forms of reason in his own writing, which he designated as "vital reason" (*razón vital*) and "historical reason" (*razón historica*). Reason in Western Europe and America has usually been confined to the inferences of logic and the explanations of the physico-mathematical sciences. Yet for Ortega these forms do not exhaust the possibilities of discursive thought. Reason is more inclusive than these, and Ortega directs us to the fact that the root of *ratio* (reason) refers to the "giving of an account" of something. Further, reason for Ortega is that thought which attempts to take possession of the principle of something, and the principle it seeks is that of human life itself. In a 1924 essay entitled "Neither Vitalism nor Rationalism" he claimed that there is a reason which is rooted in the radical reality of human life, and both its meaning and authenticity are never imposed upon it by a preestablished "pure reason." In the so-called "pure reason" of logic and mathematics thought always abandons a particular object and advances to an abstract principle or law. But in the reason that thinks human life, "vital reason," there never occurs any separation of thought and the object of thought. It is the thought form Ortega actually used in his discussions of human life. For him vital reason is "the servant of which human life is in greatest need." This reason must presuppose the radical reality of human life, the structure in which all other realities are grounded. Not a thought form of irrationalism or intuition, vital reason must think the very form and function of life. Such a reason must explain what human life is, what it does, and what it may anticipate from the radical reality of the "I" and its circumstances. It must dispel doubt and provide human life with firm belief. Vital reason is the method which provides order to circumstances and penetrates to the principle of life. For Ortega physico-mathematical reason cannot comprehend this life of ours. It is the task of present philosophy to discover the vital reason that is the help of human life in its greatest need.

In his essay "Notes on Thinking" Ortega claimed that human thought is a life form that exists in sedimented growth from elementary perceptions. The development of our mental life requires that our sense impressions get formulated into concepts through which we can interpret the possibilities of circumstances. But our perceptions are never entirely distinct from concepts, for there is always a minimal, meaningful ordering and connection in even our most elementary perceptions. The ability of human life to ascribe conceptual characteristics to circumstances is at the heart of our belief that both our life and its circumstances possess identifiable and trustworthy being. In other words, Ortega is indicating here that our ability to determine the being of something is the result of the conceptualizing possibilities of human life. In what Ortega called "the shipwreck of our life" it is vital to be able to establish through concepts a firm ideational identity to things. It is through this stable identity that human life attempts to gain a security about what it can "hold on to" in the "shipwreck" of human life.

In his 1940 essay "Ideas and Beliefs," an essay which was to be the first part of a work on "historical reason," Ortega showed that ideas and beliefs arise from the attempt to live with our circumstances. Our ideas and concepts are generated by the mind as instruments through which we attempt to comprehend and control the world of circumstances. But in our relation to circumstances it must be noted that the "I" never reacts directly to reality itself, but only to its own interpretations of reality. Such interpretations are dispersed through society as the common collective assumptions about the various possibilities of our circumstances. Such assumptions become the collective beliefs required for our survival in circumstances. Belief is at the bottom of our value formations and practical life. As we saw in the last chapter, when such beliefs are questioned, failed, or forgotten, there arises a need to replace them with new beliefs, or with new concepts that are more reasoned and objectively established in the historical flow of human life. As such, beliefs become more secure and help to provide an understanding of circumstances. For Ortega it is in *ensimismamiento*, the retreat of the thinking person into his or her interior self, that the individual produces those new principles and values needed to fill the void left by society's failed beliefs. This retreat into *ensimismamiento* is especially needed in a time of social demoralization such as our own. New principles and concepts are usually the creation of creative minorities, and when such a minority perceives a belief that is unstable or failed, then a new principle is sought which can sustain the ideas and values that our life depends upon.

Yet our interpretations of human life never seem to enjoy an absolute or eternal validity. For example, the seventeenth century's belief in the universal validity of mathematical reason has collapsed in our era. A new principle of reason must be found for the comprehension of our life and our present era. In *The Theme of Our Time* (1923) Ortega had already claimed that the great need of our time is the re-understanding of human life from the basis of vital reason. Because our vital reason is grounded in human life itself, it is never to be conceived as somehow separate from the reality it attempts to understand. In this sense vital reason is needed for our very being in the world. It is also the reason that attempts to determine the future of human life and replace the physico-mathematical reason which is an outgrown thought form for the understanding of the radical reality of human life.

Nevertheless, it seems that Ortega felt the need to supplant and redirect vital reason by a further development of the reason which is appropriate for the grasping of human life as radical reality. He called this further development "historical reason" (*razón historica*). This change seems to have come about in his thinking because he had been arriving at the conclusion that humanity does not possess a fixed or final nature, but a history. He believed that it is necessary to develop still another reasoning form, which would supplement and inform the previous vital reason. It is to historical reason that we must now turn.

Historical Reason

Ortega gave a series of lectures on historical reason in Buenos Aires in 1940. These lectures were to become part of a later book entitled "The Dawn of Historical Reason," a work that remained unfinished. After 1930 the idea of historical reason had become more and more a determinate element in his thought. While Ortega had sometimes used the term "historical reason" to be identical to his earlier idea of vital reason, it has become clear to the author that these two related ideas do not intend the same thing. We must show, in outline at least, that he developed a historical reason beyond the earlier vital reason. Historical reason extends the earlier vital reason to new dimensions. The development of historical reason was in part due to Ortega's acquaintance with Dilthey's writings after 1929. Yet both vital and historical reason were already present *in ovo* in his thought as early as his *Meditations on Quixote* (1914).

For Ortega an essential element in human life is historical reason. Historical reason is the thesis that the historicity of human life requires a thought form which is able to understand human life through historical time, how it is constituted, and how it progresses from out of the past through the present and into the future. This new thought form establishes historicity as the central and defining element of human life, and it maintains that human life in time is best understood as narration. It asks how the drama of human life happens to itself. In his "History as a System" and *Historical Reason* Ortega attempted to account for the fact that human life develops in time, and this "happening" and developing must be understood through a method adequate to its dynamic subject matter. Ortega called this thinking and method of narrative explanation historical reason. "Narrative reason is historical reason" (*y esa razón narrativa es << la razón historica*).[2] This type of reason, alone, explains how human life in time has come to be what it is.

As the narrative unfolding of human life in time, historical reason is related in part to the Heideggerean notion that the truth of Being is an expression of its temporal unfolding. Historical reason has become the *ratio* of human life, because it provides a story of radical reality as it is given in time. The thought form of historical reason is not derived from physico-deductive reason, logic, or mathematics. It is the thinking account of our temporal nature as "what we are" because of what we have been and will be. The "dawn of historical reason" is the comprehension that we exist both as what Goethe called "inheritors" and as an existence into the future. Human life must be made transparent to a reason which can address the historicity of human life in all its dimensions.[3] The previous sense of "vital reason" was retained in historical reason in that our actual existence is "vital" and cannot be explained by any method or thinking that is merely abstract, such as mathematical-deductive reason. The essence of human life is historicity, not the deductive forms of pure reason. Historical reason is never apart from human life, and it attempts to account for human life based on the supposition that human life is a *faciendum*, a self-construction of its being in and through time. As an inherited reality the being of human life exists as a cumulative synthesis of the moments in time.

Both Dilthey and Ortega believed that the intellectual theme of our time is to address the need for a historical reason focused on human life. For them rationalism and materialism have repressed and forgotten the radical reality of human life and its historical nature, by conceiving of human life only as an object at hand without historicity, creation, or possibility. The eighteenth century "age of reason" had assumed that the "pure reason" of mathematics and natural science was the very essence of man, and that all social and historical method must express this fact. But Dilthey and Ortega saw only one fundamental feature in human life, its historicity. For them historical reason is to human life what physico-mathematical and "pure" reason are to nature.

Ortega recognized that the idea of historical reason was derived from Dilthey's project of "a critique of historical reason." Yet Ortega felt that Dilthey never understood that the new continent of human life was fundamentally composed of historicity itself.[4] Dilthey's critique of historical reason was essentially devoted to the distinction between the human-historical studies and the natural sciences. He never developed a fundamental ontology of human life as radical reality. Dilthey's project remained too much in the domain of historiological science and method, especially his doctrine of *Verstehen*. Both historical reason and *Verstehen* method remained methodological ideals, programs for the *Geisteswissenschaften* and the need of those human sciences to attain a generally valid historical science. For Ortega Dilthey remained to the end a "prisoner" of historical science and method. His idea of human life remained undeveloped, and was not a basic ontology for the radical reality of human life.

Narration and Prophecy

Ortega understood historical reason as a narrative account of human life in its developing from what it has been to what it presently is and will become. Further, he sought for his historical reason the capacity to prophesy and predict the future in a manner not unrelated to the methods of natural sciences. He believed that historical reason could in a limited sense prophesy the life forms of the future. Both narrative and prophecy are central to his idea of historical reason, and these elements of his thought have not been enough examined. The historical nature of human beings refers in significant part to the fact that human life both preserves and accumulates its past within itself and exists as what it has been. Physical objects such as a stone do not possess a past in this sense, for they neither remember nor project their being in time. The possession of a past and a future is often interpreted as a characteristic of divinity, and Ortega believed that if this possession of a past could be joined to the possession of a future, our life would be an approximation of the so-called "divine nature," simultaneously possessing a past, present, and future. By means of its attempt to replicate its past through a narration of the moments of life, and to possess a future through prophecy, foresight, and prediction, our life joins all three time frames into a dynamic unity. When we understand human life as both past and future unified with the present, then for Ortega we have the basis for a "dawn of historical reason."

In the 1940 lecture series in Buenos Aires entitled *Historical Reason* Ortega said that our past is the one enduring possession in our lives. Yet humanity remains a sort of nomad in time, because our life possesses no final nature, only a history of continual change, "a being and an unbeing" that accumulates itself through time. Historical narration is the story of human events and moments up to the present. The narrative account of human life through time becomes for Ortega historical reason itself.[5] Human life becomes here what he calls a *faciendum*, a drama of self-construction. Human life exists as accumulation and "leaving off" of what has happened to it. This narration of the continual happenings of human life avoids the naturalistic and physico-mathematical thought-forms of the *Naturwissenschaften*, which constitute human life as a mere "thing at hand" in the motions of objective time. In this sense Ortega's historical reason is the attempt to grasp human being through its historicity.

It is important at this point briefly to explain historical reason as a method of explanation in contrast to other methods. Since the seventeenth century the term "reason" has tended to be identified almost exclusively with the empirico-deductive attempt to observe phenomena, form hypotheses about them, and subsume these under the covering laws of the physical sciences. But the thesis of historical reason rejects the position since Hume which states that all authentic explanation consists of providing general, covering, mathematical laws to the phenomena which are to be explained. In the twentieth century this covering-law thesis was formulated in the position presented by Carl Hempel which includes the following ideas. In a valid historical explanation there are two basic elements, (1) the *explanandum* or the event (E) which should be explained, and (2) the *explanans* or the covering law (C) which explains *E*. There is a valid explanation only when a particular event of a certain kind (E) takes place as an instance of the covering law (C).[6]

Though Ortega does not cite this article in his works, we can think of his historical reason as a counter to the positivist model. His idea of narrative explanation and subsequent prophecy is an important new element in the philosophy of history. Historical explanation is impossible without "telling the story" through which human temporal development has accumulated itself and come to be what it is in the present. In 1936 Ortega had developed a counter-positivist narration thesis in his essay "History as a System."[7] Here he argued that human life is only understandable by means of a narrative account of its progress through time, through the autofabrication in which one joins the events of human life to its prior events. We can explain our life in time by the cumulative method of relating prior and subsequent moments, a narrative method Ortega called "History as a System." By means of a narrative account of how the events, ideas, and actions of human life emerged from previous events, ideas, and actions, one can account for the reason why individual and collective human life emerged into its present status. Narration can implicitly reveal how the possibilities of actions, thoughts, and roles in the past and present actually came about in the time of human life. Historical reason has become here what Heidegger spoke of as the "revelation of the humanly possible." As a temporal concretion by which we account for the development of our being in time, historical reason is the story of the autofabrication of human life. This narration also includes a provision of the "why" element in historical explanation of human life. It rejects the positivist model which understands all "why" in terms of the covering "laws" which are supposed to govern human life. Such "laws" omit the whole of human historicality. Historical reason becomes the exact *ratio* of human autofabrication in historical time. Historical reason attempts to provide for the explanatory requirement that all antecedents of a specific kind must be understood in connection with consequences of a specified type. The narrations of historical reason reveal that in the past recognizable antecedents were followed by identifiable consequents. If some event happened, the attempt of historical reason is to show that it was followed by a response of a distinguishable and meaningful form of human life. All of this together is an accumulation of human life in time.

Yet Ortega's historical reason possesses more than a narrative and explanatory structure. It also possesses a futuristic and predictive dimension. In his *Origin of Philosophy* he argued that the past must be joined to the present and future through what he termed prophecy or foreseeing. All of these elements must be combined in a system in order for humanity to witness a "dawn of historical reason."[8] But this sense of prophecy is not predictive as a so-called general law of history would be. It means rather that it is possible to forecast general, probable forms that are not governed by any necessity such as a general law would require. Instead, prophecy refers to the elaboration of future possibilities. This kind of foreseeing is a general ability of human life. Both the present and future are founded in the tendential structures of human life. By the grasp of these structures in human life it is possible to foresee a number of identifiable possibilities, though not necessities. For example, in a military arena such as that of Iraq, it should be conceivable to determine certain behaviors, contingencies, and consequents that are possible, based on an empirical assessing of the past and present in Iraq. Provision could then be made for these possibilities. (It does not refute this example to point out that these determinations were not in fact carried out successfully.)

Historical reason is that part of human life which can anticipate some possibilities and exclude other possibilities from consideration. We may also anticipate those circumstances which would precondition and advance specific goals, and exclude others. For example, we presently have the choice between passively accepting a future of unchecked population growth or forecasting those practices and values, ends and means which experience in the past has taught us will tend to counteract such a future. While it is true that the forecasting and fabrication of the means for knowing the future are problematical and fallible, the possibilities are not nullified simply by those difficulties. It is always possible for historical reason to prescribe the possibilities that may counteract certain conditions in order to promote new conditions.

The idea of self-determination in human life is closely related to the futuristic aspect of historical reason. Self-determination refers to our understanding the fact that human life possesses the capacity for self-alterability through historical time. Human alterability is the self-making or autofabrication of human life and historical existence. Here human life assumes the responsibility for its existence in the future circumstances which it both forecasts and constructs. Human beings in this sense are technicians with respect to the circumstances which they anticipate and fabricate in their lives. In the period of the industrial revolution in the nineteenth century, for example, human beings employed both deliberation and appropriate behavior in the construction of such inventions as the Bessemer Converter, which produced steel by removing impurities from the metal by heat and air processes. The result was that the age of mass production of steel dawned upon the Euro-American worlds. This fabrication of new industrial circumstances and new means of production resulted in profound changes in human relations, consumption practices, class relations, and moral and work habits in the population. New economic, social, and moral habits in turn produced a new mentality, which produced a so-called "economic man," in contrast to the prior "feudal man" of previous eras. Thus both a new human life and circumstances were fabricated by human beings and their historical destiny. Such autofabrications were founded upon the self-alterability of both human beings and their circumstances. Our life is a human autonomy which fabricates its future in time. Our life is also the agent of transformation of its present and future circumstances. Under a threat of perishing we may become autonomous technicians creating a new future.

Human life exists as a historical system in our consciousness, and historical reason is in part the understanding of human life in terms of its systematic dimensions. This means that all human experience through time is linked in a "dialectical chain" of three temporal forms, past, present, and future. All of these forms are both meaningfully and temporally connected, as human beings accumulate the elements of past and present and from these anticipate a future. For example, the experience of the United States acting in the conflicts of the Middle East must be understood in relation to previous international relations, such as the founding of Israel and the history of oil diplomacy. The conflicts also cannot be understood apart from the history of Islamic and Christian relationships. These and many more elements are crucial ingredients in the contemporary Palestinian and Iraq situations. For Ortega these conflicts would have to be conceived as an ongoing historical process, a systematic advance of human life in time, or as a *cognitio rerum gestarum* which is the resultant accumulation of past and present into the future. In his *En torno a Galileo* of 1933 Ortega defined the historical system as human life continually making its world as a projected horizon of itself. He went on to say that every change in this horizon results in a change in the ongoing drama of human life.[9]

While historical reason is the attempt to understand the accumulation of our having-beens, it is also the anticipation of what may be generated in the future from these accumulations. As a science of the present, historical reason also becomes the intent to understand the present system as something which becomes a future. Never the imposition of laws upon historical material, historical reason becomes that thinking which connects the process of historicity to the past, present, and future. Because historical reason is the thinking of the becoming of human life, Ortega calls it "the foresight of the future," a reason which is able to anticipate the general features, vital themes, and implicit consequences from the past. The assumption here is that these future consequences are not simply accidental and causeless, for the future possesses a foreseeable structure which completes and actualizes the past. Sometimes Ortega calls this process "prophecy," by which he means that there exists a historical reason which can anticipate the general features of human life as it emerges from the past into the present and future. There is a systematic ground that prescribes how subsequent events emerge from anterior events. He claims that it would have been possible to have anticipated the future system of the Roman world at the time of Julius Caesar (100–44 BC). Caesar could have foreseen the future of Roman life from conditions before and contemporary with himself. In fact, it was Cato the Younger (95–46 BC), a contemporary of Julius Caesar, who actually foresaw the "Caesarism" that would follow the reign of Julius after his death. This does not mean, however, that Cato foresaw all the specific circumstances in the rise of Caesarism. It means that Cato anticipated the general historical systems of political life which followed. Through comprehending the vital psychological dispositions and implicit normative injunctions of the past and present in the Age of Caesar it was possible for Cato to join prophecy to narrative reason. All specific anticipations of the future must join prophecy to narrative in order to give a fully empirical account of the historical process.[10] Such historical prophecy is not the same as supplying historical laws to phenomena to determine historical events. Historical reason refers only to the prophecy of probable systems that could arise from the specific tendential structures that will eventuate in a fully developed historical system. Put another way, historical reason is the anticipation of the probable circumstances that will eventuate in and complete the tendencies that are already at work. Such a form of prophecy is to be found in Ortega's *Revolt of the Masses* (1930). He developed the ideal type of the "Mass Man" in Europe and the United States. There were three elements that allowed for the forecasting of mass man; namely, scientific experiment, technology, and industrialism. In the early nineteenth century many economic and social advances appeared which were made available to the population. The *Revolt* recounts how social, technological, medical, educational, and wealth-producing inventions improved the well-being of the average person. The masses came to assume that these advances guaranteed to them natural rights and services that society must provide to them. But these consumers would remain ignorant of the work, thought, excellence, and invention of those who made their well-being possible. The inventions and advantages which were the work of a minority belonged to everybody as their natural right. Ortega constructed the intellectual, social, and moral identity of this mass through a narrative description of where this group came from, what it expected, and what formed its final identity. His purpose here was to construct "a trajectory of experiences," the accumulation of the historical experiences of the masses. Through an understanding of this accumulated experience and behavior Ortega showed the limits and growth of the mass as an historical type. He also prophesied its future life form as the ground from which would arise the seizure of power and rank by force. The mass would be the prelude to the "false dawns" of fascism and communism.[11] There will exist a "new barbarism," violence, inauthentic vocation, and totalitarian devotion to the power and authority of the state. The unqualified will seize leadership through coercion and force. Militarism, extended violence, and repression will grow and be augmented by the state.[12]

Such a historical reason becomes in Ortega's thought an account of how previous experience gives rise to subsequent systems and forms of life. All future circumstances are understood in relation to previous ones, or the system that was "in force" in those times. In his *History as a System* Ortega claimed that only a historical reason which transcends abstract causal theory through the narration of actual development can reveal what human being actually is and what it will become.[13] All human being is the result of the previous happening of human life, even though this happening lacks a final or static identity. This process of becoming is transparent only to historical reason. For Ortega our realization of this fact is the promised "dawn of historical reason."

CHAPTER NINE

The Social Dimension

The "I" and the Other

The "I" is the term that expresses the identity and singularity of the individual human being, or the basic conscious subject. For Descartes the "I" takes the form of a simple substance which is intuitively known in our thinking existence. For Kant the "I" is the dynamic unity of all consciousness, a necessary condition of experience. For the philosophy of human life the "I" is one component of the dynamic relation between the self and its circumstances. The "I" of this bipolar relation forms its identity through the unity of its accumulation of experiences through time and circumstances. For Heidegger this thesis is developed as the assertion that the "I-myself" or "who" of human life is the temporal existence that belongs to itself and identifies itself through the personal pronoun "I."[1] The "I" of human life, in other words, is the way the human being understands itself as its own possession through its taking hold of its own past, present, and future. Here the "I-myself" is not simply a thinking substance, but an "I-world" relationship from which it can never escape or separate itself. In this relation it exists in such a way that it remains both single and unified through its ability to assume its own past, present, and anticipated future.

In the philosophy of human life there is always the need to show that our life exists as an intentional relation of an "I" to the circumstances to which it must comport itself. This status of human life is most completely expressed by Ortega's "I am myself and my circumstances." No theoretical suspension of belief in an external world can nullify the fact that we exist in a world of circumstances towards which we must exist.

There can be no theory, thought experiment, or assumption which can adequately abrogate the belief of both the plain man and the empirical sciences that there is in fact a universe, an encompassing environment which is always "there" for the "I-subject." This is to say that our life is always enjoyed or suffered in the context of a world. Yet Dilthey, Husserl, Heidegger, and Ortega y Gasset all rejected the thesis of a so-called "natural standpoint," i.e., the claim that there exists an objective world that is utterly apart from and independent of a knowing subject. The being-in-the-world of human life is a necessary condition for all objective knowledge claims; our existence as human life is never self-enclosed or self-sufficient. But neither is the "objective world" self-enclosed or utterly apart from its being known by the human subject. The world of human life relates to the universe through what Heidegger has called the present-at-hand-ness (*Vorhandenheit*) of all beings. The world exists as an instrument through which we attempt to realize our purposes and our understanding. Yet all the objects at hand in the world are "there" in various ways. They may be "right there" in front of us, or merely remote, abstract, or theoretical entities with only a dimmed-down relation to our concerns. For example, the distant Wasatch Mountains which I see from my writing desk are assumed to be "there" as only a distant fringe of consciousness. But when I refer to the mountains to illustrate a point which is a personal concern, such as writing this book, my mountains assume a closer, more vital relation to my concerns in the world.

Each human life must accept its status of being in a world of circumstances into which it has been thrown. Such an acceptance implies the recognition of the categorical conditions of human life which we may call the "facticity" and "thrownness" of human life; i.e., we are who and what we are partly because of certain facts in which we participate, or which we inherit and cannot change. Always in a particular historical situation and a temporal past it has inherited, the "who" or "I-myself" of human life has partly a social and historical identity it cannot change. The "I-myself" is more inclusive than an atomic, individuated thing. In an important passage of his *Being and Time* Heidegger has stated that the "who" of human life is more than the "I-myself."[2] Not merely solitary and subjective, our life shares an identity of Being in a common world with others. The philosophy of human life must take account of the fact that our life is "being with others," who are in turn "beings with us." Such a situation is a categorical characteristic of the way our life is in the world. While our life exists as a radical solitude, it must not be concluded that the individual is the sole radical reality. The "other" is more than a single bodily presence which covers an inward "I." In my life I come to realize that the "other" who appears to me in my solitude also possesses an "I" to which I must orient my life. The "other" is a reciprocal existence in a common world, and the categorical structure of human life must always include the element of our being with the "other," and the "other" with us.

A fundamental characteristic of this "other" is that it is always potentially able to respond to another person and that other person to it. This means that in the interaction of "I" and "other" there can occur on the part of both parties a subjective calculation of the other's response to it. From this there emerges a sort of social reciprocity between myself and the other. At this point a new dimension appears within human life: the recognition and expectation that the "other" possesses a life like my own.

But because the other's life is not my own, nor mine his, the interaction of two human lives is ultimately a "dubious communication between two solitudes," as Ortega would have it. Human social interaction does not eliminate this solitude. Because the life that is actually mine is "snug" (*atopadizo*) within me, my being with another remains always doubtful, conjectural, and even inhospitable. Also we come to recognize that the world of the "other" is not simply for our private advantage, but for the possible advantage or disadvantage of each other. We must continually wonder about the status of the other. Both "I" and the other must attempt to see the world as the other sees it, and to incorporate it into the radical reality of our lives, to "humanize" it or make of it an alter ego. We may even attempt to substitute the other's life for our own as we would want it to be, or to allow the other's interpretation of our life to replace our own. But when the life world of the other becomes questioned or doubtful, the "I" must return to the radical reality of its own solitary life to consider the situation.

This search for the inner meaning of the "other" does not cease until death. The life of the other always remains "a reality of the second order." Such a secondary life is never the radical or unquestioned reality that is my own life. When I am in the presence of another, my "lived body" is given to myself as my own, and all that is sensed of the other is an external body apart from me. The other's self is witnessed through its gestures, actions, and relations by analogical inferences. Because my coexistence with another remains inferential, Dilthey has shown that all human life must externalize itself to the other through its empirical life expressions (*Lebensäusserungen*). The "I" and the "other" may attempt to make of each other an alter ego which can be reciprocated or mutually exchanged, yet we have access to another's life only through our own life; and all history and social studies are significantly the attempt by human beings to make of each other a mutually exchanged and understandable entity. The attempt is always to make of the other something definite and concrete by reducing it to definite expectations, typicalities, and systems within the socio-historical world.

Dilthey's *Verstehen*

In our discussion of the category of the historicity of human life we argued that some common type of human nature is always assumed by those who interpret history and those who make it. The constancy and intelligibility of human nature are the fundamental provisions through which we are enabled to understand the life assertions, actions, and creations of human life in historical time. Dilthey believed that human actions and creations, transpiring in time, must both assume and depend upon the fact that they are the products of natures like our own. Such an assumption involves the question of how generally valid explanation is possible in the historical sciences in the first place. Dilthey sometimes referred to the generally valid explanation of human life in time as the issue of historicity or the critique of historical reason. The possibility of an interpretive understanding of human life in historical time rests upon the common experiential, emotional, and cognitive natures of both those who make history, the interpretants, and those who interpret it, the interpreters. In this sense the possibility of the understanding of human life is shared with living contemporaries, and implicitly with the dead and those yet to be born. This shared nature of human life is the foundation of the human studies and of history generally. Put another way, human beings make and do mutually intelligible things, constitute common meanings and will, and realize like ends. Human agents, though unlike in many ways, share common patterns of existence and meanings through historical time. Dilthey understood by his category of *Verstehen*, or understanding, the interpretive reconstruction of these patterns and meanings of human existence in both the past and present and even the future. Such an interpretive understanding occurs in the act of *Verstehen*. Here there is a transfer of the lived experiences of the interpreter into the evidences expressed in the life assertions of the other. In such a transfer the interpreter's understanding is intended to duplicate the meaningful behavioral content of the other's life through its life expressions (*Lebensäusserungen*) through time. In this sense humanity is a historical possibility of itself, because its actions and creations through time have become the central fact of generally valid interpretation of the historical past and future.[3]

Dilthey's doctrine had to address the problem that our life, the life of each one of us, exists through time as an I-world polarity, yet it always retains an internal dimension that cannot be observed from the outside. While we may perceive objects and situations outside of ourselves, the radical reality of the "I and its circumstances" is always known from within. Our life is subjective, not because it is hidden or mysterious, but because it possesses an inside. My life is presented to me in such a way that it always remains hidden to the life of another outside of it. But this hiddenness or internality of my life is more than an issue of internal and external sensations. All internal sensations are as private to me as my external sensations are to someone else. Whether my experience is of the external world or of my own inner states, it always exists as something private to myself. We are transparent only to ourselves, and the inner life of others remains significantly hidden to us. This is the issue that Dilthey addressed in his theory of life assertions and their understanding (*Verstehen*) by another.

It is through life assertions that human beings externalize and publicize the immediate and private states of their inner life in the form of language, actions, creations, gestures, cultural artifacts, institutions, and finally history itself. Such assertions of human life become present to the outer empirical world that others sense and attempt to understand. Their life assertions possess intelligibility and importance, because those who first expressed them and those who understand them both possess the common medium of human life. All human life requires the interpretive understanding of what it has put forth, and those who understand require an external agent who has expressed his or her life to the end of mutual understanding. While my life is apparent to itself, its outer expressions are always in need of interpretation by others. Others in turn are in need of interpretation by me. This means that the initial privacy of human life becomes revealed in its external expressions, which are first lived within but are revealed in the external world.

Dilthey's doctrine of *Verstehen* in this sense becomes the description and interpretation of the outer expressions of human life. Such life expressions are the outer material signs in the circumstantial world of some content in an agent's mind. They are those inner events to which agents attach meaning. These physical expressions may be purely material, such as a look of fear or rage, or they may be cultural, such as a natural language or a tool. Life expressions may also be unintentional or unconscious, such as body language or perspiration on the face. Such natural signs are meaningful, though they are usually understood in the context of our daily experiences and life associations. The question here is always one of how we are to grasp the mental state behind any experience or manifestation, and how these states may be related to our own inner life and its outer expressions.

Dilthey's discovery and promotion of *Verstehen* as a category of human life is related to the fact that after 1894 he came to believe that the psychological observation of our inner life is flawed, because it tends to "freeze" the dynamic nature of the psyche in the very process of our introspective description of our lived experience. Self-reflection (*Selbstbesinnung*) on the immediacy of human life cannot adequately comprehend lived experience in its wholeness, he thought, because psychology at best is only a supplemental study of human life. He thought an objectively valid study of humanity and its works is only possible through history, for human beings understand themselves through history, not through psychological introspection.[4] While Dilthey did not entirely abolish psychology from the human studies, he thought it must be significantly replaced by the empirical study of human historical behavior, creations, and the aggregate of their life assertions through time. Here Dilthey assumed and employed Hegel's doctrine of Objective Spirit (*Objektiver Geist*), but instead of using Hegel's stages of the growth of spirit in a philosophical theory, Dilthey developed an empirical theory of life expressions from which we can reconstruct the human past as it actually existed. It is now to be through the empirical life expressions of humanity in time that lived experience becomes objectified and generalized. In this manner objectified human experience becomes "dissolved into history,"[5] and this fact becomes central in Dilthey's critique of historical reason. The variety and fullness of human life is only revealed through history, and this revelation will ground a generally valid conception of humanity to the present stage of its development.

In ordinary German, *verstehen* is a verb which simply means in English "to understand." As an abstract noun *Verstehen* indicates understanding in general. In Dilthey's usage *Verstehen* becomes a category of human life, a *terminus technicus* which refers to the method of the interpretation of another's inner experience through his or her outward life expressions—actions, creations, symbols, gestures, utterances. Dilthey, as we have seen, called these outer empirical expressions life assertions (*Lebensäusserungen*). An interpreter of such expressions attempts to understand them by transposing them into his or her own inner life experience, then into the meanings, values, and purposes that made up the lived experience of the agent who initially asserted something. Such transposing of the interpreter's life is an attempt to relive another's life (*nacherleben*) as it is understood from the original life expression of the interpretant. Such an interpretation must then be referred to an actual individual's lived experience which supplied meanings, values, and purposes to the expression. In sum, *Verstehen* is the category of human life which is an interpretive understanding of an action, creation, or other life expression to which a meaning, value, and purpose have been assigned by an agent.[6]

We can better understand the process of *Verstehen* when we think about what happens when we interpret a signal, such as a flashing light. We may also think of how we interpret a painting, like Rembrandt's "The Philosopher." We attempt to grasp the "inner" significance of colors, emotions of the face, and the lived experience of the artist behind the overt painting. Our understanding of such a work does not refer to our awareness of the outer, quantifiable, sensory aspects of such a work. Nor do we understand it in the denominators of the physical sciences, such as its specific gravity, angstrom units of light, chemical composition, atomic composition, etc. As an object of *Verstehen* the work expresses meanings, values, purposes, art forms, and historical significance. The feature that distinguishes our understanding of such a life assertion as a painting from our explanations of a natural phenomenon is that the former requires *Verstehen* and the latter requires explanation (*Erklärung*) under the form of natural laws.[7] In the natural sciences there is always an attempt to explain physical phenomena through the hypothetical generalizations of sense experience, but for Dilthey the human studies aim at the interpretive understanding (*Verstehen*) of the lived experience that originally produced the physical life assertions in the first place. Such assertions are the subject matter of the *Geisteswissenschaften*, such subjects as history, philosophy, religion, art, social studies, pedagogy, politics, law, literature, music, linguistics, and philology, subjects which are understood by reference to their "inner" or mind-affected content. In other words, they have subjective significances, values, and purposes which have been imputed to them by their creators. Here the inner significance of the life world is more deeply sedimented than that of the natural sciences, but even the latter sciences derive their assumptions through an analogical extrapolation from the lived experience of human life itself.

While *Verstehen* is an attempt to infer another's lived experience from the empirical expressions themselves, this method is not simply the sense perception of material objects such as a stone. *Verstehen* occurs only when we have understood from objectified life expressions the meanings, values, and purposes which their creators imputed to them. The human sciences must employ *Verstehen* as a hermeneutical or interpretive method of inquiry in the sense that the human agent possesses a self-referential capacity to infer from empirical life expressions an inner significance that is not merely an outer sense experience. In this sense the *Verstehen* process approximates what the medieval philosophers designated as knowing *per causas*, i.e., understanding what an agent or group has intended or created in a given life expression. It is in such understanding that intersubjectivity is apparent in human life.

For Dilthey there are four different types of life expressions, which are ranked in terms of their relative complexity: (1) simple bodily expressions of another, such as the giving of a signal or a smile; (2) outward expressions of another's emotion; (3) expressions of another's inner cognitive content in language, symbols, imitation, acting, etc.; (4) the most complex expressions, artistic or intellectual symbols and creations. The purpose for *Verstehen* in all of these cases is to interpret the expressions by means of the empathic projection of ourselves into another's life situation, or by means of the imaginative reliving of the emotive, volitional, cognitive, and valuational intent of their creator, and to infer an abstract meaning content (*Denkinhalt*) that can be contained in judgments.

Again, *Verstehen* here becomes the method used to deal with the inner experience of another through the interpretation of the outer empirical and material expressions of human life. It is both the attempt to translate the outer into the inner, and the inner into the outer. All inner content becomes here embodied in the physical, spatial, and temporal expression of human beings living and dead. In the case of the assassination of President Lincoln, for example, there existed the outer complex of the Derringer pistol that discharged the bullet into the head of Lincoln, the overt behavior of the assassin, the crowd, the blood on the floor, etc. Yet these outer materials do not in themselves constitute an assassination. A pistol fires a bullet, but only an agent acting under an intention and an inner meaning-complex commits an assassination as a sociohistorical event. This means that the outer material aspects of such an event have a lived historical significance that resides in the inner experience of such an action. It is only through an understanding (*Verstehen*) of the historical milieu of the agent and his victim, and of the meanings, values, and purposes of the assassination that we have an adequate understanding of this event. On the other hand, such events are not simply "inner." No event can be understood apart from an outer world of objects, objective temporal sequence, and the general environment and physical behavior of the assassin. Both the inner and outer sides of the event must be understood as the necessary conditions of such historical actions. The actual historicity of this event is formulated in the use of the *Verstehen* method through the attempt to re-subjectify the outer material expressions of the life which originated them. Yet it remains the case that our grasp of the inner and outer aspects of the assassination of Lincoln is asymmetrical. In other words, our method of grasping the inner side of the life expressions of an assassination is understanding (*Verstehen*), and the means of explaining its outer material, sensate dimension is natural science and its explanations (*Erklärung*). Both are necessary for a complete understanding of such an event.

In sum, Dilthey believed that the distinction of the methods and subject matters of the human and natural sciences through their inner and outer dimensions and methods was an intellectual revolution. He also believed that his idea of human life, lived experience, and *Verstehen* had provided a generally valid basis for understanding human existence in time. The birth of the idea of human life occurred in the horizon of his attempt to establish the autonomy and general validity of the human studies. The autonomous method and subject matter of the human studies was the basis of his critique of historical reason. One goal of such a critique was to attain a generally valid theory of human life and history. This goal is necessary to the assumptions of a theory of human life and the human studies, if we are to be delivered from the metaphysics of the pre-Kantian world and the exclusive reliance upon the methods of natural science in the human studies.

Heidegger's Understanding

In German, as we have seen, *Verstehen* is a noun which means understanding. In Dilthey specifically it is the name of a method for the interpretation of the life expressions of another in the past, present, and possible future. As an *ars interpretandi* it assumes that both the interpreter and the interpretant may achieve an intersubjective unity through their common participation in human life. Such a unity can be expressed by generally valid judgments. But Heidegger's doctrine of *Verstehen* possesses an importantly different sense. For Heidegger *Verstehen* is an ontological characteristic that expresses simply what it means to be human (*Dasein*). The notion of understanding, *Verstehen*, here becomes an expression of human awareness—the awareness of one's possibilities as a being-in-the-world. Human understanding of its own able-to-beness here becomes the prior ground of any theory of knowledge or interpretation. In Heidegger's doctrine of *Verstehen* we see at work the fact that human understanding of the world exists as a possibility of existence and not simply the static actuality of objects at hand. Understanding for Heidegger becomes an element in the grasp of the very possibility of freedom. Our understanding of freedom does not arise through moral or epistemological theories, but through our grasp of what it means to be at all in an existence that is open to the future. In his 1927 lecture course entitled *Die Grundprobleme der Phänomenologie* Heidegger claimed that Dilthey's search for the general validity of historical science and the *Verstehen* method does not in fact represent a different order of understanding than that of the natural sciences. The difference between the natural and historical sciences as they are understood in the philosophies of life and the neo-Kantian schools seems defective, in that it presents no clear understanding of human being in the world.

Verstehen here is not Dilthey's method of advancing from outer life expressions to the inner experience that illuminates them with meaning. Nor did Heidegger follow Dilthey in the search for the general validity of the historical sciences or "the critique of historical reason." For Heidegger our relation to others is not one of inner and outer experience as in Dilthey's doctrine of *Verstehen*. For Heidegger it is only because *Verstehen* is the pre-thematic understanding of the world prior to all method or science or interpretation that we can be said to be able to possess. *Dasein* possesses the pre-thematic ability to deal with the past, present, and possible future, the ability to "be with" (*Mitsein*) others in an understandable relation. This is to say that the end of all historiological science is to reveal those possibilities of life which have been established by the actions and creations of previous human life. It is only because human life has been able to understand the having-been and able-to-be, the possibilities of other life, that it is capable of being with others at all. The end of all *Verstehen* is to reveal the force of the possible through the repetition of what has been established before.[8]

For Heidegger Dilthey's understanding of *Verstehen* as the interpretation of life assertions back to their meaningful grounds in inner experience is merely a reflection of the inauthentic demand of *das Man* that historical science approximate the methods and subject matter of the natural sciences. But this is neither a theory of truth nor an authentic historiography.[9] *Verstehen* becomes in Dilthey part of the Cartesian error of understanding human life and its world as the clear and distinct understanding of material things at hand. Human existence has here become in Dilthey an entity at hand represented by conceptual thinking. Dilthey used as the means of this thinking his philosophy of human life and his methodology of *Verstehen*. His work contributed to the forgetfulness of being and the inauthenticity of contemporary thought. It was Heidegger's goal to replace Dilthey's critique of historical reason with a return to originative thinking (*das änfangliche Denken*) demanded by a general ontology of human life and existence. Yet Heidegger's critique here does not address the fact that Dilthey's theories of *Verstehen* and the critique of historical reason were not intended to be ontological, but a contribution to historiological science and a quest for historical knowledge.

Interpretation

We have seen that understanding (*Verstehen*) is one of the fundamental means by which human life is disclosed to itself. What we call understanding is in fact not only the interpretation of life assertions, as we saw it in Dilthey, but also the act of the disclosure of the possibilities of life itself. Understanding is founded on the concerns we have for our being in a world of circumstances with which we must deal. This implies that all understanding is involved with anticipating how to manage or control something. Of course there may also be in our understanding a theoretical dimension, which involves a process of formal abstraction or theory. At that level of abstraction, such as working out a mathematical calculation, the practical concerns of human life are not emphasized. Yet the basic nature of all understanding is involved with human life's projection of its possibilities in the world of circumstances, especially its anticipated future. In this manner of projection human life constructs its life world and its history. This construction of our life is never complete, because our life is always ahead of itself and "on the way" to possibilities which are never complete or exhausted.

All understanding involves interpretation, or the assigning of meanings, values, and purposes to things which are at hand in our environment or implicit in our awareness. Our interpretation of these elements is then projected upon future possibilities of our life. We understand our future possibilities always in relation to our previous interpretations. We never advance into our possibilities "all at once" without a past and present conditioning our future. We anticipate a future which will bear a relation to our present and our past. Interpretation in this sense is an act of incorporation of past, present, and future in our life and its circumstances. We understand our lives and their works in a back and forth exchange between present, partial meanings and a projected whole which is never complete but always anticipated.

All acts of interpretation presuppose two fundamental structures of human life. The first of these Heidegger calls the "fore-structure" of interpretation. This means that every act of our interpretations supposes prior presuppositions or points of reference. Human life brings to all phenomena alternative ways of conceiving things and placing them in the world. The second element that all understanding presupposes he calls the "as-structure." This means that we always interpret phenomena "as" something, "as" examples of general types, entities, or situations. Both the "fore" and "as" structures are interpretive in that they bring to phenomena past, present, and future references. We understand something only in the total contexts of "fore" and "as." For example, a facial expression is seen "as" something friendly or indifferent. But our seeing something "as," in this case our interpretation of a face, must exist in the context of human life's previous, "fore"presuppositions about the implications that friendly and hostile faces have for our lives.

All of this suggests that life's meanings occur temporally. Human life always brings historical forms to its present and future worlds. Our life exists out of a past toward a future about which it must care. For example, we interpret a pencil at hand under the projection of our being able to write upon a piece of paper. This paper is the projection "upon which" the pencil receives its meaning. Our use of the pencil is a sort of transcending projection of the past and present into a possibility of our life. For Heidegger such an existence toward a future is what makes us historical beings, and is a feature of the way we are in the world.

Our life exists as constant acts of interpretation, and this is so usual and "everyday" that we normally don't notice that we are in fact doing it. We are usually conscious of hearing, seeing, and feeling the world of circumstances as already interpreted, as already past. It is ordinarily only when we witness something radically unfamiliar or startling, such as a murder, that we stop to unpack how the experience was given to us, what it means, how it came about, etc. Yet interpretation also exists at a more discursive and formal level. In the case of interpreting the motives behind an act of war, or a complicated crime, we are forced to graduate both the "fore" and "as" structures of such events into an explanation of the motives of others or into a context of a narration of life through time. Here we find that our explanation is inevitably historical in nature.

All interpretation exists as what Heidegger calls "a hermeneutical circle." Such a circle is for him the most primordial element in our understanding. It is not to be confused with a "vicious circle," or an argument which is invalid because it assumes as true or as understood something which is yet to be proved. In a hermeneutical circle there occurs an interpretation or projection or "fore" conception of something which I must connect with my present life. Here there is present an action or plan which is serviceable for my life. Such a projection becomes a part of a world of meanings already presupposed or anticipated. In the hermeneutical circle there is always a pre-understanding of something in the context of what is already part of the present and past of my life. In this sense, nothing can be understood in the absence of meanings we already assume. There is no pre-suppositionless understanding.

Language

Interpretation is a subject that suggests the question of the role of language in human life. Language is the verbal and written communication of words and statements used, and is understood within a community of users. All language must be examined in the context of human life and culture. Language for Heidegger reveals the intelligibility of the world in life expressions that communicate how users, hearers, and readers are in a common world of discourse. For him language is part of a prior realm of "Discourse," which includes, for example, certain life expressions, such as a signal to advance or retreat, or such as a crucifix, which express to a community moods, references, events, actions, creations. But our ordinary verbal or written speech expresses not only formal sentences but also the philosophical fact that human life exists as an openness to the world and its circumstances. It is through language that our understanding of circumstances can be expressed in meaningful speech and communication. We express how we are in the world in speech and writing.

Our speech consists of both talking and listening. When we listen to the speech of others, we do not simply hear a noise that is later interpreted as a meaning. Instead, we hear a message or theme which is constituted as the spoken message itself. We hear a communication that is present to us as a general meaning which is to be incorporated into the meaning structure which our life already possesses. For example, a cry for help or a swearing response is not simply a vocalization we hear, but a "message" which we must take account of in our life. Cries of help or rage contain messages that we are not in the world neutrally but as careful beings. Our language is sedimented with meanings and implications for the Care Structure of human life.

Yet language is not to be understood as simply a tool for practical responding to circumstances. It is through language that human life possesses the possibility of expressing and understanding the wonder and meanings of the world in general. Language is the "house of being" which cares for and preserves Being. It informs us what it means to be at all.

The Anonymous "They"

Heidegger poses the problem of the self as the "who of *Dasein*," that existence which stands out as its very own and which is expressed by the personal pronoun "I." This "who" exists in such a way that it is always the individual "I" of our life, the self which "takes hold" of its own past, belongs to itself in the present, and anticipates its own future. But in an important passage of *Being and Time* Heidegger suggests that the "who" of human life might not be simply the "I myself."[10] In other words, we may not be simply solitary individuals, because the individual human is always open to and with others, existing in a common world with them. This status of "being with" others Heidegger calls *Mitsein*, a life category of coexistence with others in a relation of solicitude. This relation is part of the authentic wholeness of human life. The "who" of our individual life may be more than the "I-myself;" it may be joined to another aspect of ourselves which is vague, inconclusive, and conforming. This phantom self may incorporate our individuality into an anonymous "they" or "one," an everybody-in-general yet nobody in particular. This "they" may show itself as a part of our existence which is absorbed in the meanings, decisions, and values of a vague reference group which is not our "I" itself, yet is related to ourselves. For the most part the existence of our individual life is one that gets shared with others. Our "I" is not to be understood only as a private, individuated unit, but also as a relation with others. We are specifically in the world by reference to the concept of "being with" (*Mitsein*), and this status is examined in the context of the "who" of human life.

The "who" of human life had been previously understood in the history of philosophy as ego, soul, or spirit. But the whole question of the "who" needs an elucidation of its nature. For the most part our life is not simply an "I-myself," but an "anybody self" which is available to others, and others to it. In our actual life we exist in public circumstances which are encountered as a life world of common meanings and uses. Whether we are dealing with a fork, a steering wheel, a light switch, or a common language, we assume an existence of an "anybody" who can understand and use these human creations. Human life grasps how it is in the world by the supposition of an "anybody" who can use these creations and life forms. The telephone company assumes an "anybody" who can understand and "consume" the telephone's uses. Our "being with" others here is made possible by a sort of fabricated public self who is an "anybody," an "anybody" who is always a possibility at any time for me to become.

This "anybody" self has both positive and negative senses. In the positive sense the "anybody" is a necessary and useful component of our being with others. Society is largely composed of encounterable social forms that "anybody" might relate to and share and use. The "I-myself" must conform to the expectations and relevances of the "anybody" through a commonality of significances. But there is a second, negative sense of the "anybody" which we may think of as a "being with" in an extreme and dehumanizing sense. Our public self may come to relinquish its possibilities and responsibilities to others and lose its identity to a mass. In this defective sense the "anybody" self "falls" through leveling. When this public self suppresses all differences and imposes a conformity and standardization on itself, then the self has devolved into a *das Man* in the negative sense. The term *das Man* was Heidegger's way of expressing both the authentic and defective senses of the "other" who is a categorical part of our being in the world.

The defective mode of our "being with" is also found in the writings of Kierkegaard. He was the first to write about the relation of our life to the category of the "crowd." This relationship appeared after his earlier concentration on the relation of the individual to Christianity, but by the time of his *The Two Ages* (1846) his emphasis graduated to the relation of the individual to the "crowd" or "public." In *The Two Ages* he was the first to see that the politics and sociology of the present age will be dominated by *das Man*. It is also in the thought of Kierkegaard that we find the first expression of the "crowd" as a philosophic concept. Such an idea became a significant feature in the later philosophy of life that he helped to inaugurate. His goal was to express to his contemporaries that they were foundering in a pseudo-moral collectivity which stands in contradiction to the duty of the Christian individual. The goal of the Christian life is to discover an authentic individuality as a "single one."

For Kierkegaard the crowd is born when individuals conceive of their identity in terms of number and numerical superiority. In this sense abstract numerical superiority becomes an idol, and the individual loses his or her inwardness by tending to believe what "they" believe and presuppose. An impersonal, abstract collectivity comes to replace the personal agent. The crowd emerges in different stages. First, through the "public chatter" of small talk and gossip the crowd pretends to be "in the know" about private and public matters. It is made to seem as if the crowd possesses a private wisdom or inside information. Here the public and private domains have already become blurred. The second stage appears when the individual disperses personal decisions and opinions as though they were "coming out of" a higher agency of truth. The final stage of untruth is reached when the abstract collectivity allows itself to be deified, to take the characteristics that belong to God. For the individual this self-deification of the crowd, in which he may take part, acts as a temptation to an "idolatry in secular dress." It also creates in him or her despair and loneliness. Through his or her individual despair of ever attaining inwardness or individuality the individual resigns individuality to a crowd of abstract equals. But human beings are equal only before God; otherwise they are inherently unequal. The "equality" of the crowd is but another attempt to substitute man for God.

In this state the "I-myself" is significant only in so far as there is an identification with the mentality of the other as an anonymous "they." The tendency is to dim down the identity of the "I-myself" to the vague averageness of the "they." Our personal life receives and expresses only what "they" say, and our "they" self replaces our authentic "I-myself." A personal life which decides and evaluates becomes submerged in an average life form which replaces it. But such a life is not our own, because it is a forgetful drifting into the possibilities of the crowd. In ordinary usage this expresses itself as "They are saying x" or "They are doing x." Henry David Thoreau expresses this in his *Walden* when he remarks that a clothing salesman said to him, about his clothes, "They are not wearing that anymore."

In Heidegger's examination of the fallenness of the crowd he lists three characteristics of this state: (1) idle talk (*Gerede*), (2) curiosity (*Neugier*), and (3) ambiguity (*Zweideutigkeit*). In the case of idle talk there is an interpretation of the world through the use of language, but a dimming of truth takes place when a person uses such an expression as "They say that X is a homosexual." Here there is no concern for evidence or fact. Such idle talk is a way of avoiding or preventing inquiry about the assertion while at the same time seeming to assert some definite truth. The idle talk of the crowd is promoted by curiosity. In this state we seem to seek truth through our concern or solicitude by being a spectator of the world. Yet the spectator is actually concealed and indifferent. For example, "someone" will ask, "How are you?" but he or she actually remains neutral or unconcerned. Ambiguity is a third state of inauthentic human life. Here a person takes the role of an average neutrality by dissolving into a role of theoretical indifference. For example, a psychologist may assume a clinical pose by seeming to be above a patient's mental suffering, through the role of "somebody" who does not participate in the patient's anxieties and depression. The psychologist treats the cares of the patient as "already known or thought about." The patient's self-understanding is assumed unscientific or unimportant. In such a case not only the psychologist but also the patient becomes an abstract ambiguity, an "anybody" in a role that they are expected to play. Fallenness is defined by Heidegger as the identification of our own existence with a fictional "other" who is composed of idle talk, curiosity, and ambiguity.[11] In this fictional other, which is normal and obvious in its role playing, we seek to avoid our actual existence and to become totally depersonalized and dissipated in our posture as an "anybody"(*das Man*).

At this point it is important to remember that our individual life is never totally incorporated into a "generalized other" role. A person may retrieve himself or herself from the state of fallenness through the characteristic of human life called resoluteness (*Entschlossenheit*): the capacity of a human life to call itself out of a given state or to achieve some goal or status. Here we resolve to be ourselves and to belong to ourselves alone in our actions and beliefs. It is through resoluteness that we recall ourselves from the fallenness of idle talk, curiosity, and ambiguity.

While we may ignore the call to be ourselves, we may still remain open to the possibility of freedom from the crowd, though such freedom is a state most do not often attain. Human life is always open to the possibility of performance or attainment. Such possibility is a basic category of human life through which we project our existence into the future. The world exists for us not only as static fact, but as possibility.

It is also through conscience that we extract ourselves from fallenness. Conscience is the calling of our life back to itself from its distractions and forgetfulness to the affirmation to be itself. It is through conscience that human life becomes aware of its own incompletions, its "falling short" of its resolves. Conscience recalls us to the fact that we are always in a state of finitude and potential death; conscience also stands aware of its own guilt. It is in guilt that the self calls itself back to its possibilities in the future. But we never finalize our possibilities in life. Guilt creates in our life an anxiety over our imperfections, and requests us to acknowledge what we have not become.

Finally, our resoluteness is challenged by the fact of death. It is when we realize that death is our final possibility that we come to the awareness that we cannot live in public or mass possibilities alone. It is in the full realization that we are going to die that we see most fully our "thrownness" into a world we did not choose. Our status as part of a crowd is always outstripped by the final possibility of death. We cannot here tranquilize our life as an "anybody" with the anonymity and distractions of the crowd. In this situation our resoluteness can be to death itself, and to the full realization of its implications for conscience, guilt, and fallenness in general. In other words, death may be a teacher in our lives.

The Vital Elite

In the humanization of the "other" we find that such a humanized being or circumstance may either aid us in the construction of our lives or restrict our possibilities and actual projects. My individual existence may be mediated and even appropriated by the "other." If my life is actually dominated or stupified by a system of social conformities and expectations, then for Ortega the "I" of my life is a prisoner of *alteración*, i.e., a life removed from any inwardness, due to an over-reliance on the values, expectations, and goals of the "other." *Alteración* is a necessary part of human life, because human beings are forced to be concerned with things other than themselves, if they are to survive in circumstances. Yet for Ortega we must never lose the perspective of our true inner and personal life that we must create. If we live our personal inner life always outside of ourselves in the values and expectations of others, then our life is deprived of its ownness by being "turned over" to an anonymous other, the abstraction that so often seizes our life. Our autofabrication in historical time is no longer our personal project, but a group sociality which can mislead us from our autonomy. Our creative responsibility has drifted outside of its original interiority into the vague life of the other. Yet the greatest danger of *alteración* is that it may deprive me of my prior and more authentic condition of "a life within myself," which Ortega designates as *ensimismamiento*, a "withdrawing into" my more authentic being. For Ortega it is only through *ensimismamiento* that our life can find its way to our authentic vocation. Correspondingly, it is only through those who can gain such a responsible and creative inner life that the greater social group can hope for the improvement of its human condition. It is through those who can attain a state of responsible self-creation and provision of values that human life can improve itself. The author would designate this authentic minority as "the vital elite" of human life.

In an essay entitled *Ensimismamiento y alteración* (1939) Ortega stated that it is only through the inner possession of *ensimismamiento* attained through the efforts and self-reliance of a minority that we can attain the creative and moral perspectives demanded by human life. Such a select and qualified minority can actualize itself through self-imposed demands. Ortega claimed that only a select and qualified minority is able by means of its personal, moral, creative, intellectual and executive abilities to assume the responsibilities of its generation. Such a vital elite is able to see that human life in circumstances is always in need, always insecure. It is also able to see that human life possesses a constant tendency to decline into an "invertebrate" or spineless, stupified barbarism. For Ortega the awarenesses of the vital elite are usually not possessed by the masses, who are usually fallen into *alteración* through their indifference to any self-imposed qualitative demands. This is also the case with most individuals. It is only to be hoped that the mass of humanity can be directed to support and complement the efforts and creations of a minority whose vocation is the promotion of a higher humanity. It is the ideal role of the vital elite both to invent and decide the most efficacious directions of humanity. But in our era, and perhaps always, the forms of civilization—such as philosophy, religion, education, politics, art—are seized and controlled by the very masses who are lost in *alteración*. The critical and creative capacities required in civilization are not possessed by a mass lost in a self-satisfied conformity which makes no demands upon itself.[12] The function of the vital elite must be the humanization of circumstances through the creation of new standards, norms, ideas, inventions, and behaviors appropriate to higher civilization. In the West the vital elite has declined, and it seems doomed to inadequacy. Any such elite is resisted or ignored by the masses, who want no self-demands or responsibilities of any kind. The construction of civilized forms is the very vocation of a qualified and select minority. The vital elite is the vanguard and spark plug of the ideas, values, and creations of an authentic humanity. Ortega saw the need of an elite especially in politics. In Spain, for example, such an elite was necessary to provide the leadership, reflection, and backbone which Ortega prescribed as necessary for the survival of his country, as proclaimed in his *Invertebrate Spain* (1921) and *The Revolt of the Masses* (1930).

What is the nature and identity of the masses whom the vital elite must both oppose and lead? Perhaps it is best here to indicate who the masses are not: they are not any particular social class or economic group, not working people or the poor or racial minorities, nor are they the uneducated or illiterate, immigrants, or the disadvantaged or "third world." In turn, Ortega does not mean by the elite the rich or famous, the powerful, the fashionable princesses, or the media and entertainment moguls. For him most entertainers and media persons are excluded from the "elite" designation ipso facto. The mass and the elite are neither all nor any of these types. The mass is a state of mind which Ortega delineates in his *Revolt of the Masses*. In that work he defines the mass as that group in nineteenth century Europe which claimed both rights and advantages which it did not itself create and which previously belonged only to the few. The productive technology, inventions, and creations were conceived by a vital minority of inventors, technocrats, scientists, doctors, etc., but the incipient mass came to demand that they too should possess these improvements as their right. The mass rightly asserted that the ancient regimes did not possess any superiority to themselves, but the mass also went on to assume a state of mind which refused to make demands upon itself, establish goals, or create higher civilization. While asking nothing of itself, it tended to demand equality and comfort from a world to which it claimed to owe nothing. Its needs and demands became natural rights, and it claimed that no individual or group was superior to itself. Because its opinions seemed to require no justification by reason, education, or experience, it did not admit or remember errors, but always assumed that its past behaviors and notions were obvious and true. It demanded all rights to all things with no reciprocal duties or efforts. It would enforce and justify its opinions and desires, even if they entailed the destruction of higher culture or the political order. As a creature of its own *alteración* the mass drifted and waited, in a role-assuming existence which possessed no interiority, decision, leadership, or effort. It assumed that all its thoughts and deeds were authoritative, and the trivia, vulgarity, and conformity of everyday life were considered normal and unquestionable. It identified excellence and betterment with self-gratification and distractions.

Among the mass, then, firm beliefs are so weakened that it is difficult or impossible to establish certain grounds for actions, values, or social projects. Collectively there has come to exist a nihilism of pseudo-equality of standards, values, and taste. Such a collective situation Ortega calls "demoralization." This term indicates an absence of those beliefs and standards which maintain the very tone of human life. In the state of demoralization there comes to exist the assumption that there are no adequate solutions to our problematic circumstances and personal lives. Beliefs are unable to provide a basis for actions, goals, or family life. In this situation a select and qualified minority, a vital elite, must become the agent which attempts to counteract the demoralization of mass society.

The vital elite as an effective ideology is compatible with the nineteenth century liberal tradition of parliamentary democracy and the Jeffersonian ideal of a natural aristocracy. Ortega understood liberalism as that ideology which can secure and protect permanent human rights and attempt to establish freedom from all the unnecessary constraints of the national state. But it is the final goal of liberalism to protect the intellectual freedom of the individual from both the state and the masses. Liberalism ideally will operate under the restraints of constitutionalism and disjoin itself from the extremes and inadequacy of both left and right.[13]

Ortega distinguished liberalism from all forms of egalitarian democracy, for he thought that the typical mass democrat believes in neither liberalism nor freedom. He refuses to hear that people are unequal in any significant respect, and he is traditionally indifferent or hostile to the idea of a qualified minority with any significant political influence. As early as his *The Modern Theme* (1923) Ortega sought to reveal the need of a qualified leadership for Western Europe in the early twentieth century.

Ortega believed that in the feudal era there was a legitimization of leadership through the hierarchy of the land-owning classes. In this era the individual possessed limited freedom, and beliefs were generated from church authority and traditional wisdom. The feudal era gave way to the Renaissance with its more rationalistic and individualistic political forms. The idea of secular progress was promoted, an idea which reached its height in the French Revolution. In the final stages of the nineteenth century democracy, science, technology, and industrialism developed, providing the collective life forms of the twentieth century, but *alteración* appeared in the nihilism and demoralization of the masses. Along with Nietzsche, Sorel, and Spengler, Ortega believed that nihilism and demoralization were prolonged into our own era. In the twentieth century only a vital elite could even faintly hope to repel "the diffuse authoritarianism of the mob;" they alone could hope to possess the historical awareness required for the thinking of circumstances and the creation of ideas and beliefs necessary to counteract both demoralization and *alteración*. Here liberalism bears an important relation to the vocation of the vital elite. Because freedom of thought is the precondition of effective leadership and idea formation, it is only the unrestricted thinking of a qualified minority that can effectively address our historical condition. The vital and historical reason that can foresee and address the possibilities of a given generation is best located in the hands of a qualified elite. This remains the case even though the presence of an elite is precarious and problematical in all collectives. For Ortega it is one of the vocations of philosophy to provide the ideas and beliefs which can counteract the aimlessness and failed beliefs of the masses, and provide the leadership and stability required in contemporary circumstances.

Culture

Closely related to the category of the "other" is culture. In his *Mission of the University* (1930) Ortega distinguished human culture from its near relation, the social collective of the "other." Culture, he tells us, is "the system of vital ideas by which each age transmits its active convictions about what is to be esteemed." In his earlier *Meditations on Quixote* (1914) he wrote that all the objects at hand in the world seem to us at first to be simply there, inhospitable and problematic for our life. "Culture" here refers to the human actions and creations by which circumstances are converted from mere "things at hand" to entities and ideas which are to be permanently preserved. Such a process of selection, appraisal, and preservation is called by Ortega "the reabsorbing of those circumstances" which at first seemed only brute or arbitrary objects at hand. This means that we reconstitute such objects by "humanizing" them through their ideal transformation into the customs, beliefs, concepts, values, and projects by which they are "absorbed" into human life and its culture. Here circumstances are humanized by being transformed from mere objects-at-hand to the very stuff of human life. For example, a stick found upon a forest floor may be picked up and utilized by a tribal member as a weapon, cane, or object used in a sacred ceremony, and an anthropologist may further "absorb" this stick-utilization by incorporating this life practice into an academic treatise in the life forms of cultural anthropology. An artist "reabsorbs" circumstances when he or she interprets a landscape, mountain, or farm as an example of pioneer heritage.

In this sense culture is more than ornamentation or display of the rich and educated. Culture here becomes a guide or estimate of circumstances that may be endowed with significance, value, and relative permanence. By such an act of "absorbing" circumstances human beings establish standards of estimation and clarify and affirm how they are oriented in the world. Culture has become here an activity of clarifying and saving human life and its works. All human life is an extended act of interpretation of the world at hand. Humanized circumstances become "purified" in their being related to human life as "formulae" for what is to be taken care of, clarified, and interpreted for human ends.[14] Culture preserves those beliefs and actions which were successful in the attainment of definite ends. Culture also lets drop those interpretations and projects which failed.

For Ortega it is the central mission of the university to preserve and teach those vital ideas, beliefs, and creations which the ages have attained. While the university is a place of scientific research and "pure knowledge," it is also its mission to become once more the teacher of culture that it was in the middle ages. We have the base for authentic teaching and learning exactly in proportion as the learners do not know about a world that has been reabsorbed and humanized as culture. University culture must also be able to derive from circumstances the humanized meanings, values, and purposes of circumstances in selected and hierarchical order of importance. For Ortega, however, the reabsorbing of circumstances in orders of hierarchy and importance is the concrete destiny of all human beings in their search for a place in the world. There is a constant search for strategies by which we all must absorb the unclarified immediacy of unhumanized circumstances. In this sense culture becomes part of the endless human search for a secure and lasting place in the world.

Mood

Our life is continually in one mood or another. Our moods are a permanent property of our life, in that they are the result of the ways that we relate to our circumstances with our feelings. We are always in some way moodfully related to our world. Our moods are a fundamental disclosure of our life to ourselves. Through this disclosure we are able to arrive at an estimate of the well-being or ill-being of our existence. But moods of our life are not simply "extras" which our nature may or may not possess. They reveal to us how we are in our circumstances at the actual moment. As such, they are fundamental constituents of human life which are given and inescapable and to which we are "delivered up" in the world. Our moods are part of the understanding that attends all our possibilities and projects. All our possibilities, from the attempt to achieve a profession to cutting the lawn, are never to be separated from a mood. Also our very "thrownness" into our circumstances is always joined to a mood of our life. The world into which we are thrown is simply there, and we must adjust to a world we did not choose. Such brute facts are aspects of our essential human condition which has been thrust upon us.

Facts demand of us that we do not think of our life as solely a contemplative or abstract theoretical being existing in security and effortlessness. Rather, we are possessed by mood, because one of the deepest elements in our life is its concern over how it is in both a world and time which it did not choose. Our life is a continual movement forward in time, a continual orientation to a project. No part of such an orientation is without a striving, to evade or fulfill something. Even at night in our dreams we are recapitulating such orientations. Our past has been disclosed in the moods of a world that has been there previously. We always find ourselves coming out of situations in which we have already existed moodfully. We are always concerned about how the world of circumstances will affect our lives, and our moods and dispositions are ways that our world discloses itself through past, present, and future. It is not through pure *theoria* or theoretical reason alone that our life exists, but in the generative moods of our life in time. Philosophy itself originated not in pure *theoria*, but in moods of wonder, fear, and the need for totality in our understanding.

Fear and anxiety are moods through which human beings relate their lives to the world. Fear reveals itself as a mood which approaches human beings in their awareness of concrete circumstances which threaten them and from which they can flee. Fear is possible for human life because we are by nature concerned with what threatens us in the world. Anxiety (*Angst*) is unlike fear in that it has no definite object about which it is anxious. It never encounters one object that defines what it is about. Rather, we are anxious about our being in the world of circumstances as such. Anxiety is present to us everywhere, yet nowhere. Our anxiety, however, is not nothing. We are anxious in our life because we are forever in a world of circumstances with which we must somehow deal. As a constant possibility for our life, anxiety is a basic categorical component of our existence. We cannot avoid the sense of uncanniness that results from our being in a world we did not choose and cannot fully understand.

CHAPTER TEN

The Directions of Human Life

Will, Motives, and Ends

In the philosophy of human life will is understood as the total conscious process of affecting circumstances for the attainment of ends. As such, will cannot be separated from the power to act toward ends. Yet will and power are not the same, for a given agent may have the power to act but not necessarily the will, and vice versa. Purpose is joined to both will and power, in that purpose is understood as that which we set before ourselves as an object to be attained through our ability to act toward an end. No given end or purpose can be conceptually separated from the means required for its attainment. Dilthey addressed all of these dimensions in his thoughts about motives and ends. In his *System of Ethics* he discussed teleological experience, especially motive and ends.[1] Here he began by noting that sense data are given to the psyche, and our reflex mechanisms absorb these sense data into our biological drives. The basic drives seek satisfaction through those human actions which promote survival and which are remembered and valued in the course of human life. Such select values become the ends to which reason and experience direct behavior.

For Dilthey power (*Kraft*) is not simply an external or mechanical force required for the dispersion of energy. It becomes in his thought a "lived" or "inner" force in the whole system of human life. In a baseball game, for example, one kind of power is the physical displacement of mass or energy required to move a player around bases. But the "lived" power of the game is the striving and orientation of the players to definite goals following the rules and meanings of the game. "Lived power" also includes motives, that element within an individual, rather than without, which incites him or her to action. Motives are also implicit judgments which seem to an agent an adequate ground for a given form of behavior to a desired end.[2]

Dilthey joins the concept of motives to reasons in that he believes that a motive is actually a "reason why" human beings employ one action over another. The presence of a motive in a given action is the material that the historian looks for in his explication of historical events. In other words, the historian looks for the "reasons" which prompt an action. Such reasons are in fact essential parts of all means-end behavior in human life. In so far as an agent possesses a present idea of what is required to attain a goal, he acts with respect to his motives.[3] Motives are reasons in that they are that part of behavior which is preceded by a deliberative consideration of ends and means and an explanation of why an agent does x instead of y. All motivated behavior is action in which we understand what we are attempting to do; and when we see that it is accomplished, we understand that it has conformed to our original conception of it.[4]

In all motivated means-end behavior there are two agents, one who acts and one who attempts to understand the action. We usually possess an implicit understanding of our own motivated behavior. But in trying to grasp another's motives and behaviors Dilthey believed we must use the formal method of *Verstehen*. For him motives can be inferred from another's overt actions through a process of analogical reasoning; we infer from the actions of another the motives that would obtain in ourselves performing like actions. In end-oriented behavior Dilthey believed that motives and all deliberative behavior are in fact causal agents in the historical world. But the sort of cause he referred to is not that which is used in the natural sciences. In the human sciences motive-deliberative action is understood by the reason something was done and not by the citing of physical laws. If we shake our fist at a person involved in a family argument, such an action is partly a physical motion of an arm and fist, which is explainable by the methods of physics and physiology. But it is not appropriate to explain the fist-shaking in this sense alone. The physiological explanation does not account for the meanings and assumptions present in the argument. The motive-deliberative aspect of the action is only externally and incompletely related to the physical action of the fist-shake.

Possibility and Self-Determination

In the Western tradition of philosophy since Aristotle it has been assumed that actuality not only is prior to possibility but also possesses a higher degree of reality. In the philosophy of human life it is possibility that enjoys a higher status than actuality. In the thought of Heidegger the priority of possibility over actuality is a central theme. The term "possibility" does not in this context refer to the fact that contingencies happen in human life; nor does it imply that "anything can happen." Rather, the term "possibility" refers to an open future in which it is "possible" that human beings can with understanding decide and actualize themselves.

Heidegger develops possibility (*Möglichkeit*) as an existential category or mode of human existence and history. Possibility is that mode of our life which allows for the transcendence of the actualities of the present into a future which does not yet exist. The presence of possibility in our existence expresses the fact that our being in the world need not always be limited to the restraints and prohibitions of the present actual world. We can understand the world not only in terms of actualities but as what can be projected and anticipated in the future. Possibility is our continual reminder that we are not entirely limited to those elements in our life which are simply given, not chosen or valued.

Possibilities arise in human life through what Heidegger terms "the projective character of understanding." Our understanding exists as its continual projection of the possibilities of our life on the world and on the future. Understanding in this sense allows us to be aware of our ability to be at all. For Heidegger we actually exist as creatures who understand, or attempt to understand, how we are in the world. We are aware of ourselves in terms of what is possible for us in the world. For Heidegger we are "thrown" (*Geworfenheit*) into the human condition of being aware of our ability to understand possibilities in the world and especially the future. Our understanding is not only an apprehension of facts at hand, but it is a deeper mode of awareness that allows us to be cognizant of what it means to be in a world at all. As such, understanding is the projection of our life's possibilities into a future with actualities of its own. Through its ability to project our life ahead of itself into "what could be for it," understanding opens up the possibilities that are real for it in time and history. Such projection is the manner in which we exist in the world. Our existence is a project for itself.

Human beings in their lives are able to exist as a "not yet," for our projections are not yet actual for us in the present. But by projecting ourselves into the future we become in a sense our own future anticipations. Such "not yet" anticipations have both personal and sociohistorical dimensions for our lives. For example, Martin Luther King was "thrown" into the conditions of his life, conditions which were simply given, not chosen. He was, as it were, "frozen" into the status of being black, in a given historical time, with its social, economic, educational, and class conditions. His people tended to constitute themselves in terms of the actualities of their present. Yet he was able, and he helped to make his people able, to understand both their actualities and their possibilities through an understanding that projected these into new life forms which were "not yet." These "not yet" life forms he urged could be actualized, if only in a partial way, by both him and his followers. By transcending the actuality of present racist conditions he hoped to achieve greater racial equality with new rights under the law. In this sense both King and his followers became in their lives their own future possibilities. They tended to become an "I am what I will be" life form. If he and his followers adequately understood and envisioned the future, it was through an understanding of both present actualities and future possibilities as "not yet." If his future "not yet" was actually possible and achievable, then his project was authentic. But if he had projected only the present possibilities of *das Man*, prejudice, curiosity, falling, and idle talk, then his project would have been inauthentic and without fulfillment. When agents project authentic possibilities for their lives, and when they act for the sake of these possibilities in accord with a motive, then self-determination becomes an actuality. Such a mode of becoming is the very ground of history.

Man the Technician

In his essay "Man the Technician" (*Meditación de la técnica*) Ortega understood human autonomy and human life's autofabrication in terms of historical reason. This means that human beings exist as self-making creatures; i.e., they accumulate their being through historical time in the anticipation and construction of present and future circumstances. In this sense human beings are technicians, and technology becomes an essential characteristic of human life. In asking the question "What is technology?" Ortega's essay advances to an answer by addressing another question, namely "Why should human beings rather live than die?" This is the most justified and fundamental of all life's questions and it cannot be answered by reference to an instinct of self-preservation. Human beings do not simply live by their instincts, but they govern themselves by other faculties, such as will, thought, and memory, which supervise our instincts. Human beings live because they want to, and they do this by avoiding cold, gaining warmth, and feeding themselves. These satisfactions impose a new need, namely to construct the tools for facilitating these and subsequent needs. These needs and their fulfillment are the fundamental conditions of human life. These are felt subjectively as necessities. But things are not necessary in themselves; they are necessary for the living of each human life. Constructing a home is necessary not in itself but for living. Living is the original and basic necessity of which subsequent necessities are consequences. Our life is necessary in a subjective sense: our inner need and resolve to live. But our living does not simply happen by itself. It requires a new type of activity. For the living of their lives human beings must produce, fabricate, and find what they do not presently possess.

Producing, fabricating, and finding are the materials and means of human life. These actions are different from needs such as keeping warm. When we are constructing tools, building fires, or farming land, we suspend for a time the primary actions involved in gratifications which meet needs directly. Instead we disengage ourselves temporarily from immediate "vital urgencies" and attempt to remain free for activities which in themselves are not directly and presently the satisfaction of needs. These secondary activities produce the means or tools for the subsequent satisfaction of needs or desires. For Ortega this means that part of our life does not coincide with our primary, organic needs. Because human beings are not identical with circumstances, but only placed in them, they are able to "put aside" some circumstances to withdraw from gratification for a time, and invent a series of actions, such as cultivating a field or constructing a flint for fire-making. We can manufacture the tools and perform the actions to modify nature, creating objects which did not exist before, for the satisfaction of our needs and desires. This is human life as technology in its primordial form.

Ortega, then, defines technology as the improvements placed on nature by human beings for the satisfaction of their needs. We then possess the technical acts, which are exclusively human, and in totality they are human life's means for accommodating the needs of our life. In sum, technology is man's reaction to the circumstances of nature. In this sense technology is a dialectical relation between man and nature.

Technology generates in human beings the construction of a new nature, a "supernature" that we impose between ourselves and primal nature. Technology reforms nature by its attempt to abolish need by assuring human satisfaction in all possible circumstances. Technology is the human way of not resigning ourselves to the world of need and nature as they are in themselves. Human nature is present whenever we find original nature altered with tools and artifacts. Thus technology is an essential part of human being in a world of circumstances. Yet technology goes beyond necessities; it may also produce objects of pleasure or well-being. Not simply raw existence but human well-being is perhaps the most desired end of technology.

Another end of technology is increased security, yet Ortega believed it is the very feeling of security which is threatening Western civilization. For example, a belief in progress, which is a major article of faith of the Western world, gives us a feeling of false security, for it seems to suggest that a great reversal in prosperity or peace will not happen. Technology has allowed us to forget or shun "things that ought to be done" (*pragmata*) in our circumstances for our survival and well-being. Also overlooked is the possibility of technology becoming not a servant of need but a master of human life, which creates an unwanted and dangerous destiny for all of us.

We must "earn" our existence in circumstances and in our history. We are at once akin to nature, yet not akin to nature. We are partly biological animals and partly the possibility of transcendence. Our natural part realizes itself, as our hair grows on our head, without our effort or plan. This is why human beings do not consider our natural part our true nature or being. But our self-transcendent part is an aspiration, a project in the construction of our lives. We feel that our life as an autofabrication through time is our true being. This is the life about which we tell a story, a narration. The autofabricated life is a program, a project of our existence, an aspiration to overcome something or to be something through historical time.

The issue here is the distinction between our life as a voluntary, transcending construction, as radical reality, and our life as our biological nature. Our historical and fabricated being and our biological being are not identical. Our self-transcending and historical being is a denaturalized existence which cannot be discerned by exclusive reference to our anatomy, sensations, or physiology. This means that our biological nature is relatively fixed as *homo sapiens*. Our invariable organic structure traverses our bodily life, but is of a different being from our life as radical reality; our species nature is not our historical being. While our biological existence, of course, is a necessary condition of our life as embodied, it is not a sufficient condition to explain our life as radical reality, and it is not anything radically real.[5] Our human being is both natural and extra-natural; we are thus "ontological centaurs." Our body, of a given and fixed nature, does its work automatically, through biological laws of growth and decay, but our extra-natural life as radical reality is not given ready-made or realized according to laws; it is achieved in historical time, an existence which accumulates and fabricates itself toward its own future. Ortega's thesis, that human life has no fixed nature but a history, never denies that human beings possess a biological identity. It only affirms that our real being is the radical historicity of human life.

For Ortega the first task of philosophy is the description and interpretation of what he sometimes calls our biographical life. This was an element in his thought from at least the time of *En torno a Galileo* (1933), in which he referred to the idea of human life in its biographical sense. In his *Meditación de la técnica*, which appeared as a lecture course in 1933, biographical life and its autofabrication were central in his thinking. In these works the term human life is identical to its biographical story. Our biological life is an automatic advance produced by fixed laws, but our biographical life is always lived in the face of the demand to transform itself into something it is to become. Human life is a bipolar relation, demanding of us that we adjust to circumstances. Our life is a constant technological demand for its autofabrication in time. Here again technology is an intrinsic component of human life, this time as a vital component of our self-making. We must transform our circumstances, not merely accept them. It is our extra-natural part, our biographical life, which transforms itself in the natural and historical environment. Because our life is always needful in problematic circumstances, we must constantly reconstitute our environment and ourselves.[6]

According to Ortega, Dilthey made the mistake of understanding our biographical life as *Geist,* or pure consciousness. Dilthey's idealism, he thought, was a mistaken philosophical enterprise. His idea of the *Geisteswissenschaften* had become a "failed belief" which Europe had ceased to trust. Idealism, the thesis which holds that idea or spirit is fundamental reality, does not include the world component, nor does it see that both "I" and my circumstances are radically real. "Spirit" (*Geist*) is not the radical reality in which all other realities are grounded, and from which they derive their meaning. Human life is this radical reality. Ortega believed Dilthey's idealism only reinforced the bifurcation of man into body and soul, making human life "a thing at hand," instead of the aspiration and self-making of biographical human life. Only the idea of human life as radical reality can save the human condition from the mistakes of both materialistic reductionism and idealism. Later (in Chapter 11) we will show reservations and limitations to these criticisms of Ortega about Dilthey.

For Ortega Dilthey's thought was largely directed to forming the general validity of the *Geisteswissenschaften,* yet Dilthey was the one who had discovered the "continent" of the idea of human life, and Ortega understood this original position to include the following elements of the historicity of human life: (1) human life most fundamentally is historicity; (2) our human nature is understood basically through its diverse manifestations in history, and not through empirical psychology; (3) historical science (*Historie*) is the interpretation of human life in time by *Verstehen* from the universal perspectives of mankind as they have revealed themselves.[7]

For Ortega Dilthey's greatness was in his discovery of human life and its fundamental historicity. Yet Ortega added to Dilthey's thought the themes of circumstances, autofabrication, and biographical human life. There also appears in Ortega's thought the existential theme asserting the great paradox of human biographical life, that it consists never only of what it already is, but also of what it has not yet become. Human life is always incomplete. This incompletion appears in Ortega's claim that our life possesses no final nature, only a history. Our historicity is the great fact of our life, for we are the beings that we are today and tomorrow only because yesterday we were something else. Our final identity, our "ownness," is the "drama" of our biographical life. Humanity is the technological being who is responsible for the construction of its life.

Historical reason is the attempt to understand human life as a biographical happening, a *res gestae,* and our understanding of this happening he termed a *cognitio rerum gestarum,* "a thinking of human life as a radically historical event." Our biographical life is our self-making as we advance into the future. The final end of biographical being is to humanize circumstances through the construction of our life in time. To describe this happening is the task of historical reason. Here the basic end of reason is to understand how the fact of human life has affected the fabrication of circumstances. Through the transcendence of the old life and its circumstances our living nature is a "drama" which "fills in" our possibilities through time. Such a historicity of human life makes us always in advance of our biological being, a sort of "fugitive" from our present status. Human life in this sense is always incomplete, a "not yet" which surpasses its former self in historical time. From Nietzsche Ortega has taken the idea that we may will our human life to "rise" and advance itself. All the beauty and meaning we grant to imaginary beings must be understood as a possibility of human life. Our incompleteness is our very being and opportunity. In this sense our life is in part the past through which it has achieved what it presently is. It is also the possibility of its transcendence into the future. The solitary and disillusioned thing I call my life is actually a prelude to a new form of life yet to be born. In a posthumous work entitled *Man and People* Ortega claimed that human life is never a static originality but an "inheritor" which becomes its own future. This idea, he claimed, is a new dimension of historical reason.[8] Such a reason is the authentic *Realdialektik* which explains the past, present, and future of human life. This reason both narrates what we have been and projects our life's irreversible advance into the future. Historical reason, then, thinks of human life as the transcending of our biological nature and as the being which creates history.

It will be helpful at this point to bring in Heidegger's contribution to the subject of technology and to compare his position with that of Ortega. Both thinkers wrote about the nature of technology, its role in human life, and its relation to Western philosophy. For Heidegger the question of technology was always understood in the context of the prior question of Being. The question of Being is the fate of the West, and this fate is for him closely related to the triumph of technology. Yet Heidegger never saw the fateful path of technology as something that should be reversed. For him both technology and the contemporary will to power of secular society are only phases in the revelation of Being. For better or worse, contemporary humanity must pass through the era of mass technology as part of the fate of our era. Heidegger's position with respect to technology takes the form of a passive acceptance of the unfolding of Being in the West. Contemporary nihilism must also await the fate of the historical destiny of Being, in the hope that history will deliver us from the distractions and problems of contemporary technology and its circumstances.

After his so-called "turning" from an emphasis on *Dasein* or human being in his *Being and Time*, Heidegger's philosophical emphasis turned largely to the question of Being itself and away from the "regional ontology" of *Dasein*. After *Being and Time* Heidegger came to distrust technology for a resolution of the circumstantial problems of human life. He also saw in contemporary Humanism a tendency to venerate change and to develop a materialism of mass production through the overuse of natural resources and the conquest of nature. He saw these as becoming the ends of human life, and the whole issue of technology for him came to be associated with threats to our survival. Heidegger's response to the issues of survival, technology, and even war seems to have taken the form of advocating our "releasement" (*Gelassenheit*) to the fate of Being itself.

Heidegger and Ortega seem divided on the question of what is required for "our age in need." Heidegger's tendency was to take the path of what has been designated in German intellectual history as a "knowledge by acceptance and devotion" (*Wissen als Hingebung*), whereas Ortega took the path referred to as "mastery and control of circumstances" (*Wissen als Herrschaft*). For Ortega the way to understand and resolve our contemporary condition is historical reason, with technology as one means for dealing with our circumstances. Ortega's intent here was the autofabrication of human life and its circumstances through what can be called a "technological imperative;" i.e., we must meet and master circumstances through the technology required to autofabricate our existence in its circumstances. Our human life must exist in the circumstances of the present and the future through an activist responsibility for ourselves and our environment. Our life is in fact a technological being which must address the crises of our existence and environment. For Heidegger it seems that these factors must be resigned to the fate of Being in the West. His position is passive acceptance, while Ortega's is a technological imperative to the autofabrication of our life in its circumstances.

There is a further ambiguity in Heidegger's thought. On the one hand, there is in him the assumption that the Enlightenment's myths of secular progress and human perfectability are failed beliefs. On the other hand, his passive response to history in the idea of releasement to Being seems inadequate. He lacks any doctrine of engagement or *praxis* with respect to problems and their circumstances. Nothing seems to be required of an engaged humanity. Our human historicity is not supplied with a historical reason or an imperative to actively construct our lives and meet problems. There is no executive function of human life or any theory of *praxis* available to our "time in need."

Ortega's notion of the historicity of human life comes to the claim that our life possesses no fixed nature, only a history. Also, human life exists under the imperative of the autofabrication of human life in circumstances. These conditions demand that we cannot resign ourselves to any "releasement" that would not require us to construct our lives and address ourselves to a responsible fabrication of circumstances, to "humanize" them through historical time. The human being is an "ontological centaur" and does not possess a fixed or final nature. This means that our historical nature is always unfinished in time. We seek constantly to realize our historical nature as a self-creation. It is technology, in part, that aids in our self-construction. It is through our very technicity that we are able to construct our unfinished nature. The idea of human life presupposes a "technological man" for both our adjustment to circumstances and the autofabrication of our life. The term that Ortega used to express the need for the transformation of our life is *quehacer* or "that which must be done."[9] Our historical nature must be oriented to the transformation of circumstances, for our life is a task, a "thing to be done." We are the "unhappy beings" who must construct our lives by engaging circumstances. This is our historical destiny and the basic requirement of our lives. For Ortega technology is seen as part of the fundamental nature of human being. Yet the very quality of our life may fall below what it has constructed itself and its circumstances to be, for example, as in "the decline and fall of the Roman empire." There are implicit standards below which we may fall, such as in protecting our environment for the health and safety of the next generation. It is imperative for our survival that we maintain certain standards for ourselves and our environment, that we attain real ends and fabricate the means necessary to those ends. This is the technological imperative that enjoins us not to fall below the "level of the times." Contrary to Heidegger, Ortega understood that technology is a fundamental property of our being. The human being is *homo faber*, and our very historical existence depends upon the levels of attainment achieved in history. Because technology is a means of sustaining human well-being, we must use it to master the circumstances which surround us. Our life for Ortega is understood by the metaphor of a "shipwreck." It is required of us in this shipwreck to follow the technological imperative to resolve life's tensions and achieve its goals. The passive waiting for Heidegger's dispensations of being is not enough for the present human condition. It is a failure of nerve and resolve. It is "below the level of the times."

Generations

Presently we measure time in terms of seconds, minutes, hours, days, and years. Yet in the past it was not always so. In the Hebraic tradition there was another unit of temporal measurement which had an important relation to human life: the generation. Ortega revived this notion in his theory of time, and one of his contributions to historiography was his idea of generations. Julián Marías has claimed that Ortega's theory is the first adequate interpretation of generations.[10] By the time of his *History as a System* (1936) Ortega's theory of generations is part of his idea of historical reason, as an explanatory device in understanding the historical process and establishing links between the actions, values, and meanings which connect different periods of time.

Ortega was actually not the first to propose a modern theory of generations. It was an important element in Dilthey's study entitled *Über das Studium der Geschichte der Wissenschaften vom Menschen, der Gesellschaft und dem Staat* (1875).[11] Dilthey understood a generation as a collection of individuals who are joined in time by their mutual relations to significant events, and who instruct their successors in the interpretation of circumstances. But Ortega extended this thesis, and in his *El tema de nuestro tiempo* the generation becomes the basic element in his theory of historical becoming. Generations are a composition of leaders, followers, creators, and minorities who live according to significant beliefs, values, goals, and aspirations (or lack of them). These individuals supply to their generation its group identity. Common beliefs and goals are established as the legacy of a group of individuals in a given time and place, and these remain relatively constant as ideal types. For Ortega each generation moves on a definite "vital trajectory" in a given historical era. Generations become a synthesis of typically significant individuals, a unit of those who advance on the trajectory and carry the thrust of historical evolution and destiny. Each generation possesses its own destiny and mission in its individual development.

Ortega not only attempted to identify the nature of generations, but he supplied a chronological designation for them. A generation is a zone of dates between which identifiable and significant individuals live. The zone of dates that a given generation inhabits is one of fifteen years in length, and the individuals born within this span are alike in values and beliefs. A given generation also exists alongside other generations, which it often sees as an obstacle to be avoided or overcome. Ortega saw one specific generation to be composed of those between the ages of thirty and forty-five. This group attempts to impose its beliefs, values, and goals on its era and its reference group. Yet this imposition is counteracted by the generation between the ages of forty-five and sixty, who, according to Ortega, possess the significant power and end-orientation in a given society. There are also two less active and vital groups of generations: first, those who are older than sixty, who are on their way out of power and authority; second, those from one to fifteen, who are too young to be able to impose their vital trajectory on those above them. Each of the above-mentioned generations possesses not only its own zone of dates, but its own power configuration and vital sensibilities. When we think of these characteristics as an aggregate, we get a sense of the historical mission and destiny of the generational unit in question.

Each of us as an individual is born into a particular zone of dates and thrown into its particular historical circumstances. Generations share these circumstances and they, like individuals, die and pass into memory and oblivion. With each generation the drama of human life changes, and each plays out its vital theme. Each generation will have a different identity from those which went before it, and from those which come after it; each will end with its own definite characteristics and particular zone of dates.[12]

All living individuals at a particular time are contemporary with other living individuals at that time. Ortega refers to these as "contemporaries," even if they differ widely in age. Individuals who differ in their zone of dates, their generational ages, he designates as "coevals," and these possess different vital and historical characteristics. Each coeval contributes differently to the formation of historical systems, and it tends to understand the past and future differently according to how it forms perspectives on its vital interests and prospects. In this sense each generation possesses its own destiny. Of course, it remains true that coevals and contemporaries possess in common the great identifying reality of human life. This great similarity is so significant that it makes generational differences seem small by contrast. In our common humanity we are alike; in our generations we differ to the extent that our particular "story" or life's "drama" will be identifiably different. Each individual will also relate differently to his or her circumstances and to the sociohistorical world of predecessors and successors.

The generations which have gone before us have created a "world in force" for Ortega. This world is composed of powers, prerogatives, and achievements of its own, but it will expect of those who follow it to "live up" to what it has achieved or to repair its failures. All generations and individuals must confront the particular circumstances which compose their present and prefigure their own possibilities. But it is the generation which is always the unit to be addressed by historical reason. A generation is the concrete, vital, and efficacious element in all historiography. As such it is a concrete structure of human life in definite circumstances. All individuals must actualize their most vital possibilities through their generations. The generation becomes the heart of historical science. As a methodological idea the theory of generations rejects both a massivist and individualistic interpretation of the historical process. The theory, as part of the historical system, aids in the construction of the narrative of the past and present and the anticipation of the future.[13]

Death

The question of death arises within our life and takes its meaning in that context. Just as each of us must live his or her own life, death is our own and cannot be shared. There is only one thing more mysterious and significant than death, and that is life itself. Death is a compelling fact for many reasons, but it is examined in the philosophy of human life for the perspective it generates in our existence. In other words, death is necessary to the proper interpretation of our life. But death cannot be approached only through a dictionary definition, which states that "Death is the cessation or privation of existence, the opposite of life." A thinking approach to death is required here, and the philosopher of human life who has most deeply and fully sounded the significance and interpretation of death is Martin Heidegger. For him human beings do not fully understand the implications of the fact that they are going to die, nor do they want to understand them. What does it mean to a human life that it is going to die? This question is of great import to all of us and significant for the understanding of what it means to be at all.

Heidegger first points out that we are beings unto death (*Sein zum Tode*).[14] Death is something about which human life must be concerned, and this concern is expressed as a wonder and awareness of what it means not to be, and to be unable to be. Heidegger is not here concerned with death out of any morbid interest, philosophical sensationalism, or moral-religious interest. Heidegger is concerned with death as an existential category of our very being in the world, and the implications of what it means to be an authentic human being in the face of death. He also examines what it means to live an inauthentic life in the face of death. All of these meanings are for him part of the question of the meaning of Being. In other words, the fact of our death can help us to understand the meaning of our human being.

Our death is the reality that may be able to allow a more complete perspective on our life than any other existential category. Yet there is a problem about our understanding of death: we cannot actually experience or know the state of being dead. Death is not available to us in the way a thing at hand is available for us to experience. In this sense death seems to be something we should not bother about. Death is not identical to the process of dying and suffering in the approach to death itself. We cannot know the status of death itself, for it cannot appear within our life, yet the question for Heidegger is what the possibility of death can mean to our life as it is lived. His concern here is with our life's being toward death (*Sein zum Tode*) as a certain fact. The goal is to examine human life in the face of a death it cannot actually experience, to reveal what death can mean for individuals who are in the radical reality of life itself. This is quite a different thing from having a morbid interest in death or the psychology of dying. He wants to ask what it means to confront death as a fact of our existence.

Death is the thing that our life finds it impossible to be. We may be dying and finally terminated, but we are not death as a thing in itself. Plato in his dialogue *Phaedo* attempts to demonstrate that the form of life logically excludes the form of death. This is why Heidegger says that we are "beings toward death," not the final mystery of death as it is in itself. Death is seen as a limit of life's understanding of its own possibilities, and for Heidegger we can only understand that which is a real possibility of our life. What, then, shall we do with the question of death? His answer is that we must deal with it as something that is coming, yet not actually present. He asks what it could mean to be a "being toward death." He notes that we cannot approach the question of death by reflecting upon the death of others. Such a death is not our own death, and we cannot completely grasp its significance by knowing that others have died. We can only approach our own possibility of death as something "not yet."

When we approach the question of death, we are forced to remember that death is a fact that is "thrust upon us" without our consent. But this tyrannical fact of death is related to what Heidegger calls the fallenness of human life. We are fallen beings in the sense that we take inauthentic refuge from the fact of death in *das Man* as a they-self. In this state we attempt to avoid any understanding or confrontation of the question of death. While the concern about our coming death is perhaps the chief object of human care, we tend to avoid an authentic care about death. Mass man in a state of fallenness wants to understand death on his own terms, through such devices as "idle talk." In such a state the mass wants to convince itself and others that death is someone else's fortune, and "not yet" really our own. The mass man wants to avoid all thinking of death and finality in human life by avoiding any experience that is unpleasant or threatening. It always seeks the commonplace idle talk that "everybody" can share in a light manner. It also sustains the idea of death as trivial and worthy only of curiosity. Death is for *das Man* only a thing at hand in the form of a human corpse. This is another way of saying that death is actual only in the form of another's deceased body. This actuality is always someone else's, and only faintly a possibility for ourselves. To understand death in any other form is a threat to our tranquillity and indifference. It becomes necessary to seek equilibrium in the crowd, in pop culture, and in the general stupification of the masses. Death will only be tolerated as a spectacle for the crowd, an object of curiosity. The "they self" of the crowd is a possibility for all of us. In the status of the crowd death becomes a fear of an actual event that belongs to someone else. Yet death is not a fear that the dead entertain. It is only a fear possessed by the living.

When death is authentically understood as the real possibility of the fullness of human life, it is for Heidegger not given as fear, but as dread (*Angst*). Fear is given in our response to some object at hand. Dread comes to us in the mode of possibility. Here death is seen as a universally shared possibility of all human life, especially our own. Inauthentic man always seeks the at-handedness of the fear that understands death as gossip, idle talk, and the presence of the corpse of another. Dread is the authentic grasp of the deeper and more pervasive and mysterious possibility of the universality of death. In fear we can flee, avoid, or hide from death in the crowd, but we cannot avoid dread, the uncanny awareness of what is the real possibility for all human life. The flight from death in fear is the fallen life of human beings. Dread is a categorical aspect of authentic human life. In the authentic attitude of dread Heidegger tells us that we must be resolute to death as our very own. It is in the mood of dread that we come to a knowledge of our authentic being in the world. Death brings us to an awareness of our freedom to transcend the fearfulness of death as a thing at hand and to be resolute to our real possibility of death. In this sense death loses some of its absolute dominion over the deeper mystery and wonder that is human life.

CHAPTER ELEVEN

Summary of Human Life as Radical Reality

Dilthey's Idea of Human Life

Dilthey's greatest contribution to philosophy was the idea of human life. For him human life is revealed as the most fundamental experience that can be given to human beings, because it is the source in which all subsidiary realities must appear. Ortega claimed that we owe more to Dilthey than to anyone else for the idea of human life, yet Dilthey's idea was part of a more extended project, which he called "the critique of historical reason." Such a critique would consist of a critical analysis of the philosophical foundations of history and the human studies. The idea of human life, then, became the horizon in which all experience and knowledge appear. The *Lebensphilosophie* movement of which Dilthey was a part had its roots in the organic idealism of Goethe and Schlegel, yet it was Dilthey who more than any other was the parent of the idea. By the term human life Dilthey intended a non-biological concept that distinguished him from both Nietzsche and Bergson. Dilthey often referred to human life as the whole of history, and not to the psychological or personal life of the individual.[1] He also distinguished human life from what he considered the various irrationalisms of modernism, such as in Nietzsche and Bergson, for he thought of himself as a pure philosopher of human life.[2] Human life was considered a common medium of history and the human studies, including literature, poetry, religion, education, and art, but his end was to transform the intuitive status of human life into a discipline that would underlie all of these subjects and their elaboration. For Dilthey philosophy must understand our life in terms of the properties presented in human life itself.[3]

It was not until around 1860 that Dilthey's generation began to assume the reality of subjective phenomena as a subject fit for philosophical analysis at all. As we have shown, the *Lebensphilosophie* movement was opposed to the so-called "natural system" school, which grew from the mathematical sciences of the seventeenth century. There the standard of knowledge was the "physical reason" of the mathematical sciences themselves. In the face of this the question for Dilthey became how history and the human studies were to be given a general validity and theory of knowledge through what he called "the critique of historical reason." Physical reason would no longer be the model for the human studies, as it had been for French and German positivism in the late nineteenth century.

It was the work of the historical school in the nineteenth century, then, to show that human life could be considered real. They, along with Dilthey, believed that human life cannot be understood from the sense appearances of the physical world alone. Dilthey followed Hegel in the desire to see human life as a historical reality, but he replaced Hegel's Absolute Spirit with the claim that all history is the expression of human life in time. He also rejected Hegel's notion of "Reason" as the basic characteristic of history. Hegel's entire system, Dilthey maintained, must be replaced by the idea of human life.[4]

Dilthey was the first to distinguish human life from biological life, in his claim that the term "human life" referred not to the biological status of human beings but to a historical world, which he first called the *Menschenwelt*. Our life is given to us subjectively, as lived from within, and not given through external sense experiences (*Erfahrung*). It is experienced by us in such a manner that the part of it which knows and the part which is known must be considered a unity. It possesses an experiential capacity for reflective self-awareness (*Selbstbesinnung*) of its own inner status. Yet we cannot go behind this life to a reality behind our own. Human life is our ultimate presupposition. Our life is our fundamental experience.[5] Because the world can only be known from the context and finality of our life, we cannot pretend to know Kant's so-called "thing in itself" as the real or even as an ingredient of our experience. Further, Dilthey would see human life as the dynamic interaction between the "I" and its world (*Welt*). This is not an exclusive subject-or-object relation, but an inclusive reality of both. Human life for him was real and fundamental, but it remained for Ortega y Gasset to designate human life as radical reality. Nevertheless, Dilthey's human life remains perhaps the greatest philosophical contribution of the latter half of the nineteenth century.

For Dilthey neither human life nor its categories can be deduced from any transcendental presuppositions, as in the case of Kant. Both life and its categories are derived from the self-reflection of human life upon itself. Our thought and judgment arise from within our life, and our capacity for thought is not so much a source of truth as a self-reflective activity that arranges and classifies what is already present in our life. Because thought cannot go behind the reality of the human life in which it arises, we can only operate within the thought system (*Seelenstruktur*) present in our life. Further, any rational or scientific inquiry cannot go behind the mental system already established in life itself. Any attempt to construct a system of meanings, judgments, and emotive-volitional content would presuppose what is already given in the original system of life. Not only can we not see behind the original system of our life, but we cannot understand what a further a priori system would mean. In sum, an inquiry behind life to its transcendental sources is ruled out from the beginning. It can be known from within only by those who already possess it.

Our conscious life is the totality of experiences we have lived through, and our mind is seen as the agent through which our past and present experience is arranged, in a way that can relate to present and future states of awareness. It is the task of self-reflection to bring to self-awareness what is already contained in our life. Human life becomes here conceived as the historical stream of the inner and outer, the "I" and its world. Our life through historical time becomes the context of first principles, a sort of pre-thematic awareness of how we are in the world. As the general context in which human actions and creations are born, exist, and die, human life becomes the biography of the human race, which can never be separated from its history, and the human studies can never be separated from human life. As the subject matter of history human life is nothing less than the story of what we have done and what we have suffered through time.

Ortega y Gasset and the Radical Reality of Human Life

In his *The Idea of Principle in Leibniz* and in his essay "Wilhelm Dilthey and the Idea of Life" Ortega acknowledged that his fundamental philosophical principle had been Dilthey's idea of human life, an idea he would develop into the concept of radical reality.[6] Earlier he had examined human life as a biological concept in a 1911 article on Jakob Uexküll's *Umwelt und Innenwelt der Tiere*, but he later came to mean by the term human life the pre-theoretical, prescientific reality of each human life as it is lived by an individual human being. He thought of human life as radical reality, because it is prior in all senses of gradation, meaning, status, and reference to realities of secondary status. It is important once again to recall that he did not mean to imply here that no other realities, such as matter, the universe in its totality, or even Deity, do not qualify as real. He only meant to claim that all other candidates for the real are in fact "secondary realities" which must appear in the context of human life's needs, meanings, frames of reference, language, culture, and history. Put another way, human life is "radical" not because it negates or transcends other realities, or because it possesses greater importance, age, or power than they, but because all else that calls itself real must appear within its perspectives, assumptions, history, and prediscursive life world. Human life is a "radical reality" in so far as such reality can be given to human beings at all.

For Ortega our life is a bipolar reality composed of two interrelated elements: "I" and circumstances. This bipolar relation becomes for Ortega a sort of insignia of his thought: "I am myself and my circumstances" (*Yo soy yo y mi circumstancia*). I am myself, he says, but the world around me forms the other half of my being. My circumstances are everything in which I find myself and through which I compose my life. I must relate to circumstances from the interiority of my "I" and experience them as the outer half of my complete being. Even while reaching out from my interiority to other people, physical objects, or social facts, I must perceive from within the circumstances which surround me and which form the exteriority of the world. Here everything which perceives itself from within is an "I," and an "I's" apprehension of what is apart and outside of it is its world.

In his posthumously published essay *What Is Philosophy?* Ortega defined human life as "what we are doing now" and "what is happening to us now." These doings and happenings belong to us as our very own, and as such they are also transparent to us. Human beings experience many happenings and doings through many perspectives, but our life itself is prior to all others; all other perspectives and realities are secondary to it and receive their meanings and interpretations through it. It is through the needs, powers, presuppositions, and expectations of our life that our circumstances are interpreted, remembered, evaluated, and given place and meaning. This life over which we preside and which is transparent to us is the arena in which the drama of self and circumstances takes place.

While our life is our closest and dearest possession, perhaps our only real one, it is possessed by us only under the proviso that we orient it, use it, "do something with it." It is required in our life that we act in circumstances which forever surround us. Our life is a continual, implicit self-interrogation which seems to ask, "What shall I do, I who live in the world?" In this situation "not doing anything in particular" is itself a sort of "doing something." Even such an act as suicide is the most dramatic "doing something" that we may choose. To be at all is both to be doing and suffering many things in the face of what is other than ourselves. As early as 1910 in his essay *Adam in Paradise* Ortega pointed out that even Adam had to be in circumstantial relation to God, Eve, serpents, Eden, Cain, and divine injunctions. In his *Meditations on Quixote* (1914) this theme of "being with and alongside something other than ourselves" is developed, and this work Ortega believed had predated Heidegger's *Being and Time* by thirteen years. In the *Quixote* he claimed that human life is a bipolar dialogue between an "I" and what surrounds it, helps it, threatens it, bores it, etc. Life and its circumstances are constitutive of each other, and in need of each other in the sense that there is no "I" pole of human life exclusively; nor is there a circumstantial pole simply and exclusively. Each is needed to complete the other by forming its other half.

For Ortega it is our fate to "humanize the circumstances" which stand over against us. To "humanize circumstances" is to bestow meaning, value, and purpose upon them, and utilize them for the "projects" which compose our lives. For example, if a primitive man were to find a stick on a forest floor, he might utilize it as a tool or decide that it was of no use or significance in his life. In either case, the stick was brought into a primitive life world of prior significances and human intents and purposes. Here a "circumstance at hand" in the form of a stick was constituted as a definite form of life, an index of how the primitive existed in a world of intersubjective significance. As an activity which begins at birth and does not end until death, the humanization of the world is required of all human life in the circumstantial world. The humanization of circumstances is an action and a meaning so profound and so needed in human life that it must be designated as one of life's categorical qualities.

As the projection of use and significance upon the world at hand, humanization refers to the meanings and purposes through which we "absorb the circumstances" which were previously unnamed, ambiguous, and unclear for human life, by converting them into what is useful for life's security and satisfaction. Through the absorbing of circumstances the human being constructs the world. By the use of a life form which ancient Greek philosophy designated as *pragmata*, human beings perform the actions which "must be done" for the uses and needs of human life. Such humanization of circumstances allows us to develop our lives in the "system of importances" which surrounds us. Our life is a continual reabsorption of circumstances, a continual working out of our lives through them. In this respect human beings are doomed to achieve themselves through something else, to become human through the absorbing of the non-human.

One of the circumstances which we must somehow humanize is other people. Such a circumstance is a problematical one in the sense that my life is for me a primary reality, but the life of another is not. My life, too, can never be a primary reality for another. The life of another can only appear to me within the context of my own life and vice versa. To give an account of the collective existence of the "I" and the "other" was one of Ortega's chief goals in his posthumously published *Man and People* (1957). In this work he wanted to show how the "I" and the other are integrated in social reality. The socialization process begins when an individual "I" constructs the life of another as an alter ego, and it does this by borrowing the materials of this construction from its own life. All sociohistorical science is for Ortega the attempt to make of others an alter ego that is interchangeable with our own. We must construct and humanize the other to the ends and purposes of our own life, and vice versa. It is out of a mutual need that we construct the other, and the other us, into a system of social significance and expectations. It is in this humanization of each other that the social arises. This dimension comes into being when the other has become a system of definite possibilities toward which we may behave. Also, it is through the expectations of behaviors and meanings of the alter ego that we anticipate others through the commonly assumed usages (*vigencias*) in society. In other words, we are given in social interaction a formula for how to behave to others. In this sense the radical reality of human life does not remain simply personal but is socially shared. With the idea of the "other" Ortega presents his theory of human life in its social dimension. Without such shared aspects of human life no study of the social or historical world is possible.

The New Being of Human Life

Ortega associates the radical reality of human life with the philosophical concept of being itself. In classical metaphysics being (*on*) was opposed to either change, becoming, or non-being. For Parmenides and the Eleatic School everything real belonged to that conception of being as the only possible object of thought. For Ortega this notion tends to restrict the real to that which is changeless and eternal. Modern thought in both science and philosophy requires that being be understood not as *stasis*, the changeless and eternal, but as process.[7] The new being of human life must also replace the Parmenidean concept of being as a *plenum* which is total and eternal. The assumptions of Parmenides have "sealed the fate of Western thought for two thousand years." In the modern era it is the process and history of human life which must assume the title of the radically real. Plato had contributed to this fate by equating truly real being with the changeless forms (*eidos*). In the medieval period being was understood as *Ens*, a noun which signifies the most general and simple predication that anything may have. For Ortega the modern period must understand being as human life, the model for all future philosophy. No final being or radical reality can be located outside its appearance in human life. Further, the idea of human life is the only idea that will reverse the medieval notion of *operari sequitur esse*, i.e., the claim that the nature of an "act" of being is dependent upon the prior nature of the being in question. This medieval position affirmed that the actuality of a being is always prior to its possibilities. This is to say that what something becomes is in fact dependent upon and posterior to what it presently is. The new being of human life would reverse this by the contrary idea of *esse sequitur operari*, i.e., the nature of an entity, in this case the self-construction of human life in time, is the product of the temporal changes through which it has passed. Priority here is placed upon the possibilities, as opposed to the changeless actualities, of the real. In other words, human life possesses a tendential structure of developmental possibilities that accumulate themselves on the path to the future. Our human life constructs the future through decision, labor, technology, and will. Human life is a constructive process which must be seen as "a gerundive, not a participle, a *faciendum*, not a *factum*," as ongoing, not sealed by the past. Here the real being of human life has been understood as its history.[8] Human life is the new being, the fundamental being which encloses its nature and validity in the claim that human life is the bipolar reality of "I am myself and my circumstances."[9]

Our life, the life of each one of us, cannot be understood simply as a thing in place or as an idea. Rather, the idea of human life tends to save the partial truths of both realism and idealism. It recognizes the realist claim that the external world is "real," that any philosophy of human life must account for the brute presence of a world of circumstances with which it must deal. This world of circumstances is not simply a property or constituent of an idea. On the other hand, the idea of human life also saves the truth of idealism which claims that my ideas and my subjectivity possess both meaning and value. Nothing exists for us which is more primary and transparent to itself than our life, yet we live in the process of its continual clarification. This "new being," this life of ours, is in continual need. It is not a self-enclosed or independent thing. Our life stands in need of both an "I" and circumstances for its completion. It is given to us as a problem that we must solve from out of the endless decisions about what to do with our life. My life is not simply a determined thing, but a continual possibility in circumstances in which I find myself forced to choose, within prescribed limits, what I shall do. The fateful and even oppressive question "What now, little man?" becomes the badge of my limited possibilities and my finitude. It is our human fate to be forced to fabricate our life in time, to be compelled to hold up the weight of our being in time. Our life here consists not so much of what we presently are as of what we are going to do. The demand to decide what we are going to do or be implies that time is at the very root of our being. We are forced in our life not to be inert, but to be engaged in our circumstances. Yet our circumstances greatly limit all possibilities. The demand to decide ourselves does not imply that we are not also surrounded by unalterable or causally determined circumstances that transcend choice or decision. We are not free to be determined, or to be in a non-circumstantial situation, to be always young or old, or to become anything we desire. Finally, we are not free to escape or nullify our death, a debt which Shakespeare thought we owe to God.

A Comparison of Dilthey, Ortega y Gasset, and Heidegger

In his "Preface for Germans" (1934) Ortega stated that without Dilthey he could not have come to be a philosopher of human life,[10] the idea which was the theme of his life's work. Ortega thought of Dilthey as a "knight-errant of the spirit" who battled positivism and materialism with a new conception of the human studies in distinction to the natural sciences. The entire critique of historical reason, including the idea of historicity, was Dilthey's greatest contribution. But Ortega was not greatly interested in Dilthey's distinction between the natural and human studies, and he contributed nothing to Dilthey's method of *Verstehen*. Ortega also noted in his "Preface for Germans" that up to 1913, two years after Dilthey's death, no one suspected that Dilthey had a philosophy of life. Dilthey even seemed to his students to stand for the opposite conviction, that such a philosophy was impossible.[11] Ortega believed that his idea of human life was developed on his own lines without imitation of anyone; that his idea was taken not from Dilthey but from the issues that face philosophy.[12]

For Ortega one of Dilthey's greatest errors was his thesis of idealism, which is found developed in his 1890 essay entitled *Beiträge zur Lösung der Frage vom Ursprung unseres Glaubens an die Realität der Aussenwelt und seinem Recht* ("Contributions to the Origin of our Belief in the Reality of the External World and its Justification"). Dilthey there maintained that both the external world and our self-awareness are comported as consciousness, whereas Ortega maintained that such a thesis is idealism, and the notion of consciousness generally is a philosophical fiction, an "unjustified hypothesis." Ortega held that Dilthey believed implicitly in consciousness, something that is neither primary being nor radically real. Ortega also denied that "the intentionality of consciousness" of Husserl and Brentano is our fundamental relation to things. The primary fact of human life is not "consciousness" but the coexistence of "I and circumstances." While for Ortega our circumstances are both perceived and thought, there exists no "consciousness of" as a fact. The only "given" in this respect which can be phenomenologically described is that of "I am myself and my circumstances in the radical polarity of human life." We can no longer rely on the failed belief of "consciousness of" as a radical reality in the world. The purported "idealism" of Dilthey must dissolve into a description and interpretation of human life as the primary reality given to human beings.

Yet Ortega's critique of Dilthey's "idealism" must be taken *cum grano salis*. Dilthey's position on consciousness is not quite what Ortega maintained it was. First, Dilthey never held the idealist position that nothing can exist independently of consciousness. Dilthey rejected such a notion. Also Dilthey's purported idealism is too general. Dilthey's actual position in his *Beiträge* is called the "phenomenality of consciousness," which maintains that "all that exists for me is always subject to the state of being a fact for consciousness."[13] It is important here to note that Dilthey did not insist that nothing can exist outside of consciousness, nor did he claim that the external world is only consciousness. Dilthey always maintained a firm belief in the independent reality of the external world. In fact, the external world is fundamentally given to us in "a feeling of opposition" to both our will and our sensations. From such a sense of opposition we derive the idea of the fundamental separation of subject and object. Here Dilthey's position is not substantially different from Ortega's idea of "I and my circumstances."

While Dilthey's work was in the tradition of post-Kantian German idealism, Ortega held that Dilthey's thought was a reaffirmation of the Cartesian dualist tradition which had misled European philosophy into the overestimation of the theory of knowledge and the underestimation of ontology and the reality of human life. Also Dilthey's emphasis upon *Geist* (spirit or mind) tends to conceive human life as a spiritual substance, a subject matter in opposition to the methods and materials of natural science. His science of self-reflection (*Selbstbesinnung*) was supposed to possess the general validity of Galileo's science of nature.[14] For Ortega all of this is misleading. If we understand human life as *Geist*, then there is created the tendency to conceive human life as a substance or as consciousness. The circumstantial world, in this case, also tends to be comported into consciousness, something it is not. For Ortega neither our life nor our circumstantial world is consciousness but the bipolar relation of "I and circumstances."

Ortega's philosophical position seems not to recognize the term "consciousness" at all. He substituted for this term the Spanish *vivencia* as a translation of Dilthey's *Erlebnis* or "lived experience." He concluded that *vivencia* would best indicate human experience without the assumptions of consciousness, idealism, or dualism. The term *vivencia* for him indicated everything which arrives at my "I" with enough presence to become part of it. Our life is composed of a unity of connected *vivencias*, but it is not consciousness, spirit, or soul. Instead, *vivencia* is a term that refers to the fact that "Awarenesses enter our body, become organized in the brain, and leave our body."[15] For Ortega this position does not commit us to Descartes' misconception of consciousness as a substance, or Dilthey's *Geist* as a spiritual entity. It is not consciousness, soul, or thinking substance (*res cogitans*) but human life which is the proper object of philosophical investigation. Human life is the radically real and, as such, the object of fundamental ontology.

Both Dilthey and Ortega seem to some to be advocates of historicism. But both thinkers made substantial deviations from this position, as we have argued earlier. Ortega seems a historicist when he asserts that "Man has no nature, but a history," but with this phrase Ortega does not mean to imply that human beings have no biological identity nor a constant identity as human life. Rather, his claim is that the very nature of human beings is their historicity. Because our nature is itself historicity, human identity is both defined and accumulated through historical time.[16] On the other hand, Ortega's position does not allow for any philosophical thesis which understands man as an eternal substance above historical change. Human life is a *species temporis*, not a *species aeternitatis*. Human life exists as historical duration and the autofabrications that have accrued to human life. The historicity of our being is not a strange or unusual element of our nature but a basic category of human life itself.

Not only was Dilthey the originator of the idea of human life, but he understood historicity as the most basic attribute of our nature. In a sense Dilthey possessed a certain ideological priority over Ortega, which Ortega seemed to acknowledge. But for him Dilthey's position was undeveloped, and the historicity of man is still something that needs to be "enunciated with vigor." For Ortega our human life is fundamentally historical in the sense that our present is always an accentuation of our past experience. We presently exist as an accumulation of all our past moments. All that we have been in the past exists as a structure that upholds our present. In this sense we not only carry the past within us but we are the present products of it. The past is an indicator, a heritage for our memory, and the ground of meaning for our present. It cannot be amputated from the present or future, except in abstraction and utopian thinking. Yet it is interesting to note that Ortega's idea of human historicity makes no mention of Dilthey's claim that we are historical beings also in the sense that those who have made history in the past share with present human beings a common cognitive nature which is constant and understandable to agents in both the past and the present. In Dilthey's thought this is the basic fact and meaning of human historicity. This notion has been identified elsewhere as "epistemic historicity," in the author's *Dawn of Historical Reason*.[17]

Ortega believed that Dilthey's work remained in the Cartesian tradition of a theory of knowledge, a criticism Heidegger also made of Dilthey. For Ortega Dilthey's whole project was essentially a "critique of historical reason," and his theory of knowledge was essentially an *autognosis*, a theory of life gained through psychological reflection and internal observation (*Sebstbesinnung*). Dilthey had sought a generic description of human consciousness as *Seelenstruktur*. He had searched for a descriptive psychology until late in his career, yet his psychological accounts of human nature were usually supplemented by the overarching thesis of a critique of historical reason. Dilthey wanted to construct the idea of human nature empirically through a historical science of knowledge (*Historie*). But Dilthey never developed any historical science that would significantly conflict with any of his previous psychological writings. His two differing themes of psychological versus historical man remained distinct and unreconciled tendencies in his thought. Ortega's position here was to avoid Dilthey's two explanatory models, and he simply maintained that man has no final being, only a history.

The human being possesses a fixed natural body as our species nature, yet we also possess a historical nature as our life. Ortega considered the latter as our true being. Such a nature is an autofabrication through time, and the seat of human freedom. Freedom here refers to the ability of human life to construct its history in accord with a capacity to achieve a possibility of its nature and circumstances.

Dilthey's critique of historical reason was a complex and challenging enterprise, and Ortega understood Dilthey's critique to have many dimensions. Yet he tended to understand Dilthey as a philosopher of historical science (*Historie*). The epistemology of this position is one that seeks to provide a unique and generally valid explanation of human life in time by means of historical science. Such an epistemological account would also provide the grounds for distinguishing historical science from the assumptions and methods of the natural sciences. His whole approach may be termed "epistemic historicality," i.e., the thesis that human life is a historical being in its essential nature. His critique of historical reason was his attempt to understand history and the human studies through the assumptions of epistemic historicity; i.e., the deepest sense in which we are historical beings has to do with the fact that those who create history and those who attempt to understand it both possess a knowing nature which is mutually understandable. Also the term refers to the purported fact that "I" and the "other" in time possess the same historical nature. These two aspects of historicity make possible historical science generally. This is the thesis that human life and its works cannot be understood apart from the common manner in which they exist and are known in historical time.

Ortega had definite and generally justified opinions of Dilthey's work. He recognized the originality and depth of Dilthey's idea of human life, especially the critique of historical reason, but he claimed that Dilthey did not actually understand his own authentic and revolutionary discovery, the reality of human life, or he kept his discovery hidden, such that his students were not fully aware of or interested in it. It sometimes seems to the author that even Dilthey was not greatly interested in his own discovery. For Ortega the idea of human life seemed muted and hampered by the "epistemological mania" or the "Kantian ontophobia" which could not understand philosophy's task as anything more than a theory of knowledge which presupposes the reality of human life. Dilthey seems too much mired in Cartesian assumptions which are no longer adequate to the modern philosophical enterprise of the philosophy of human life. Because of such assumptions as these Ortega believed that he must appropriate and redirect Dilthey's enterprise to a stage of evolution that would be up to the intellectual level of the times.[18] He believed that more is needed than Dilthey's attempt to provide a generally valid foundation to the theory of knowledge for the cultural-historical sciences of man. A whole new ontology of human life as radical reality must be provided to his tradition. What must be supplied to Dilthey's new continent of human life is historical reason, the thinking of human life as a story, a "drama" through time. Dilthey's idea of a critique of historical reason failed in adequately thinking a reason that was derived from human life itself. Perhaps these purported lacunae would account for Ortega's later contention that while Dilthey was constantly oriented to the provision of a historical science (*Historie*), Dilthey's own writings revealed that he believed that human life was fundamentally irrational.[19] Dilthey's idea of human life "never rose above a vital irrationalism," and he never developed a historical reason from the radical reality of human life itself.[20]

But it must be noted here that while Ortega's philosophical goals were different from Dilthey's, it does not allow him to conclude that Dilthey's life and work are inferior or unimportant. In my reading of Ortega I have concluded that he often ignored or inadequately discussed the methodological and epistemological advances that Dilthey actually achieved. Also, Dilthey's goal was seemingly not to provide a fundamental metaphysical foundation to the idea of human life. Ortega's cry for a "historical reason" was derived from human life itself, and his claim that historical reason is a vital need of our time is significantly programmatic and undeveloped. Yet it still remains a fact that Ortega's work is a cockcrow of a dawn of a historical reason that is derived from the reality of human life. Ortega must be regarded as one of those in the twentieth century who changed, in part at least, the focus of philosophy from the Cartesian epistemic tradition to a theory of the radical reality of human life.

Ortega claimed that many Heideggerean ideas had appeared *in ovo* in his own works prior to the publication of *Being and Time* in 1927. He stated in a 1928 lecture series which was later published posthumously as *What Is Philosophy?* (1957) that the thesis "to be is to be in a world" was present in his work by 1914. His concept of existence, he also claimed, was thirteen years prior to the publication of *Being and Time*. But he also admitted that Heidegger, Hartmann, and Scheler aided him in the development of his thinking.[21]

Ortega felt the need for a more systematic statement of his own position. He introduced such a statement in his *What Is Philosophy?*, where he asked after the very nature of philosophy itself. Since Descartes, he said, philosophy has been largely restricted to the theory of knowledge and the justification of natural science. But this trend has ignored the reality of human life. One of the primal elements of philosophy is being. Since Parmenides philosophy has sought for the meaning of being. But for Ortega being, or that which truly is, can only be ascribed to the radical reality of human life. In his *What Is Philosophy?* and *Some Lessons in Metaphysics* Ortega claimed that human life is fundamental being, because all else that claims to be real must appear within it and presuppose it. His attribution of the "truly real" to human life was intended by Ortega to replace the traditional conception of being as a self-sufficient and eternal One.[22] The reality of human life is neither of these traditional conceptions. It is incomplete, a process, finite, radically temporal, and forever in need. All philosophy and all thinking are grounded in human life and not in Parmenides' pure reality of being itself. The Parmenidean being does not adequately designate reality at all, for it is only an abstract hypothesis about totality and transtemporal reality. But such a status does not exist.

In the modern and contemporary periods, as in the case of Heidegger's *Being and Time*, the goal is quite unlike Parmenides' enterprise. The goal here is the understanding of the question of the meaning of being in the horizon of time. The interpretation of human life (*Dasein*) was only a preliminary one through which he would approach the final question of the meaning of Being-as-such (*Sein*). The question of the reality of Being was to be understood as the final horizon of human being or human life.

It was in his *Leibniz* that Ortega expressed his reservations about Heidegger's project. For him Heidegger's notion of Being (*Sein*) was both unclarified and undeveloped. Further, Heidegger's term *Dasein* had only replaced the simpler, clearer term "human life." His Being (*Sein*) is in fact a modern equivalent of the scholastic conception of *Ens* (being). For the scholastics the term *Ens* designated the most basic predicate that could be ascribed to anything. Heidegger had derived his conception of

Being-as-such from *Ens*, but he had in fact posited *Dasein* as a subordinate type of being below Being-as-such. *Dasein* (human life) for him was a preliminary field of analysis through which we must pass on our way to understanding Being. Heidegger's posing of the question of being is an unclarified re-asking of the meaning of the scholastic term *Ens*. But Heidegger never actually comprehended Being itself in his writing; he only added a new type of being which he termed *Dasein*. For Ortega this new designation never seemed to add anything of substance or method to the idea of human life. It would have been more fruitful if Heidegger had confined the question of Being to human life. Heidegger's question of the meaning of Being leaves his project only a postulated and unfulfilled question. For this reason Ortega predicted (correctly) that there would be no second half of *Being and Time*. Heidegger's Being question had entered a "blind alley," and his search for Being was only a *furor teutonicus* which had inflated the question of the meaning of being beyond its natural place as the idea of human life (*Dasein*). Further, when we understand *Dasein* as only a preliminary question to the meaning of Being itself, there is a tendency to forget how the human sciences are related to the empirical questions of human life. Heidegger's project tended to avoid the questions posed by the methodological and empirical concerns of the *Geisteswissenschaften* and to concentrate on the abstract metaphysics of Being itself. This move placed the issues of human life in an inferior status to the question of Being-as-such. Heidegger seems to have believed to the end of his life that the human sciences had a real purpose in his thought only if they added to the prior ontological conceptions necessary for their establishment.[23]

Heidegger from the beginning was hostile to *Lebensphilosophie*. He saw this movement not as fundamental ontology but an empirical, anthropological-psychological labor.[24] For him the philosophy of life movement did not enough emphasize the differences between the factual-empirical sciences and historicity as an ontological component of *Dasein*. It did not enough recognize the unique manner in which human life (*Dasein*) is in time. Historicity must be understood as the existential ground that makes history and the human sciences possible. The philosophy of human life did not do this. Dilthey's goals were inadequate, because they sought only the methodological and epistemological bases for the historical sciences, and they did not reveal the deepest metaphysical ground of *Dasein*.[25]

Ortega does not make specific reference to Heidegger's critique of Dilthey, but he would emphasize the "historical" in his idea that man has no final nature but a history. In Ortega's view it is only by placing primary emphasis on human life as radical reality that we can save Heidegger's analysis of Being from dead-endedness. Yet Heidegger believed that *Lebensphilosophie* generated historicism by its contention that *Dasein* is in perpetual change without any conception of final Being.[26] His *Being and Time* is in part an attempt to counteract this tendency with his doctrine that *Dasein* is an unchanging structure that transcends the flux and relativity of history. For Ortega human life as a biological nature is fixed, but as a historical nature it is development as autofabrication. Human life is a *species temporis*, never a *species aeternitatis*. Because we are radically historical beings, all we finally possess is our life in its history.[27] We are a "drama" of what we have done, changed from, and will become. The transformative reality of human life is the new being itself. Ortega believed that it is always in the context of human life that questions arise and are resolved in one way or another, but our life is never finally resolved until death. He expressed the actual living of our life with the Spanish verb *existir*, the putting of our life "into force." The "shipwreck of human life" must be salvaged and "put into force" for human survival and betterment. We can only put into force the life we have. Yet this life is no little thing. It is reality itself in its engagement of the world of circumstances. The construction of our life is our permanent possibility. Human life is "the sight of divinity" by whose light we construct the meaning and destiny of our world. This is the authentic dawn of historical reason.

CHAPTER TWELVE

Conclusions on the Fundamental Datum of Human Life

The problem for philosophical thought in the area of human life is not to determine what in the universe is most important or most rational, but to locate a fundamental datum that is most beyond doubt. This exemplary datum is "my life, the life of each one of us." Yet the term "my life" presents an immediate ambiguity. It can refer to an individual life, or it can be a generic expression for the shared properties that are possessed by all human life through time. In the history of ideas both senses of the term are used. Human life is understood by Dilthey to mean not so much the personal or psychological life of the individual, but a historical life whose nature is both known and shared by the entire human race. Here the emphasis is upon human life in general, and such generality is the datum which the term assumes. But for Ortega the authentic datum is not human life as a general historical reality, but "my life, the life of each one of us" (*la vida de cada cual*). Here the radical reality of the term "human life" is understood as an individual entity. For Ortega the primary datum is always the individual sense of "my life," and for him the general and historical sense of the term always presupposes this primary and individual reality of "my life."

All of the other candidates for the status of radical reality, such as matter, space, "the universe in its totality," or "that which is conceived in and through itself," etc., must presuppose a "my life" as a definite subject. The other candidates are in fact secondary realities which all presuppose a "my life" as the ultimate datum in which they must appear. These candidates cannot exist unconditionally, as it is supposed by the "natural standpoint." Rather, they exist in the context of a subject which is designated as "my life." Yet this thing we call "my life" is never independent of the ensemble of circumstances which surround it. Circumstances act upon my life, and my life acts upon circumstances, which first acted upon it. For example, a steering wheel reacts to my turning it, and I react to its presence by driving an automobile by means of it. Yet the steering wheel would not be for me what it is designated to be unless I were a human life for whom such a thing possesses meaning, value, and purpose. The steering wheel in this sense presupposes the radical datum of "my life," but "my life" always presupposes the data of circumstances as the objective pole of the mutual interaction of "I and my circumstances." The "I" and its circumstances are so closely interdependent, so presuppositional of each other, that they cannot be separated in the radical reality of human life. Even the body must appear within "my life." The fingers and toes of a baby must first appear in and take meaning from the primary life of the child as part of its circumstances. According to some psychologists, the overhead light in the hospital delivery room was probably the first circumstance of which my life was aware. Circumstances in this sense are the other half of our being which we presuppose and count on until our death.

Human life is the reciprocal event of an "I" and its circumstances. To comport this life of mine I act toward my circumstances by living the tension between myself and them. Circumstances are never apart from my life, but they are the things and events with which I compose my life. My awareness of myself depends in part upon my awareness of what is other than myself. The constant coexistence of myself and my circumstances is not a static situation; rather, these two poles constitute the dynamic event of my life. Things happen to me, and I happen to them. Neither enjoys an exclusive posture over the other. Yet human beings invent forms of life that seem to reconcile the apparent separation between themselves and their circumstances. We mutually construct imaginary possible relations that might obtain between ourselves and what is around us. Dilthey called this process a *Realdialectik*. Through this interaction we attempt to fabricate our lives by deciding what is possible and impossible in our ceaseless quest for what we may become.

We can neither describe nor understand any circumstance that is not in some way related to human life, for our life enters into all judgments, appraisals, assumptions, and expectations that we make of anything. All human life presupposes the condition that a judgment is somebody's judgment; that all facts are in some way facts for someone. Any fact or judgment must in principle possess the possibility of some kind of incorporation into human life. Even to imagine a fact that is entirely divorced from human life is impossible. Could we speak of it, refer to it, affirm or deny its existence or nonexistence? Such a postulated entity is ipso facto excluded from the domain of reference. All that is "real" must in some way possess the possibility of being "kept in view" by at least one human life. Human life is the radical fact which is the presupposition of any subsequent fact. Everything, absolutely everything, that can be real must be something that we can come across in our living. Neither an "I" nor a circumstance is a substance in itself which needs nothing else for its completion. Both "I" and my circumstances in dynamic polar interaction are required for the establishment of the radical reality that is human life.

A new philosophical thought form is needed to express the reality of human life. For Ortega philosophers are not on earth to flex the muscles of their talents, but to produce ideas which human beings require to live. The present philosophical need is to reveal and to complete the foundations required for the idea of human life.[1] Previously there have been only two authentic philosophical eras. For Ortega the first was established by the presocratics through Plato and Aristotle in their search for fundamental reality in the multiplicity of appearances. The second was in the seventeenth century when Descartes contended that thinking is its own evidence for the establishment of truth, especially in mathematics and mathematical science. Here philosophy was fundamentally considered a theory of knowledge. The third era was inaugurated by Dilthey's idea of human life. We are still in the process of understanding this new era in philosophy. Philosophy is the elaboration and critique of our fundamental presuppositions. It is also needed to supply through these presuppositions a basic orientation into our circumstances. Human life is usually significantly disoriented, and human beings think in order to rescue themselves from the normal doubt and disorientation of their lives in circumstances. Yet our life is not decided automatically or unconditionally. There is always a need for intellectual clarity and security in our deciding what to do and what to be in our circumstances. There is always a need to elaborate and criticize the vital presuppositions of our lives. Such provisions will not appear or arise outside of human life, and science is not oriented to the whole issue of the life world. For the concept of human life, as we have developed it here, science has too little to say. Its judgments are limited to the biological body and the natural objects of the world at hand. It is the mission of philosophy to explore the new thought form of human life, its presuppositions, orientation, and decision-making, its possibilities for "my life, the life of each one of us."

If our general description of human life is accurate, if our claims are valid, then each category of human life will be experienced within the greater perspective of the whole of human life. Perspective is not only a characteristic of our lives, but it is the very organization of reality.[2] Each individual human life is a point of view on the universe, a vantage point not possessed by any other life. And yet anything we call real inevitably reaches our minds only through a plurality of possible perspectives. For Aristotle the categories were the common properties which every real being carried within it, such as the occupation of space and production of change, but human life is considered a new being which possesses its own unique categories, only some of which are shared with the Aristotelean enumeration. One uniquely human characteristic is our transcendence over brute nature when we humanize our circumstances and fabricate our history. The fabrication of history is a task so inclusive and demanding that it cannot be simply described by the Darwinian struggle for survival. All such deterministic theories fail to describe how human life actually deals with circumstances, and they tend to nullify personal volition. But human beings are in fact causal products of the past in the sense that they are accumulations of the past which human life preserves in the form of its "having-been" nature. This "having-been" human nature is the result of the fact that we are compelled to "store up" what we have been, and to advance upon ourselves in time. Yet we accumulate a past not because our previous life is over and done with forever. Even though we cannot go back to what we have been, our "having-been" nature is a categorical part of what we presently are and will be. Added to this historical nature is the fact that we develop in a forward manner. The future exerts demands upon us in the here and now, and we must keep doing something to keep afloat "forwardly." I am forced, as it were, to advance from my present into a future that is not yet, not ready made, for I must fabricate it for myself.

History is not only my life in the past, but a collective drama upon a larger stage. Each individual abides within a larger group drama with its own unique past, present, and future. In such a group we live largely as anonymous subjects within a greater "world in force." Our survival requires that we occupy ourselves with group projects and with goals that were decided for us. We must respect the boundaries of such a "world in force" yet still fabricate our personal history. We must also communicate with others and they with us, and it is in this context that we must decide by what criteria we can deal with others. One of the possibilities of our life is that we can decide criteria for our various behaviors. Such a decision is a constitutive possibility of human life. We must constantly decide our life, yet our decisions are always fallible, always unfinished, always open to the possibility of being "one way or another." There exists in human life an implicit imperative which commands the following: if we are to live in circumstances and attain specific goals, including moral ones, then we must in fact "do what ought to be done" for their attainment. All rational behavior must obey the injunction to act toward specifiable ends through specifiable means. Ortega calls this situation the *quehacer* or *pragmata* of human life. This means that human life is to a considerable extent a rational-deliberative matter which states that if we would attain such and such an end, then we should or must do x, y, or z. This situation is implicitly one of "ought implies can." It implies that only what is possible for human life can act as a ground of behavior, moral or otherwise. If we fail to decide in the face of "what ought to be done," then we remain lost in our vague trust in historical drift. The imperative to decide is our human destiny, a destiny composed of three elements: circumstance, vocation, and chance.[3]

It is life's destiny to "humanize the world," which means that we in part conduct our lives by projecting upon circumstances meanings, values, and purposes. Human life here acts as a "presence over things" at hand which may be inert, even meaningless and valueless. Human beings incorporate these into their lives and "humanize" them through the endowment of certain meanings, values, and purposes. If, for example, there is an unused plot of earth at hand, a human being may "humanize" it by first determining that the land is "unused," a word that possesses meaning, value, and purpose only in human life. We may "absorb" this piece of land by creating a vegetable garden, or preserving it for conservation purposes. Such a piece of earth at hand becomes "mine" or "ours" not only in a legal sense, but as a human project laid upon by a sort of human endowment. By such an endowment we affect our circumstances, and they us, in a dialectical relationship between a human life and one of its circumstances. Both poles must be present in any act of humanization. Such a "humanizer" was Don Quixote, a hero who assumed a magical being for himself as a "knight-errant" and as one who transformed his plain, everyday circumstances into giants and maidens, which provided the Don with expectations and possibilities for his own life. Like Don Quixote we are "ontological centaurs," dual beings who are at once biological bodies and a role or project in a world which we "humanize."

My life is the fact of all facts, and such an insubornable fact is given to me as a problem to be solved. While there is no absolute clarity or security granted to me, I more or less manage to carry out the project of my life so that I may rightly assume that there is something trustworthy in it. The world more or less "fits" my projects, and my circumstances are secure enough for me to conceive and order the relative importances that make up my possibilities. My life is understandable enough that I am able to live a metaphysical reality called "my life," the oldest reality that human beings have known, the most immediate and transparent thing there is. Yet any life is so elusive, mysterious, and deep that it is difficult to describe or systematize it. Sometimes that which is closest to us may be furthest away. Because it is elusive and difficult, human beings tend to look beyond their lives to theories and explanations that are themselves derivative and problematical. The problem is one of "seeing" "the things themselves" in description and interpretation. Yet my life is mysterious not because it is a deep secret, but because it is a reality that is given to me from the "inside," while it is given to others from the "outside." We must interpret the life and works of others through the process called *Verstehen*. Yet our life possesses the possibility of being aware of itself and describable to itself as an immediate presence in the reciprocity of circumstances. It is required of me to solve the question of what I will do in the next moment, hour, or year. I am the being who is always in advance of myself, preoccupying myself with matters great and small which are ahead of my present doing. I attempt to decide something which is possible for me, a "not-yet" for which I am concerned. My life, your life, the life of each one of us, reveals itself as concern (*Sorge* or *cura*) about its possibilities, concern about what will aid or foil our decisions, concern about circumstances great or small. My life is essentially fallible, finite, even defective with respect to many of its projects. It is dependent upon causes and circumstances outside of myself, and I must respond to them through a body which is a circumstance for my inner life.

As lived time I am a duration, from beginning to end living in material circumstances which are understood through cosmic time outside of my lived time. As a living being I am in constant need of living through the outer manifestations which are my "life assertions." All of us must take the assertions of other people into our own lives through the interpretations of *Verstehen*. We must incorporate others' assertions into our own life's meanings, values, and purposes. While my body is a particular being, it becomes a generalized being through culture and history. While my life is "a point of view on the universe," I am confined by my very condition to experience the world through discreet and limited perspectives. The great problem of life's perspectival nature is to find within all the possible perspectives given to us an exemplary idea or cognitive experience which captures a form of truth or authentic being for us.

My life is its history, an aggregate of past experience that exists in the suspicion that it is lost or disoriented, or may become so. My life presses me for its betterment and survival to be oriented to and clear about future circumstances and expectations. It is difficult to be authentically clear. We are usually clear only about the fact that others seem clear about their beliefs and expectations. Yet human life possesses a "vital reason" that is capable within limits of comprehending the temporal-historical reality of human life. To live is to have no other recourse than to reason in the face of circumstances in their temporal flow. To reason is to relate our life as it has been already lived and understood to the totality of human life and its circumstances. We place our individual experiences in the larger perspective of others' experiences. It is at this point that philosophy becomes apparent as a vital need of human life. It was so for Plato, and it is so for the philosophy of human life. Philosophy is not an educational luxury, an intellectual decoration, or a "wonder," but a need of the species. Philosophy may be here defined as the thoughtful search for a valid orientation of human life through the elaboration and critique of our ultimate presuppositions about reality, truth, and value. For the philosophy of human life the reality and primacy of human life must now replace the philosophical thesis of Descartes' era, *Cogito ergo sum*." "I think, therefore I am" must give way to the deeper and more adequate thesis that "I think because, and only because, I first live."[4] It is human life which selects through time the ideas and values by which it lives or fails to live. The criteria of truth and value are always given to human beings through their life in circumstances. There can be no moral or normative values that are not founded in human life in time.

Three cautionary notes are in order here. First, the idea of human life neither proves nor disproves the existence or nonexistence of God. The significant thing is that God, however defined, has somehow managed to be a presence within the perspectives of human life, and an issue for it. The idea of human life, in fact, suggests at least the possibility of a search for theology. Second, the idea of human life is not a revival of the presocratic notion of "*homo mensura*, the claim that "man is the measure of all things." Rather, the idea of human life states that for something to be real, it must somehow appear within and be kept in view of at least one human life. Ortega's claim that it is the destiny of human beings to "humanize the world" is neither an anti-environmental notion nor an anthropocentric one. Human beings cannot avoid understanding circumstances in terms of the nature and understanding they actually possess. Even the idea of a non-anthropomorphic environmentalism is in fact a humanization of circumstances by human life itself. We cannot avoid imparting meanings and values that are not human meanings and values. We cannot attain ends that have not somehow arisen within human life. Finally, this essay is at very best only a collection of abstract and skeletal thought forms that have been generated within my life in its relation to its circumstances. Human life as a thing in itself can in the end only be lived by an individual. Human life is finally a mystery that can never be fully expressed or rationalized, but only lived in an immediate present, and approached with a thankful "Yes," as James Joyce would have it. About more than this we are forced to be silent.

The prow of the ship of human life is forever cutting into the future as it attempts to decide what it is going to do or be. The course is never given automatically; circumstances act at the crossroads of life's possibilities and decisions. Suffering, dissatisfaction, anxiety, ignorance, and need permeate all of life. The essence of life seems all too often to be only a craving for more life; yet this is not its essence. The essence of

Conclusions on the Fundamental Datum of Human Life

human life is self-transcendence through historical time, to think and act at or beyond the level of the times, and to "humanize" the world. This is the vital vocation of human beings, a vocation that must happen in a hostile, dangerous, and indifferent world. We must always live in the country of "the enemy." Human life is not neutral, but points to possibilities and projects that can result in some kind of realization. Yet humanity is surfeited with fanaticisms, ideologies, and "false dawns." As Nietzsche once remarked, "Civilization has existed for five thousand years, and there is still no goal for mankind." Such a goal must arise within the fragility and care and wonder of human life. We are our life and nothing more.

Notes

Introduction

1. *Obras* 12, 326. All references to the work of Ortega are from José Ortega y Gasset, *Obras Completas*, First Edition, 12 vols. (Madrid: Alianza-Revista de Occidente, 1983). Citations will be by volume and page, and the author we refer to as "Ortega" after the Spanish usage.

Chapter One

1. The best scattered discussions of human life in general are to be found in Vol. VII, *Der Aufbau der geschichtlichen Welt in den Geisteswissenschaften*, pp. 3–245, of the collected works of Wilhelm Dilthey, *Gesammelte Schriften*, 20 vols., 1914–1982. Vols. I–XII (Stuttgart: B.G. Teubner, and Göttingen: Vandenhoeck und Ruprecht 1958–present); Vols. XIII–XX (Göttingen: Vandenhoeck und Ruprecht). Hereafter these will be cited in abbreviated form with the volume number in Roman numerals and the pages in Arabic numerals, e.g., *G.S.* VII, 105. Many of Dilthey's important works have been published independently of the 1914 Teubner vols. These include: *Leben Schleiermachers* (Berlin: Vereinigung wissenschaftlicher Verleger, 1922); *Das Erlebnis und die Dichtung* (Leipzig: B.G. Teubner, 1906); the biographical source *Briefwechsel zwischen Wilhelm Dilthey und dem Grafen Paul Yorck von Wartenburg, 1877–1897*, ed. Sigrid von der Schulenburg (Halle: M. Niemeyer, 1923); a volume of letters and notes of the young Dilthey, *Der junge Dilthey. Ein Lebensbild in Briefen und Tagebüchern, 1852–1870*, ed. Clara Misch (Stuttgart: B.G. Teubner, 1933).
2. Eduard Spranger uses this expression in his *Wilhelm Dilthey* (Berlin: Borngräber, 1912), p. 7.
3. Dilthey, *G.S.* VIIII, 184; V, 4, 83.
4. *G.S.* V, 198.
5. *G.S.* VII, 261.

6. *G.S.* VII, 261.
7. *G.S.* VII, 130–166.
8. *G.S.* VI, 314.
9. *G.S.* VII, 228–245.

Chapter Two

1. Heidegger, *Sein und Zeit*, Seventh edition (Tübingen: Max Niemeyer Verlag, 1979), pp. 27–39. All references to *Sein und Zeit* will be abbreviated as, for example, *SZ* 27. The present English translation of *Being and Time* is by John Macquarrie and Edward Robinson (New York: Harper & Row, 1962). The appropriate English material is in this book correlated with the German citation.
2. For Heidegger's relation to both Descartes and Kant, see the letter which Heidegger wrote to Father William Richardson, which was reprinted in his *Heidegger. Through Phenomenology to Thought* (2nd ed., The Hague: Martinus Nijhoff, 1967), p. xiv. For the genesis of the priority of our actual existence in historical time over the Husserlian search for a pure transcendental consciousness, see Martin Heidegger, *Platons Lehre von der Wahrheit: Mit einem Brief über den Humanismus* (Bern: A. Franke, 1947), translated by Edgar Lohner as "Letter on Humanism" in *Philosophy in the Twentieth Century*, ed. William Barrett and Henry D. Aiken (New York: Random House, 1962), Vol. III, p. 287.
3. See for example Ortega, *Obras* 8, 270–280.
4. *SZ* 394–395.
5. Ortega summarized his claims to originality in many places, but the most prominent source is *Leibniz*, *Obras* 8, 270–279. In his *What Is Philosophy?* Ortega presented perhaps his best systematic statement of his philosophy of human life.
6. For a further discussion of these issues see the author's *The Dawn of Historical Reason: The Historicality of Human Existence in the Thought of Dilthey, Heidegger and Ortega y Gasset* (New York: Peter Lang, 1994), pp. 249–256.

Chapter Three

1. *G.S.* VII, 261.
2. *G.S.* VII, 229.

Chapter Four

1. *G.S.* VII, 267.
2. *Obras* 12, 105.
3. *Obras* 7, 402–413.

Chapter Five

1. *G.S.* V, 370.
2. *G.S.* VII, 71–74.
3. *G.S.* VII, 248.
4. SZ 326.
5. SZ 329.

Chapter Six

1. *G.S.* V, 364; VII, 261.
2. *G.S.* VII, 161.
3. *G.S.* VIII, 85.
4. *G.S.* V, 180; VII, 135.
5. *G.S.* XIX, 66.
6. *G.S.* V, 180.
7. For a further explanation of historicism see Dwight E. Lee and Robert Beck, "The Meaning of Historicism," *American Historical Review* LIX, April, 1954, 568–577.
8. *G.S.* VIII, 85.
9. SZ 398.
10. SZ 375.
11. SZ 49–50.
12. SZ 384.
13. SZ 395.
14. *Obras* 6, 32, 203.
15. *Obras* 1, 413.
16. *Obras* 7, 169.
17. *G.S.* VII, 192.

Chapter Seven

1. *G.S.* I, 261, 418.
2. *G.S.* VII, 261.
3. *G.S.* VII, 248.
4. *G.S.* VII, 192, 196–197.
5. *G.S.* VII, 122.
6. *G.S.* V, 171.
7. *G.S.* VII, 71–74.
8. *G.S.* VII, 234.
9. *G.S.* VII, 261–262.
10. *Obras* 3, 199.
11. *Obras* 3, 199.

Chapter Eight

1. *Obras* 6, 46.
2. *Obras* 8, 274.
3. *Obras* 6, 49.
4. *Obras* 9, 365.
5. *Obras* 12, 237.
6. This classical position was first presented by Carl Hempel in his 1942 article "The Function of General Laws in History"; see Patrick Gardiner, ed., *Theories of History* (Glencoe: The Free Press, 1963), pp. 344–356.
7. *Obras* 6, 13–50.
8. *Obras* 9, 362.
9. *Obras* 6, 43; 5, 37.
10. *Obras* 3, 151–156.
11. *Obras* 4, 193–200.
12. *Obras* 4, 221–228.
13. *Obras* 6, 35–41.

Chapter Nine

1. *SZ* 47–48, 114.
2. *SZ* 115.
3. *G.S.* VII, 135, 234.
4. *G.S.* VII, 279.
5. *G.S.* VII, 278.
6. Dilthey's *Verstehen* has been assigned as a method to history, sociology, economics, and psychology by Max Weber, Werner Sombart, Ferdinand Tönnies, Ernst Troeltsch, and Eduard Spranger. Max Weber employs *Verstehen* in his assumption that social actions are the basic elements of explanation. See also *G.S.* VII, 210.
7. *G.S.* V, 254.
8. *SZ* 224, 395.
9. *SZ* 39, 153, 395.
10. *SZ* 115.
11. *SZ* 175, 220.
12. *Obras* 3, 152.
13. *Obras* 4, 221–228.
14. *Obras* 1, 319–321.

Chapter Ten

1. G.S. X, 13–124.
2. Max Weber also proposed this definition of motives in his *The Theory of Social and Economic Organization*, trans. A.M. Henderson and Talcott Parsons (Glencoe: Free Press, 1947), pp. 98–99.
3. G.S. VII, 17.
4. R.G. Collingwood has argued the same in his *The Idea of History*, Oxford University Press, 1951, p. 308.
5. Obras 9, 396–398.
6. Obras 5, 338–339.
7. Obras 6, 198.
8. Obras 7, 100–101.
9. Obras 5, 341–342.
10. Julián Marías, *Generations: A Historical Method*, trans. Harold Raley (Tuscaloosa: The University of Alabama Press, 1970), p. 69.
11. See for example G.S. V, 36–41.
12. Obras 5, 37.
13. The author is indebted for the concept of generations to Oliver W. Holmes' *Human Reality and the Social World: Ortega's Philosophy of History* (Amherst: University of Massachusetts Press, 1975), pp. 116–123.
14. SZ 45–53.

Chapter Eleven

1. G.S. VII, 261.
2. G.S. VI, 314.
3. G.S. IV, 517; VIII, 163.
4. G.S. VII, 130–166.
5. G.S. V, 5.
6. Obras 7, 100, 401; 6, 165–167.
7. Obras 8, 270–292; 12, 26–38, 97–101.
8. Obras 5, 40.
9. Obras 7, 338–406.
10. Obras 6, 165ff.
11. Obras 8, 45–46.
12. Obras 8, 45–46.
13. G.S. V, 90.
14. G.S. II, 259.
15. Obras 6, 257–258.
16. Obras 8, 52.
17. Howard N. Tuttle, *The Dawn of Historical Reason* (New York: Peter Lang Press, 1994), pp. 21–38.

18. *Obras* 6, 213–214.
19. *G.S.* VII, 218.
20. *Obras* 6, 25–32, 193–197.
21. See Chapter Two, Endnote 5.
22. *Obras* 7, 243; 12, 36–37; 7, 388.
23. *SZ* 46, 397–404.
24. *SZ* 394–395.
25. *SZ* 400.
26. *SZ* 396.
27. *Obras* 6, 49–50.

Chapter Twelve

1. *Obras* 5, 28.
2. *Obras* 3, 199.
3. *Obras* 3, 432.
4. *Obras* 4, 58.

Bibliography

Dilthey: Selected Bibliography

I Dilthey Bibliography
There is a chronological bibliography by Ulrich Herrmann entitled *Bibliographie Wilhelm Dilthey: Quellen und Literatur.* Weinheim, Berlin and Basel: Julius Beltz, 1969.

II Dilthey's Works
Gesammelte Schriften. 20 vols. Stuttgart: B. G. Teubner; Göttingen: Vandenhoeck und Ruprecht, 1914–90-present.
G.S. I *Einleitung in die Geisteswissenschaften: Versuch einer Grundlegung für das Studium der Gesellschaft und der Geschichte.* Edited by B. Groethuysen. 4th ed., 1959.
G.S. II *Weltanschauung und Analyse des Menschen seit Renaissance und Reformation.* Edited by G.Misch. 5th ed., 1957.
G.S. III *Studium zur Geschichte des deutschen Geistes: Leibniz und sein Zeitalter. Friedrich der Grosse und die deutsche Aufklärung. Das achtzehnte Jahrhundert und die geschichtliche Welt.* Edited by P. Ritter. 2d ed., 1959.
G.S. IV *Die Jugendgeschichte Hegels und andere Abhandlungen zur Geschichte des deutschen Idealismus.* Edited by H. Nohl. 2d ed., 1959.
G.S. V *Die geistige Welt: Einleitung in die Philosophie des Lebens. Erste Hälfte: Abhandlungen zur Grundlegung der Geisteswissenschaften.* Edited by G. Misch. 2d ed., 1957.
G.S. VI *Die geistige Welt: Einleitung in die Philosophie des Lebens. Zweite Hälfte. Abhandlungen zur Poetik, Ethik und Pädagogik.* Edited by G. Misch. 3d ed., 1958.
G.S. VII *Der Aufbau der geschichtlichen Welt in den Geisteswissenschaften.* Edited by B. Groethuysen. 2d ed., 1956.
G.S. VIII *Weltanschauungslehre: Abhandlungen zur Philosophie der Philosophie.* Edited by B. Groethuysen. 2d ed., 1960.
G.S. IX *Pädagogik: Geschichte und Grundlinien des Systems.* Edited by O. F. Bollnow. 2d ed., 1960.
G.S. X *System der Ethik.* Edited by H. Nohl. 1st ed., 1958.

G.S. XI *Vom Aufgang des geschichtlichen Bewusstseins: Jugendaufsätze und Erinnerungen.* Edited by E. Weniger. 2d ed., 1960.
G.S. XII *Zur preussischen Geschichte: Schleiermachers politische Gesinnung und Wirksamkeit. Die Reorganisatoren des preussischen Staates. Das Allgemeine Landrecht.* Edited by E. Weniger. 2d ed., 1960.
G.S. XIII *Leben Schleiermachers. Auf Grund des Textes der 1. Auflage von 1870 und der Zusätze aus dem Nachlass.* Edited by Martin Redeker, 1970.
G.S. XIV *Leben Schleiermachers. Zweiter Band: Schleiermachers System als Philosophie und Theologie.* Edited by Martin Redeker, 1966.
G.S. XV *Zur Geistesgeschichte des 19. Jahrhunderts: Portraits und Skizzen. Quellenstudien und Literatur berichte zur Theologie und Philosophie im 19. Jahrhundert.* Edited by Ulrich Herrmann, 1970.
G.S. XVI *Zur Geistesgeschichte des 19. Jahrhunderts: Aufsätze und Rezensionen aus Zeitungen und Zeitschriften 1859–1874.* Edited by Ulrich Herrmann, 1972.
G.S. XVII *Zur Geistesgeschichte des 19. Jahrhunderts: Aus Westermanns Monatsheften: Literaturbriefe, Berichte zur Kunstgeschichte, verstreute Rezensionen 1867–1884.* Edited by Ulrich Herrmann, 1974.
G.S. XVIII *Die Wissenschaften vom Menschen, der Gellschaft und der Geschichte: Vorarbeiten zur Einleitung in die Geisteswissenschaften (1865–1880).* Edited by Helmut Johach and Frithjof Rodi, 1977.
G.S. XIX *Grundlegung der Wissenschaften vom Menschen der Gesellschaft und der Geschichte.* Edited by Helmut Johach and Frithjof Rodi, 1982.
G.S. XX *Logic und System der philosphischen Wissenschaften. Vorlesungen zur erkenntnistheoretischen Logik und Methodologie 1864–1902.* Edited by Hans Lessing and Frithjof Rodi, 1990.

III Other Writings
Das Erlebnis und die Dichtung: Lessing, Goethe, Novalis, Hölderlin. 13th ed. Stuttgart: B. G. Teubner; Göttingen: Vandenhoeck und Ruprecht, 1957.
Leben Schleiermachers. Vol. 1. Edited by H. Mulert. 2d ed. Berlin: de Gruyter, 1922.
Aus Schleiermachers Leben: In Briefen. 4 vols. Berlin: G. Reimers, 1858–63.
Briefwechsel zwischen Wilhelm Dilthey und dem Grafen Paul Yorck von Wartenburg. 1877–97. Edited by Sigrid von der Schulenburg. Halle: M. Niemeyer, 1923.
Der junge Dilthey: Ein Lebensbild in Briefen und Tagebüchern, 1852–1870. Edited by Clara Misch, née Dilthey. 2d ed. Stuttgart: B. G. Teubner; Göttingen: Vandenhoeck und Ruprecht, 1960.

IV English Translations of Dilthey's Writings
Descriptive Psychology and Historical Understanding. Translated by Richard M. Zaner and Kenneth Heiges, with an introduction by Rudolf Makkreel. The Hague: Martinus Nijhoff, 1976.
"The Dream." Translated by William Kluback. In *Wilhelm Dilthey's Philosophy of History.* New York: Columbia University Press, 1956. *Gesammelte Schriften,* Vol. V, 339–416.

Patterns and Meaning in History: Thoughts on History and Society. Translator unacknowledged. H. P. Rickman, ed. New York: Harper & Row, 1962.
Wilhelm Dilthey: Selected Writings. Translated by H. P. Rickman. Cambridge University Press, 1976.
Makkreel, Rudolf A. and Rodi, Frithjof, eds. *Wilhelm Dilthey. Selected Works.* Princeton, NJ: Princeton University Press. Volumes in selected works include:
I *Introduction to the Human Sciences*
II *Problems of the Human Sciences*
III *Foundations of the Human Sciences*
IV *Hermeneutics and the Rise of Historical Consciousness*
V *Poetry and Experience*
VI *Philosophy and Life*

V Selected Secondary Works
Abel, Theodore. "The Operation Called Verstehen." American Journal of Sociology 54 (1948): 211–18.
Aron, Raymond. *Introduction to the Philosophy of History.* Boston: Beacon Press, 1961.
Bergstraesser, A. "Wilhelm Dilthey and Max Weber: An Empirical Approach to Historical Analysis." *Ethics. An International Journal of Social, Political and Legal Philosophy* 61 (1947): 92–110.
Bollnow, Otto F. *Dilthey. Eine Einführung in seine Philosophie.* Stuttgart, Berlin, Köln, Mainz: Kohlhammer, 1967.
Bulhof, Ilse N. *Wilhelm Dilthey: A Hermeneutical Approach to History and Culture.* The Hague: Martinus Nijhoff, 1980.
———. "Structure and Change in Wilhelm Dilthey's Philosophy of History." *History and Theory. Studies in the Philosophy of History* 15 (1976): 21–32.
Collingwood, R. G. *The Idea of History.* New York: Oxford University Press, 1946.
Dilthey-Jahrbuch für Philosophie und Geschichte der Geisteswissenschaften. Göttingen: Vandenhoeck und Ruprecht, Vol. 4 (1986–87), Vol. 6 (1989).
Diwald, Hellmut. *Wilhelm Dilthey.* Göttingen: Musterschmidt Verlag, 1963.
Donoso, A. "Wilhelm Dilthey's Contributions to the Philosophy of History." *Philosophy Today* 12 (1968): 151–63.
Ermarth, Michael. *Wilhelm Dilthey: The Critique of Historical Reason.* Chicago and London: The University of Chicago Press, 1978.
Ebbinghaus, Hermann. "Über erklärende und beschreibende Psychologie." *Zeitschrift für Psychologie und Physiologie der Sinnesorgane* 9 (1895): 161–205.
Engel-Janosi, Friedrich. *The Growth of German Historicism.* Johns Hopkins University Studies in Historical and Political Science. Baltimore, 1944.
Friess, H. L. "Wilhelm Dilthey: A Review of His Collected Works." *Journal of Philosophy* 26 (1929): 5–25.
Habermas, Jürgen. *Knowledge and Human Interests.* Translated by Jeremy J. Shapiro. Boston: Beacon Press, 1971.

Hirsch, Eric Donald, Jr. *Validity in Interpretation*. New Haven: Yale University Press, 1967.
Hodges, Herbert A. *Wilhelm Dilthey: An Introduction*. 2d ed. London: Routledge & K. Paul, 1949.
———.*The Philosophy of Wilhelm Dilthey*. London: Routledge & K. Paul, 1952.
Holborn, Hajo. "Wilhelm Dilthey and the Critique of Historical Reason." *Journal of the History of Ideas* 11 (1950): 93–118.
Hughes, Henry Stuart. *Consciousness and Society: The Reorientation of European Social Thought, 1890–1930*. New York: Knopf, 1958.
Hughes, Stuart. *History as Art and Science*. New York: Harper & Row, 1965.
Husserl, Edmund. "Philosophie als strenge Wissenschaft." *Logos* 1 (1911): 289–341.
Iggers, Georg. *The German Conception of History*. Middletown: Wesleyan University Press, 1968.
Kluback, William. *Wilhelm Dilthey's Philosophy of History*. New York: Columbia University Press, 1956.
Kornberg, Jacques. "Wilhelm Dilthey on the Self and History: Some Theological Roots of *Geistesgeschichte*." *Central European History* 5 (1973): 295–317.
Krausser, Peter. "Dilthey's Revolution in the Theory of the Structure of Scientific Inquiry and Rational Behavior." *Review of Metaphysics* 22 (1968): 262–80.
Kremer-Marietti, Angèle. *Wilhelm Dilthey et la anthropologie historique*. Paris: Seghers, 1971.
Lee, Dwight, E., and Beck, Robert. "The Meaning of Historicism." *American Historical Review* 59 (1954): 568–77.
Makkreel, Rudolf A. *Dilthey: Philosopher of the Human Studies*. Princeton: Princeton University Press, 1975.
Mandelbaum, Maurice. *The Problem of Historical Knowledge*. New York: Liveright Publishing Corporation, 1938.
Marcuse, Herbert. "Das Problem der geschichtliche Wirklichkeit." *Die Gesellschaft internationale Revue für Sozialismus und Politik VIII*, 1931.
Masur, Gerhard. "Wilhelm Dilthey and the History of Ideas." *Journal of the History of Ideas* 13, no. 1 (1952): 94–107.
Meinecke, Friedrich. *Die Entstehung des Historismus*. 2d ed. Munich, Berlin: R. Oldenbourg, 1946.
Misch, Georg. *Lebensphilosophie und Phänomenologie*. Leipzig, Berlin: B. G. Teubner, 1931.
Nagel, Ernest. "On the Method of *Verstehen* as the Sole Method of Philosophy." *Journal of Philosophy* L, no. 5 (1953): 54–157.
Ortega y Gasset, José. "History as a System." *Philosophy and History*. Edited by R. Klibansky and H. J. Patou. New York: Harper & Row, 1963.
———. "Wilhelm Dilthey and the Idea of Life." *Concord and Liberty*. Translated by Helene Weyl. New York: W. W. Norton, 1946.
Palmer, Richard E. *Hermeneutics: Interpretation Theory in Schleiermacher, Dilthey, Heidegger, and Gadamer*. Evanston: Northwestern University Press, 1969.

Rickert, Heinrich. *Die Grenzen der naturwissenschaftlichen Begriffsbildung.* Tübingen: J. C. B. Mohr, 1902.
———. *Die Philosophie des Lebens.* Tübingen: J. C. B. Mohr, 1929.
———. *Kulturwissenschaft und Naturwissenschaft.* Freiburg: J. C. B. Mohr, 1899.
Rickman, H. P. *Understanding in the Human Studies.* London: Heinemann, 1967.
———. *Wilhelm Dilthey. Pioneer of the Human Studies.* Berkeley: University of California Press, 1979.
———. *Wilhelm Dilthey, Selected Writings.* Cambridge: Cambridge University Press, 1976.
Ricoeur, Paul. "The Task of Hermeneutics." In *Heidegger and Modern Philosophy.* Edited by Michael Murray. New Haven: Yale University Press, 1978.
Rile, Gilbert. *The Concept of Mind.* New York: Barnes and Noble, 1965.
Spiegelberg, Herbert. *The Phenomenological Movement.* 2 vols. The Hague: Martinus Nijhoff, 1960.
Spranger, Eduard. *Wilhelm Dilthey.* Berlin: W. Borngräber, 1912.
Stein, Arthur. *Der Begriff des Verstehens bei Dilthey.* 2d rev. ed. Tübingen: J. C. B. Mohr, 1926.
Suter, Jean-Francois. *Philosophie et historie chez Wilhelm Dilthey.* Basel: Verlag für Recht und Gesellschaft, 1960.
Topper, Bonno. "Dilthey's Methodology of the *Geisteswissenschaften.*" *Philosophical Review* 34 (1925): 332–49.
Troeltsch, Ernst. *Der Historismus und seine Probleme.* Tübingen: J. C. B. Mohr, 1922.
Tuttle, Howard. "The Epistemological Status of the Cultural World in Vico and Dilthey." In *Giambattista Vico's Science of Humanity.* Edited by Giorgio Tagliacozzo and Donald P. Verene. Baltimore: Johns Hopkins University Press, 1976.
———. *Wilhelm Dilthey's Philosophy of Historical Understanding: A Critical Analysis.* Leiden: E. J. Brill, 1969.
Wach, Joachim. *Das Verstehen: Grundzüge einer Geschichte der hermeneutischen Theorie im 19. Jahrhundert.* 3 vols. Tübingen: J. C. B. Mohr, 1926–33.
Weber, Max. *The Methodology of the Social Sciences.* Translated and edited by E. A. Shils and H. Finch. Glencoe: Free Press, 1949.
Windelband, Wilhelm. "Geschichte und Naturwissenschaft." *Präludien.* Tübingen: J. C. B. Mohr, 1915. Vol. II, pp. 136–60.

Heidegger: Selected Bibliography

I Heidegger's Bibliography
The best general bibliography is Hans-Martin Sass, *Martin Heidegger: Bibliography and Glossary.* Bowling Green, Ohio: Philosophy Documentation Center, Bowling Green State University, 1982. W. J. Richardson provides a list of Heidegger's works in his *Heidegger: Through Phenomenology to Thought.* The Hague: Martinus Nijhoff, 1967. (Pp. 675–80 lists Heidegger's works in order of composition, and pp. 663–71 lists his lecture courses and seminars at Marburg and Freiburg.) A Bibliographical Guide is

found in Michael Murray, ed., *Heidegger and Modern Philolosophy: Critical Essays*. New Haven: Yale University Press, 1978, pp. 355–65. Martin Heidegger's complete works are presently being published in the *Gesamtausgabe*. Frankfurt: Klostermann, 1972 ff.

II Selected Works of Heidegger with Current English Translations

"Aletheia (Heraclitus, Fragment B 16)." In *Martin Heidegger, Early Greek Thinking*. Translated by Frank A. Capuzzi. New York: Harper & Row, 1975, pp. 102–23.

"Aristoteles-Einleitung." In *Dilthey-Jahrbuch für Philosophie und Geschichte der Geisteswissenschaften*. Göttingen: Vandenhoeck & Ruprecht, Vol. 6 (1989).

Beiträge zur Philosophie (Vom Ereignis), Gesamtausgabe. Vol. 65. Edited by Friedrich-Wilhelm von Herrmann. Frankfurt am Main: Klostermann, 1989.

"Building, Dwelling, Thinking." In *Martin Heidegger, Poetry, Language, Thought*. Translated by Albert Hofstadter. New York: Harper & Row, 1975, pp. 145–61.

"Der Satz vom Grund." In *Der Satz vom Grund*. Pfullingen: Neske, 1971. Translated by Keith Hoeller in *Man and World* 7 (1974): 207–22.

"Der Zeitbegriff in der Geschichtswissenschaft." In *Zeitschrift für Philosophie und philosophische Kritik* 161 (1916): 173–88. Translated by H. S. Taylor and H. W. Uffelmann, "The Concept of Time in the Science of History." *The Journal of the British Society for Phenomenology* 9 (1978): 3–10.

Die Frage nach dem Ding (1962). Pfullingen: Neske, 1962. Translated by Barton and Vera Deutsch, *What is a Thing?* Chicago: Regnery, 1969.

Die Grundprobleme der Phänomenologie (1927). Frankfurt: Klostermann, 1975. Translated by Albert Hofstadter as *The Basic Problems of Phenomenology*. Bloomington: Indiana University Press, 1982.

Einführung in die Metaphysik (1935). Tübingen: Niemeyer, 1953. Translated by Ralph Manheim, *An Introduction to Metaphysics*. New Haven: Yale University Press, 1959.

Gelassenheit (1959). Pfullingen: Neske, 1959. Translated by John M. Anderson and E. Hans Freund, *Discourse on Thinking*. New York: Harper & Row, 1966.

Identität und Differenz (1957). Pfullingen: Neske, 1957. Translated by Joan Stambaugh, *Identity and Difference*. New York: Harper & Row, 1969.

Kant und das Problem der Metaphysik (1927). Frankfurt: Klostermann, 1951. Translated by James Churchill, *Kant and the Problem of Metaphysics*. Bloomington: Indiana University Press, 1962.

"Logos (Heraclitus, Fragment B 50)." In *Martin Heidegger, Early Greek Thinking*. Translated by David Farrell Krell. New York: Harper & Row, 1984, pp. 59–78.

"Moira (Parmenides VIII, 34–41)" In *Martin Heidegger, Early Greek Thinking*. Translated by Frank A. Capuzzi. New York: Harper & Row, 1984, pp. 79–101.

Nietzsche (1931–1946). 2 vols. Pfullingen: Neske, 1961.

Nietzsche, Vol. I: *The Will to Power as Art*. Translated by David Farrell Krell. New York: Harper & Row, 1979.

Nietzsche, Vol. II: *The Eternal Recurrence of the Same*. Translated by David Farrell Krell. New York: Harper & Row, 1982.

Nietzsche, Vol. III: *The Will to Power as Knowledge and as Metaphysics.* Translated by Joan Stambaugh, David Farrell Krell, and Frank Capuzzi. New York: Harper & Row, 1987.

Nietzsche, Vol. IV: *Nihilism.* Translated by Frank A. Capuzzi and David Farrell Krell. New York: Harper & Row, 1982.

"'Only a God Can Save Us': *Der Spiegel's* Interview with Martin Heidegger." Translated by M. P. Alter and J. D. Caputo. *Philosophy Today* 20 (1976): 267–84.

"Overcoming Metaphysics." In *Martin Heidegger, The End of Philosophy.* Translated by Joan Stambaugh. New York: Harper & Row, 1973, pp. 84–110.

Platons Lehre von der Wahrheit (1942): Mit einem Brief über den "Humanismus" (1946). Bern: Francke, 1947. These are translated in William Barrett and Henry D. Aiden, eds., *Philosophy in the Twentieth Century,* 2 vols. New York: Random House, 1962. Vol. II, pp. 270–340.

"Poetically Man Dwells...." Translated by Albert Hofstadter. New York: Harper & Row, 1975, pp. 213–29.

Prolegomena zur Geschichte des Zeitbegriffs (1925). Edited by Petra Jaeger. Frankfurt: Klostermann, 1979. Translated by Theodore Kisiel, *History of the Concept of Time.* Bloomington: Indiana University Press, 1992.

"Science and Reflection." In *Martin Heidegger, The Question Concerning Technology and Other Essays.* Translated by William Lovitt. New York: Harper & Row, 1977, pp. 155–82.

Sein und Zeit (1927). Tübingen: Niemeyer, 1927. Translated by John Macquarrie and Edward Robinson, *Being and Time.* New York: Harper & Row, 1962. With marginal pagination of the German edition of *Sein und Zeit* (Seventh edition).

"The Age of the World Picture." In *Martin Heidegger, the Question Concerning Technology and Other Essays.* Translated by William Lovitt. New York: Harper & Row, 1977, pp. 115–54.

"The Thing." In *Martin Heidegger, Poetry, Language, Thought.* Translated by Albert Hofstadter. New York: Harper & Row, 1975, pp. 165–86.

Unterwegs zur Sprache (1957). Pfullingen: Neske, 1959. Translated by Peter Hertz and Joan Stambaugh, *On the Way to Language.* New York: Harper & Row, 1966.

Vom Wesen der Wahrheit (1930). Frankfurt: Klostermann, 1961. Translated by John Sallis, "On the Essence of Truth." In *Martin Heidegger. Basic Writings.* New York: Harper & Row, 1977, pp. 117–41.

Vom Wesen des Grundes (1928). Frankfurt: Klostermann, 1928. Translated by Terrence Malick, *The Essence of Reasons.* Evanston, IL: Northwestern University Press, 1969.

Vorträge und Aufsätze (1936–53). Pfullingen: Neske, 1954. This is a collection of eleven essays which includes the following English translation: "The Question Concerning Technology." In *Martin Heidegger, The Question Concerning Technology and Other Essays.* Translated by William Lovitt, pp. 3–35.

Was ist das-die Philosophie? (1956). Pfullingen: Neske, 1956. Translated by William Kluback and Jean Wilde, *What is Philosophy?* New Haven: College and University Press, 1958.

Was ist Metaphysik? (1929). Frankfurt: Klostermann, 1955. Translated by David Farrell

Krell, "What is Metaphysics?" In *Martin Heidegger, Basic Writings*. New York: Harper & Row, 1977, pp. 91–112.

"What are Poets For?" In *Martin Heidegger, Poetry, Language, Thought*. Translated by Albert Hofstadter. New York: Harper & Row, 1975, pp. 91–142.

"Who is Nietzsche's Zarathustra?" Translated by Bernd Magnus. *Review of Metaphysics* 20 (1967): 411–31.

Zur Sache des Denkens (1969). Tübingen: Niemeyer, 1969. Translated by Joan Stambaugh, *On Time and Being*. New York: Harper & Row, 1972.

III Selected Secondary Sources

Alderman, Harold. "Heidegger's Critique of Science and Technology." *Heidegger and Modern Philosophy*. Edited by Michael Murray. New Haven: Yale University Press, 1978, pp. 35–50.

Alleman, Beda. *Hölderlin und Heidegger*. Zurich: Atlantis, 1956.

Arendt, Hannah. "Martin Heidegger at Eighty." *New York Review of Books* 17, 21 (October 1971): 50–54.

Barash, Jeffrey A. *Martin Heidegger and the Problem of Historical Meaning*. Dordrecht: Martinus Nijhoff, 1988.

Biemel, Walter. *Heidegger*. Translated by J. L. Mehta. New York: Harcourt Brace Jovanovich, 1976.

Brentano, Franz. *On the Several Senses of Being in Aristotle*. Translated by Rolf George. Berkeley: University of California Press, 1975.

Caputo, John D. "Time and Being in Heidegger." *Modern Schoolman* 50 (1973): 325–49.

Gadamer, Hans-Georg. "The Historicality of Understanding as Hermeneutic Principle." In *Heidegger and Modern Philosophy*. New Haven: Yale University Press, 1978, pp. 161–83.

———. "The Problem of Historical Consciousness." *Graduate Faculty Philosophy Journal* 5 (1975): 8–52.

———. *Truth and Method*. New York: Continuum, 1975.

Gethmann, Carl F. *Verstehen und Auslegung. Das Methodenproblem in der Philosophie Martin Heideggers*. Bonn: Bouvier, 1974.

Gillespie, Michael A. *Hegel, Heidegger, and the Ground of History*. Chicago: University of Chicago Press, 1985.

Gray, J. Glenn. "Splendor of the Simple." *Philosophy East and West* 20 (1970): 227–40.

Guignon, Charles B. *Heidegger and the Problem of Knowledge*. Indianapolis: Hackett Publishing Company, 1983.

Harries, Karstur. "Heidegger as a Political Thinker." *Review of Metaphysics* 29, no. 4 (June 1976): 642–49.

Hoy, David C. "History, Historicality and Historiography in *Being and Time*." In *Heidegger and Modern Philosophy*. New Haven: Yale University Press, 1978, pp. 329–53.

Husserl, Edmund. "Phänomenologie und Anthropologie." In *Philosophie und Phänomenologische Forschung*. Vol II (1941): 1–14.

Kierkegaard, Søren. *Concluding Unscientific Postscript*. Translated by David F. Swenson. Princeton: Princeton University Press, 1968.
Kisiel, Theodore. "The Missing Link in the Early Heidegger." In *Hermeneutic Phenomenology: Lectures and Essays*. Edited by Joseph J. Kockelmanns. Washington, DC: University Press of America, 1988.
Ladriere, J. "History and Destiny." *Philosophy Today* 9 (1965): 3–25.
Lampert, Lawrence. "On Heidegger and Historicism." *Philosophy and Phenomenological Research* 34 (1974): 586–90.
Landgrebe, Ludwig. *Major Problems in Contemporary European Philosophy from Dilthey to Heidegger*. Translated by Kurt Reinhardt. New York: F. Ungar, 1966.
Löwith, Karl. *Heidegger: Denker in dürftiger Zeit*. 2d ed. Göttingen: Vandenhoeck und Ruprecht, 1960.
———. *Nature, History, Existentialism*. Edited by Arnold Levison. Evanston: Northwestern University Press, 1966.
Lukàcs, György. *The Destruction of Reason*. Translated by Peter Palmer. Atlantic Highlands, N.J.: Humanities Press, 1980.
Macquarrie, John. *An Existential Theology*. New York: Harper & Row, 1965.
Magnus, Bernd. *Heidegger's Metahistory of Philosophy: Amor Fati, Being and Truth*. The Hague: Martinus Nijhoff, 1971.
Makkreel, Rudolf A. "The Genesis of Heidegger's Phenomenological Hermeneutics and the Rediscovered 'Aristotle Introduction' of 1922." *Man and World* 23 (1990): 305–20.
Marcuse, Herbert. "Contributions to a Phenomenology of Historical Materialism." *Telos* 4 (1969).
———. *Hegel's Ontology and the Theory of Historicality*. Translated by Seyla Benhabib. Cambridge: MIT Press, 1987.
———. "Über konkrete Philosophie." *Archiv für Sozialwissenschaft und Sozialpolitik* 62 (1929): 111–28.
Marx, Werner. *Heidegger and the Tradition*. Translated by Theodore Kisiel and Murray Greene. Evanston: Northwestern University Press, 1971.
Meissner, W. W. "The Temporal Demension in the Understanding of Human Experience." *Journal of Existentialism* 7 (1966–67): 129–60.
Morrison, Ronald P. "Kant, Husserl, and Heidegger on Time and the Unity of Consciousness." *Philosophy and Phenomenological Research* 39 (December 1978): 182–98.
Murray, Michael, ed. *Heidegger and Modern Philosophy*. New Haven: Yale University Press, 1978.
Pöggeler, Otto. "Heideggers Begegnung mit Dilthey." *Dilthey Jahrbuch*, Vol. 4 (1986–87).
———. *Martin Heidegger's Path of Thinking*. Translated by Daniel Megurshak and Sigmud Barber. Atlantic Highlands, NJ: Humanities Press, International, 1987.
———. "Heidegger Today." *The Southern Journal of Philosophy* 8 (Winter 1970): 173–308.
———. "Historicality in Heidegger's Late Work." *Southwestern Journal of Philosophy* 4 (1973): 53–73.

Richardson, William J. *Heidegger Through Phenomenology to Thought.* 2d ed. The Hague: Martinus Nijhoff, 1967.
Rodi, Frithjof. "Die Bedeutung Diltheys für die Konzeption von *Sein und Zeit.* Zum Umfeld von Heideggers Kasseler Vorträgen (1925)." *Dilthey-Jahrbuch,* Vol. 4 (1986–87).
Rollin, Bernard. "Heidegger's Philosophy of History in *Being and Time.*" *The Modern Schoolman* 49 (January 1972): 97–112.
Rotenstreich, Nathan. "The Ontological Status of History." *American Philosophical Quarterly* 9 (1972): 49–58.
Sallis, John, ed. *Heidegger and the Path of Thinking.* Pittsburgh: Duquesne University Press, 1970.
Schrag, Calvin O. "Heidegger on Repetition and Historical Understanding." *Philosophy East and West* 2 (1970): 287–95.
———. "Phenomenology, Ontology and History in the Philosophy of Martin Heidegger." *Revue International de Philosophie* 12 (1958): 117–32.
Schürmann, Reiner. "Anti-Humanism: Reflections of the Turn Toward the Post Modern Epoch." *Man and World* 12, no. 2 (1979): 160–77.
Sherover, Charles. *Heidegger, Kant, and Time.* Bloomington: Indiana University Press, 1971.
Spiegelberg, Herbert. *The Phenomenological Movement.* The Hague: Martinus Nijhoff, 1965.
Tuttle, Howard. "An Explication, Critique, and Application of Heidegger's Doctrine of Historical Temporality." *Southwest Philosophical Studies* 8, no. 3 (1983): 66–72.
———. "Algunos puntos de la crítica de Ortega y Gasset a la Teoría del Ser de Heidegger." *Revista de Occidente* 108 (Mayo 1990): 61–69.
Wren, Thomas E. "Heidegger's Philosophy of History." *The Journal of the British Society for Phenomenology* 9 (May 1978): 126–30.
Vycinas, Vincent. *Earth and Gods: An Introduction to the Philosophy of Martin Heidegger.* The Hague: Martinus Nijhoff, 1961.
Zimmerman, Michael E. *Eclipse of the Self.* Athens, Ohio: Ohio University Press, 1986.
———. "Heidegger and Marcuse: Technology as Ideology." *Research in Philosophy and Technology.* Volume II. Edited by Paul T. Durbin and Carl Mitcham. Greenwich, Conn.: Jai Press, 1979.
———. "Heidegger and Nietzsche on Authentic Time." *Cultural Hermeneutics* 4 (1977): 234–64.
———. *Heidegger's Confrontation with Modernity. Technology, Politics, Art.* Bloomington: Indiana University Press, 1990.

Ortega y Gasset: Selected Bibliography

I General Bibliography
Antón Donoso and Harold Raley have published a general bibliography of secondary sources entitled *José Ortega y Gasset: A Bibliography of Secondary Sources.* Bowling

Green, Ohio: Bowling Green State University, Philosophy Documentation Center, 1986. It contains over 4000 entries and includes books, essays, journal and newspaper articles, encyclopedia entries, dissertations, recordings, and films. It also has an extensive subject index. 449 pages. The complete works of Ortega in Spanish are published as
Obras completas. 4th ed. Vols. 1–6. Madrid: Revista de Occidente, 1957.
Obras completas. 3d. ed. Vol. 7. Madrid: Revista de Occidente, 1969.
Obras completas. 2d ed. Vols. 8–9. Madrid: Revista de Occidente, 1965.
Obras completas. 1st ed. Vols. 10–11. Madrid: Revista de Occidente, 1969.
Obras completas. 1st ed. 12 Vols. Madrid: Alianza Editorial-Revista de Occidente, 1983.
Epistolario. Edited and introduced by Paulino Garagorri. Madrid: Revista de Occidente, 1974.

II Ortega's Selected Works in English Translation in Alphabetical Order
Concord and Liberty. Translated by Helene Weyl. New York: W. W. Norton, 1946.
The Dehumanization of Art and Other Essays on Art, Culture and Literature. Translated by Helene Weyl et al. Princeton: Princeton University Press, 1968.
Historical Reason. Translated by Philip W. Silver. New York: W. W. Norton, 1984.
History as a System. Translated by Helene Weyl and William C. Atkinson. New York: W. W. Norton, 1941.
The Idea of Principle in Leibniz and the Evolution of Deductive Theory. Translated by Mildred Adams. New York: W. W. Norton, 1971.
An Interpretation of Universal History. Translated by Mildred Adams. New York: W. W. Norton, 1973.
Invertebrate Spain. Translated by Mildred Adams. New York: Howard Fertig, 1974.
Man and Crisis. Translated by Mildred Adams. New York: W. W. Norton, 1958.
Man and People. Translated by Willard B. Trask. New York: W. W. Norton, 1957.
Meditations on Hunting. Translated by Howard B. Wescott. New York: Scribner's, 1985.
Meditations on Quixote. Translated by Evelyn Rugg and Diego Marín. Introduction by Julián Marías. New York: W. W. Norton, 1961.
Mission of the University. Translated by Howard Lee Nostrand. New York: W. W. Norton, 1966.
The Modern Theme. Translated by James Cleugh. New York: W. W. Norton, 1933.
On Love: Aspects of a Single Theme. Translated by Toby Talbot. Cleveland: World Publishing, 1957.
The Origin of Philosophy. Translated by Toby Talbot. New York: W. W. Norton, 1967.
Phenomenology and Art. Translated and with an introduction by Philip W. Silver. New York: W. W. Norton, 1975.
Psychological Investigations. Translated by Jorge García-Gómez. New York: W. W. Norton, 1987.
The Revolt of the Masses. 25th anniversary ed. Translator anonymous. New York: W. W. Norton, 1957.
Some Lessons in Metaphysics. Translated by Mildred Adams. New York: W. W. Norton, 1969.
What is Philosophy? Translated by Mildred Adams. New York: W. W. Norton, 1960.

III Selected Secondary Sources

Acuna, Hernan Larrain. *La Genesis del Pensamiento de Ortega*. Buenos Aires: Compañia General Fabril, 1962.

Adams, Mildred. "Ortega y Gasset." *Forum and Century* 90 (July-December 1933): 373–78.

Alluntis, Felix. "Radical Reality According to Don José Ortega y Gasset." In John Ryan, ed., *Studies in Philosophy and the History of Philosophy*. Washington: Catholic University of America, 1969.

———. "The Vital and Historical Reason of Ortega y Gasset." *Franciscan Studies* 15, no. 1 (1955): 60–78.

Aranguren, José. *La ética de Ortega*. 2d ed. Madrid: Taurus Ediciones, 1959.

Armstrong, A. Mac C. "The Philosophy of Ortega y Gasset." *Philosophical Quarterly* 2, no. 7 (1952): 124–38.

Artola, Miguel. "En torno al concepto de historia." *Revista de estudios politicos* 62, no. 99 (1958): 145–83.

Bareo, Arturo. "The Conservative Critics: Ortega and Madariaga." *University Observer* I (Winter 1947): 29–36.

Benítez, Jaime. *Political and Philosophical Theories of José Ortega y Gasset*. Chicago: University of Chicago Press, 1939.

Borel, Jean-Paul. *Introduccíon a Ortega y Gasset*. Translated by Laureano Perez Latorre. Madrid: Ediciones Guadarrama, 1969.

Ceplecha, Christian. *The Historical Thought of José Ortega y Gasset*. Washington, D.C.: Catholic University Press of America, 1958.

Curtius, Ernst R. "Ortega." *Partisan Review* 17 (March 1950): 259–71.

De Kalb, Courtenay. "The Spiritual Law of Gravitation: Minority Rule as Analyzed by Ortega." *Hispania* 14 (March 1931): 81–88.

De Puy, Ida B. *The Basic Ideology of José Ortega y Gasset: The Conflict of Mission and Vocation*. Palo Alto: Stanford University Microfilms, 1961.

Díaz, Janet W. *The Major Themes of Existentialism in the Work of José Ortega y Gasset*. Chapel Hill: University of North Carolina Press, 1970.

Donoso, Antón. "The Influence of José Ortega y Gasset in Latin America." *Filosofia* (Sao Paolo) 3 (1974): 43–49.

Dray, William. *Laws and Explanation in History*. Oxford: Oxford University Press, 1957.

Duran, Manuel. "Tres Definidores del Hombre-Masa: Heidegger, Ortega, Riesman." *Cuadernos Americanos* 90, no. 6 (1956): 115–29.

Fernández, Pelayo H., et al., ed. *Ortega y Gasset Centennial/University of New Mexico*. Madrid: José Porrua Turanzas, 1985.

Ferrater Mora, José. *Ortega y Gasset: An Outline of His Philosophy*. New rev. ed., New Haven, Conn.: Yale University Press, 1963.

———. *Studies in Modern European Literature and Thought*. New Haven: Yale University Press, 1957.

Gaete, Arturo. *El sistema de Ortega*. Buenos Aires: Compañia General Fabril, 1962.

Gaos, José. *Sobre Ortega y Gasset*. Mexico City: Imprenta Universitaria, 1957.

Garcia, Astrada A. "Filosofía social y sociología in Ortega y Gasset." *Humanities,* Ano VII, no. 11 (1959): 79–90.
Giner, Salvador. *Mass Society.* New York: Academic Press, 1976.
Goyenechea, Francisco. "Lo individual y lo social en la filosofía de Ortega y Gasset." Zürich: *Studia Philosophica* 2 (1964).
Gray, Rockwell. *The Imperative of Modernity. An Intellectual Biography of José Ortega y Gasset.* Berkeley: University of California Press, 1989.
Guy Alain. *Ortega y Gasset, ou la Raison Vital et Historique.* Paris: Editions Seghers, 1969.
Heidegger, Martin. "Encuentros con Ortega y Gasset en Alemania." *Clavileno* 7, no. 39 (1956): 1–2.
Hempel, Carl. "The Function of General Laws in History." In Patrick Gardiner, ed., *Theories of History.* Glencoe: The Free Press, 1963, pp. 344–56.
Holmes, Oliver W. *Human Reality and the Social World: Ortega's Philosophy of History.* Amherst: University of Massachusetts Press, 1975.
Kern, Robert W. *Liberals, Reformers and Caciques in Restoration Spain, 1875–1909.* Albuquerque: University of New Mexico Press, 1974.
Klibansky, Raymond and Paton, H. J., eds. *Philosophy and History. Essays Presented to Ernst Cassirer.* Oxford: Clarendon Press, 1936.
Maldonado-Denis, Manuel. "Ortega y Gasset and the Theory of the Masses." *Western Political Quarterly* 14 (September-December 1961): 676–90.
Marías, Julían. *Generations: A Historical Method.* Translated by Harold C. Raley. Tuscaloosa: University of Alabama Press, 1970.
———. *History of Philosophy.* Translated by Stanley Appelbaum and C. C. Strowbridge. New York: Dover Publications, 1967, pp. 442–62.
———. *José Ortega y Gasset. Circumstances and Vocation.* Translated by F. M. López-Morillas. Norman: University of Oklahoma Press, 1970.
———. *Las Escuela de Madrid: Estudios de Filosofía Española.* Buenos Aires: Emece, 1959.
———. *Metaphysical Anthropology: The Empirical Structure of Human Life.* Translated by Frances López-Morillas. University Park: Pennsylvania State University Press, 1971.
Mattei, Carlos Ramos. *Ethical Self-Determination in Ortega y Gasset.* New York: Peter Lang, 1987.
McClintock, Robert. *Man and His Circumstances: Ortega as Educator.* New York: Columbia University Teacher's College Press, 1971.
Morón Arroyo, Ciriaco. *El sistema de Ortega y Gasset.* Madrid: Alcalá, 1968.
Nicol, Eduardo. *Historicismo y Existencialismo.* Mexico: El Colegio de Mexico, 1950.
Ouimette, Victor. *José Ortega y Gasset.* Boston: Twayne Publishers, 1982.
Orringer, Nelson R. "Life as Shipwreck or as Sport in Ortega y Gasset." *Romance Notes* 17 (1976): 70–75.
———. *Nuevas fuentes germánicas de ¿Qué es filosofía? de Ortega.* Madrid: Consejo Superior de Investigaciones, 1984.
———. "Ortega's Dialogue with Heidegger in *What is Philosophy?*" *Ortega y Gasset*

Centennial/University of New Mexico. Madrid: José Porrua Turanzas, 1985, pp. 45–56.

———. *Ortega y sus fuentes germánicas*. Madrid: Editorial Gredos, 1979.

Piña Prata, Francisco. *Dialectica da razao*. Lisboa: Edicoes da Revista Fílosofia, 1961.

Raley, Harold C. *José Ortega y Gasset: Philosopher of European Unity*. Tuscaloosa: University of Alabama Press, 1971.

Ramirez, Santiago. *La filosofía de Ortega y Gasset*. Barcelona: Herder, 1958.

Sánchez Villa, Jose. *Ortega y Gasset, Existentialist: A Critical Study of His Thought and His Sources*. Chicago: Regnery, 1949.

Sharkey, James. "Ortega, Einstein and Perspectivism." *Romance Notes* 12 (1970): 21–25.

Silver, Philip W. *Ortega as Phenomenologist: The Genesis of Meditations on Quixote*. New York: Columbia University Press, 1978.

Tuttle, Howard. "Algunos puntos de la crítica de Ortega y Gasset a la teoría del Ser de Heidegger." *Revista de Occidente* 108 (Mayo 1990): 61–69.

———. "Ortega's Vitalism in Relation to Aspects of *Lebensphilosophie* and Phenomenology." *Southwest Philosophical Studies* 6 (1981): 88–92.

———. "The Idea of Life in Wilhelm Dilthey and Ortega y Gasset." *Ortega y Gasset Centennial/University of New Mexico*. Madrid: José Porrua Turanzas, 1985, pp. 105–17.

Walsh, W. H. *Introduction to the Philosophy of History*. London: Hutchinson, 1951.

Weintraub, Karl. *The Value of the Individual: Self and Circumstance in Autobiography*. Chicago: University of Chicago Press, 1978.

Wohl, Robert. *The Generation of 1914*. Cambridge, Mass.: Harvard University Press, 1979.